JOHN ROLLIN RIDGE

James W. Parins

John
Rollin
Ridge

HIS LIFE & WORKS

University of Nebraska Press: Lincoln and London

The paper in this book meets
the minimum requirements of American
National Standard for Information
Sciences—Permanence of Paper for Printed
Library Materials, ANSI Z39.48–1984.

Library of Congress Cataloging-in-Publication
Data
Parins, James W.
John Rollin Ridge : his life and works /
James W. Parins.
p.   cm. – (American indian lives)
Includes bibliographical references and index.
ISBN 0-8032-3683-2 (alk. paper)
1. Ridge, John Rollin, 1827–1867.   2. Cherokee
Indians – Biography.
3. Authors, Indian – 19th century – Biography.
4. Authors, American –
19th century – Biography.   I. Title.
II. Series.
E99.C5 R547   1991
973'.0497502 – dc20   [B]   90-40464   CIP

For Bernice and Roger LeFevre

Contents

ILLUSTRATIONS

Following page 94

Acknowledgments

I wish to thank the following individuals and institutions for providing access to materials I needed in the research for this volume: Nathan Bender, Western History Collections, Oklahoma University; Michael Gannet, Cornwall Historical Society, Cornwall, Connecticut; David Farmer and Rennard Strickland; Houghton Library, Harvard University; State Historical Society of Wisconsin; Oklahoma Historical Society; University of Tulsa Library; Tulane University Library; Arkansas History Commission; California State Library; Marysville Public Library; Yuba Public Library; Yuba County Clerk's Office; Nevada County Clerk's Office; and Archives, Ottenheimer Library, University of Arkansas at Little Rock.

Special thanks go to my wife, Marylyn Jackson Parins, and to my colleague and friend Daniel F. Littlefield, Jr.

1

Introduction

In the annals of American Indian literature of the nineteenth century, few names are as famous as that of John Rollin Ridge. He was a romantic figure in a romantic era, a man well aware of his image. During his California days, he was as protective of his carefully crafted persona as Lord Byron and Oscar Wilde were of theirs, and he cultivated the idea of himself as a misunderstood, passionate genius. This image has had considerable influence on his literary reputation.

In many respects his life *was* romantic. He was born into an influential family, one that helped shape the destiny of the Cherokee people. When his father and grandfather were assassinated because they advocated the removal of the Cherokee Nation to the West, he and his family were forced to flee for their lives. An eyewitness to his father's violent death, the teenaged Rollin harbored a deep desire for revenge and expressed his feelings in various ways. He supported, at least vicariously, the exploits of the Starr boys and others involved in the bloody warfare between rival Cherokee factions that raged in the 1840s in the Cherokee Nation and Arkansas. At the same time, he was intelligent and precocious, a fact recognized by his teachers in Arkansas and Massachusetts. He received a surprisingly good education on the frontier and was steeped in the traditions of history and literature. Ridge began publishing early, both works of poetry and political essays, and was to continue on this double literary track for the rest of his life.

In 1847 he settled down to a life of farming and stock raising, but he still was determined to pursue a literary career. The tranquil existence he had planned was not to be, however; within two years he was forced into a fight with a man from the rival Cherokee faction and gunned down his opponent. Again forced to flee his family's adversaries, he made his way to Missouri and then to California, where he tried mining during the great gold rush. But he soon began working as a journalist, a calling he followed until his death. He also wrote poetry, a popular romance, and historical essays, but the main impetus of his life was politics. His fiery editorials and sometimes heavy-handed partisanship brought him equally passionate defenders and detractors. During the Civil War, particularly, his politics became more and more radical; Ridge eventually became a Copperhead organizer and a recruiter for secret antiabolitionist societies.

Ridge's character embraced a series of contradictions. For example, he was very conscious of his Cherokee identity, yet he wrote in favor of assimilationist policies to settle the "Indian question." He took great pains to establish a personal image as a firebrand cavalier while he clearly sought middle-class respectability for himself and his family. These and other anomalies make the story of his life an interesting one. The impact of his writing, too, especially his romance novel *The Life and Adventures of Joaquín Murieta, the Celebrated California Bandit*, make his life a suitable subject of study. But most of all, it is the way John Rollin Ridge found himself in the position of American Indian writers before and since—"wandering between two worlds," in Matthew Arnold's phrase—that makes his story relevant.

When John Rollin Ridge was born on March 19, 1827, the Cherokee Nation in the East was in a state of turmoil. Like other American Indian groups in the Southeast, the Cherokees were being pressured by the federal government to leave their lands and emigrate to territories in the West that had not yet been settled by whites. In fact, some of their number had already settled in Arkansas and other areas to the west, but the great majority opposed the government's removal policy. Compounding the problem was friction between the state of Georgia and the Cherokee Nation. White citizens of that state cast envious eyes on Cherokee lands, especially after the Indians had worked hard to improve their farms and plantations. State officials, too, wished to bring the land the Cherokees lived on under their sovereignty. White Georgians pressed the federal government to implement a removal policy that would free the Nation's lands for white settlement and exploitation. Most Cherokees resisted removal, including John Rollin Ridge's father and grandfather. Major Ridge and his son John were both important leaders in the Cherokee Nation at the time of John Rollin's birth. Both made important contributions to their people, especially as advocates of education and literacy.

Major Ridge, known in his early life simply as The Ridge, was born in 1771 at Hiwassee, a Cherokee settlement on the Hiwassee River in what is now Polk County, Tennessee. His mother was half Cherokee and half white, her father being a Scots frontiersman. Affiliated with the Deer clan, she was married to a noted Cherokee hunter named, variously, Oganstota or Dutsi.[1] While The Ridge was still very young, the Cherokees were engaged in a series of fights with whites from Virginia, Georgia, and the Carolinas stemming from raids the Indians had made on white settlements. In the face of attacks by large groups of whites, The Ridge's father decided to move his family to a safer location. Accordingly, they journeyed by canoe to Sequatchie Mountain, or Walden Ridge, where they settled. Here the boy and his brother, David Watie or Oo-watie, were raised in the traditional manner. Their father taught them to hunt with blowpipes and bows and arrows; they also were taught the customs and lore of their people.

Sometime during a peaceful period between 1781 and 1788 the family moved again, this time to the settlement of Chestowee, near their former home at Hiwassee. While they were living there, hostilities again broke out between the whites and Cherokees, instigated by white intruders into Cherokee territory who violated the terms of the Hopewell treaty of 1785. One of the leaders at Chestowee called for volunteers for a war party, and The Ridge, then seventeen years old, joined the group. For several months Cherokee warriors engaged the whites in a series of raids and skirmishes. The Ridge conducted himself well in the fighting during the winter of 1788–89. When he returned to his home in March 1789, he found that his father and mother had both died. It was now his responsibility to look after his two brothers and his sister, since he was the eldest. He spent the next few years on hunting expeditions to provide food for his family, but he also spent much time with the war parties, since the border skirmishes continued until 1794.

In 1796 The Ridge's leadership abilities were recognized by his people when he was chosen to represent his town of Pine Log at the tribal council at Oostanaula. He continued as emissary the next year when the council, at his urging, revised the ancient blood law. The blood law called for retaliation whenever a Cherokee took another's life, even if the death was accidental. If the killer fled to escape punishment, one of his close relatives would be killed. The Ridge proposed that the council amend the law to allow the mitigating circumstance of accidental death. The other members agreed with the change and declared that a death must be intentional before it fell under the provisions of the blood law. From this time on The Ridge asserted his leadership and became a progressive voice among his people.

In 1792 or thereabouts The Ridge married Susanna Wickett, whose Indian name was Sehoya. At the time, American agents were urging the Cherokees to intensify their farming and to add cotton to their traditional crops of corn, pumpkins, squash, beans, melons, and sweet potatoes. The women were also encouraged to learn to spin and weave so their cotton could be made into cloth. The men were urged to leave the pursuit of game and expand their garden plots into farms and plantations. With Susanna's approval, The Ridge decided to clear land for a farm and to build a house like those of whites. The couple left Pine Log to settle in a valley along Oothcaloga Creek, where they built a log house and began to raise livestock and crops, including cotton and corn. The Ridge's efforts to live like his white neighbors and to amass material wealth were encouraged by his wife, who apparently had ambitions for herself, her husband, and her children. Success, as measured by the family's economic and social position in the Cherokee Nation, was Susanna's chief goal and would be shared by her son John and grandson Rollin. Thurman Wilkins calls Susanna a "powerful driving force behind her husband";[2] this doubtless applies to her relationship with her son as well. Women were to play an important role in the lives and fortunes of father, son, and grandson.

While the Ridges were improving their plantation and raising their children, disturbing events were taking place to the south among the Creeks, neighbors of the Cherokees. Two factions had formed among the Creek Nation, the split caused mainly by pressure to cede land to the Americans and related efforts to bring white civilization to the Indians. Some Creeks were loath to resist the Americans while others, the Red Stick faction, were ready to go to war over what they saw as threats to their way of life. Finally civil war broke out between the two factions, with the Red Sticks attempting to remove every vestige of white culture from the Creek Nation. The other side requested help from the federal government, which in turn recruited Cherokees to fight the insurgent Red Sticks. In 1813 The Ridge raised a group of Cherokee volunteers who, in accord with troops under General Andrew Jackson, went into action against the Red Sticks. He distinguished himself in the battle of the Horseshoe, the decisive action in the Creek War. The Ridge attained the rank of major during the hostilities and later adopted the title as his name. After the war, he returned to Oothcaloga.

It was at Oothcaloga that all the Ridge children were born. First was Nancy, followed by John, Rollin's father. A third baby died and was followed by Walter, nicknamed "Watty," who was mentally retarded. Finally another girl was born, some seven or eight years after John, named Sarah or Sally. Both parents realized that if their dream of prosperity for themselves and their children was to come true, the children would have to be educated. They were especially eager for their son John to learn all he could about how to survive and succeed in their fast-changing world. This special attention was probably due to two factors: their general confidence that education was the path to take, and the fact that John was slight, "delicate," walked with a limp owing to a "scrofulous" condition, and perhaps would find it hard to earn a living in an occupation where physical strength was important.[3] Watty's problems made it clear that only one of the sons would be able to follow The Ridge as a leader of the Cherokees. Despite the couple's attention to John's education, they did not neglect their daughters. Nancy had been sent to school when she was eight, and Sally grew up to be a bright and articulate woman.

The Ridge and his wife had been early advocates of educational efforts among the Cherokees, seeing the whites' schools as important for the advancement of not only their own family but the entire Nation. The Ridge spoke at councils in favor of missionaries' requests to establish schools among his people. Missionaries had conducted schools in the area since April or May 1801, when Abraham Steiner and Gottlieb Byhan started a Moravian mission and school at Spring Place. Steiner left in the fall, but Byhan stayed until about 1812. In 1805 John Gambold and his wife joined the mission, bringing new enthusiasm and energy to the school. Earlier, a Presbyterian mission and school had been opened in 1803 by Gideon Blackburn. Blackburn had secured approval for his enterprise from the federal government, the principal chiefs of the Nation, and Colonel Return J. Meigs, the American agent to the Cherokees. The school, situated near the Hiwassee River, had forty-five to fifty students. At the Cherokees' request, another school opened in the Lower Cherokee Nation in the same year. Both schools lasted until the War of 1812.[4]

John and Nancy Ridge entered the Gambolds' school in 1810. Although the Moravian institution was primarily a boys' school, the Gambolds agreed to take Nancy as well. She could not board at the school, however, so she stayed with Margaret Vann, a widow who lived nearby. Nancy and two female classmates helped Mrs. Vann around the house in exchange for their meals and beds. The male scholars all rose at dawn to begin their daily regimen, which started with morning prayers followed by breakfast, after which the girls joined them for school. Mrs. Gambold was in charge of secular instruction, while her husband directed religious studies. The boys and girls were taught to read and write and to pray and sing hymns. After the noon meal, the boys generally worked in the fields or chopped wood. Prayers followed the evening meal, and bedtime came shortly after. On Sundays Mr. Gambold preached at the school, the service being open to Cherokees from the surrounding area.

The Ridge children apparently made good progress and were quick to pick up the English language. The reports reaching Oothcaloga from Spring Place were so good, in fact, that soon Oo-watie, Major Ridge's brother, sent his son Gallegina, or Buck Watie, to the school as well. Buck, who later adopted the name of a white benefactor, Elias Boudinot, took to the school too, and he soon became one of the Gambolds' favorites. The children remained at Spring Place until 1815, when Ridge decided to hire one of the itinerant teachers who traveled through the area. His motivation was not displeasure with the Gambolds or the school, apparently, but Susanna's concern for John Ridge's ailing hip. The mother wanted John near so she could nurse him.[5] The experiment failed, however, when the new schoolmaster turned out to be an incompetent drunk who left the Ridges after three months. Buck returned to Spring Place, taking his younger brother Stand Watie with him, but Nancy and John Ridge did not go along.

About this time Cyrus Kingsbury, a Congregationalist minister, approached the Cherokee delegation in Washington with a plan to expand education in their territory. The delegates reacted favorably to the plan, so Kingsbury approached the War Department for support. The government agreed to help set up the first school and directed Colonel Meigs to build a school and a house for the teacher. He was also to supply two plows, six hoes, and six axes to introduce the students to the "art of cultivation." When female students arrived, Meigs was to furnish the school with a loom and six spinning wheels.[6] This combination of study and work was to permeate American Indian education for the next 150 years. With this promised support, Kingsbury traveled to the Cherokee country, arriving in September 1816. He made his proposal to the fall council, and the chiefs approved the plan. Kingsbury then set out in search of a site for his new school, settling on one along Chickamauga Creek in Tennessee. Construction began immediately on what was to be called Brainerd School, and Kingsbury was joined by Moody Hall and Loring S. Williams in 1817. By July of that year twenty-six Cherokee students attended the school, among them John and Nancy Ridge, aged fourteen and sixteen.

Major Ridge traveled the sixty miles to Brainerd to enroll his children, arriving on May 14, 1817. They were placed at the highest level of the Lancastrian method, the plan by which the school was organized. This method of instruction, also known as the monitorial system, allowed one teacher to instruct a number of students at different levels simultaneously by using "monitors"—older, more advanced students—as tutors for the younger ones. At Brainerd the students learned reading, spelling, writing, arithmetic, grammar, and of course religion. Instruction was given in English at this time, and though it might have been easier to teach in a child's native language, the missionaries reasoned that assimilation in language leads to assimilation in habits and manners.[7] One of the drawbacks of the Lancastrian system, however, is that often the monitors are too busy with the younger or slower children to keep up with their own studies. John Ridge apparently thought the system was retarding his own progress and let his father know. Before Major Ridge could act, however, Elias Cornelius, from the American Board of Commissioners for Foreign Missions (ABCFM), arrived in the Cherokee Nation.

Cornelius arrived at a time when the Cherokees were protesting the idea of removal to Arkansas. Cherokee leaders, among them Major Ridge, offered a countermeasure in the form of a petition to the federal government for more aid to education in the Nation. The carefully written petition demonstrated the need for the aid and also showed that the Cherokees were sincere in their efforts to accept white civilization. Cornelius was so impressed by the plan that he asked the Cherokee council for permission to expand the efforts of the ABCFM among their people. After Major Ridge spoke in favor of such an expansion, the council agreed. Cornelius also proposed to enroll promising Cherokee students in the new ABCFM school at Cornwall, Connecticut. The school, designed to instruct "foreign youth," wanted representatives from the southern American Indian groups, ostensibly to complement the "foreigners" already enrolled: one Abnaki, two Chinese, two Malays, one Bengali, one Hindu, several Hawaiians, two Marquesans, and three white Americans.[8] Cornelius invited John Ridge, Buck Watie, and Leonard Hicks, son of the Cherokee assistant principal chief, to travel with him to the school. Watie's and Hicks's parents agreed, but Major Ridge did not consent to John's matriculation at Cornwall at that time, since Susanna was still concerned about the boy's hip. In May 1818 Cornelius and his young charges left for Cornwall, with stops at Monticello to meet Thomas Jefferson and at Washington, where they greeted President Monroe. The party also visited with Elias Boudinot, president of the American Bible Society and former president of the Continental Congress. Boudinot took a special interest in Buck Watie and urged the young Cherokee to adopt his name. When Buck enrolled at Cornwall, he did so as Elias Boudinot.

John Ridge made the journey to the ABCFM school the following fall. With John were Darcheechee, a full-blood Cherokee who would later take the name David Steiner, and John Vann. The students were under the protection of Dr. Dempsey of New York City. John had been given a horse by his father, plus a saddle and bridle, post bags, and $44 in cash.[9] The students left Spring Place late in September 1818 and arrived at Cornwall in late November, when the school had been in session for some time. As in most mission schools of the time and since, the curriculum included a heavy dose of religious training as well as "instruction" in agriculture, which consisted largely of labor on the school's farm. The rest of the educational program was much like that of white American schools; Rev. Herman Daggett, the headmaster, reported that his best students, Watie and Ridge, studied geography, history, rhetoric, surveying, Latin, and natural science.[10]

In spite of his rapid progress in school, John Ridge's physical constitution did not bear up well in the northern climate. His scrofulous hip, a condition involving malfunction of the lymphatic system, worsened in the cold winters, and by the third year there he had placed himself under the care of a physician, Dr. Samuel Gold. He also wrote to his parents about his problems; they responded that perhaps he should return home. By the spring of 1821 he was so ill that Dr. Gold removed him from the attic dormitory at the school, sending him to a private room and assigning Mrs. John Northrup as his nurse. When his condition did not improve, Gold sent him to a specialist in New Haven, but his ministrations seemed to have no effect. Major Ridge was informed of the worsening of his son's illness and determined to travel to Cornwall. He set out for the North on September 4, 1821, with his interpreter. After a month's travel Ridge reached Cornwall, entering the town dressed in resplendent clothes and riding in a fine carriage drawn by four horses. He stayed two weeks, making a great impression on the townspeople. The North made a great impression on Major Ridge as well; on his return to the Cherokee Nation he told stories about all the friends he had made, saying he liked all the people in Connecticut except the "chief" in Litchfield, who, according to Ridge, "talked too much about land." [11] While there, he was told that John was not well enough to make the long journey home.

It was not until Major Ridge returned south that John began to make his recovery. Mrs. Northrup's chores with the other students dictated that at times she delegate the care of the sick young Cherokee to her daughter, Sarah Bird. As soon as the fourteen-year-old began her visits, Dr. Gold noted an improvement in John's condition. After a short time it was apparent to all that the two were in love. The Northrup family reacted by sending Sarah to New Haven to stay with her grandparents. John wrote to his parents asking permission to marry Sarah. His mother, who apparently had her heart set on his marrying a Cherokee woman, consulted one of the missionaries at Brainerd and refused to give her consent. Undaunted, John wrote again, and Susanna, not willing to make her boy unhappy, agreed to the marriage. Still there was opposition from the Northrups. When John proposed to Sarah, her family took the stand that young Ridge should return south, recover his health, and come back to Cornwall within two years to receive their blessing. John agreed, really having no choice, since the ABCFM had decreed he could not stay on as a student as long as his hip continued to give him trouble. At the end of summer 1822, John Ridge headed south.

He spent the rest of that year and most of the next regaining his health. By December 1823 he was well enough to throw away the crutches he had needed since the onset of his hip problems. At that time he accompanied his father to Washington. Major Ridge was one of a delegation—the other members were John Ross, George Lowrey, and Elijah Hicks—sent to the capital to lobby for the Cherokee position that no more land should be ceded to the whites. This policy was one Major Ridge and his son were to champion for the next nine years. John stayed with the Cherokee group in Washington for a few days and then traveled on to Cornwall, determined to press his case with the Northrup family. When he arrived, he found the Northrups friendly and ready to consent to their daughter's marriage.

The wedding was held, but only after many of the citizens of Cornwall objected. According to reports, the couple was denounced by area newspapers and castigated on racial grounds by preachers from their pulpits; people in Cornwall did not want one of their white daughters to be carried off by an Indian, no matter how well educated and civilized he was. The couple and the family held their ground, however, and the wedding took place on January 27, 1824, at the Second Congregational Church, presided over by Rev. Walter Smith. After the ceremony the pair was in danger of being mobbed, so they decided to leave Cornwall immediately.[12] A year or so later, when Elias Boudinot and Harriet Gold were also married in Cornwall, more intense violence was loosed on the town. Harriet was forced to hide from her own townspeople and was burned in effigy. Boudinot had to disguise himself to get past the angry crowds unharmed. The Cherokees, long used to white men marrying Indian women, were dismayed at the actions of the Christian citizens of Cornwall.

John and Sarah Bird Northrup Ridge traveled to the Cherokee Nation, where they took up residence at Ridge's Ferry on the Oostanaula River. But more trouble was brewing on the border between territory settled by whites and land still held by the Indians. The latest problems had their origin in a treaty signed by MacIntosh, a Creek leader, that ceded the Creek lands and provided for the removal of the Creeks west of the Mississippi. The treaty, signed on February 12, 1825, at Indian Springs, Georgia, was not honored by the Creeks, who had lately removed all MacIntosh's authority to act on their behalf. The Creeks assassinated MacIntosh and took on John Ridge and David Vann as agents to help them abrogate the treaty. For the next two years Ridge and Vann maneuvered and bargained with federal officials and representatives of the various Creek factions. Although the Indian Springs treaty was renegotiated successfully for the Creeks, John Ridge made many enemies during this period, including Creeks who disagreed with him, Cherokees who were jealous of his ability and influence, and federal officials whom he outmaneuvered. After this foray into Creek affairs, John turned his attention to his own business and to Cherokee politics. Despite his preoccupation with making a living and the bad feelings engendered by the reaction to his marriage, Ridge did not cease to champion the cause of the missionaries, especially their educational efforts. In 1826 he wrote to the secretary of the ABCFM requesting that a missionary school be established near David Vann's house. He proposed that Sarah's father be introduced to the Nation, citing his experience as a steward of the Cornwall school. Ridge said that Northrup had served in that capacity "with credit and benefit to the institution until the crime was committed in the act of marriage with his daughter and myself."[13] To John Ridge, it is clear, education was still the means by which the Cherokees could survive.

By this time the Ridges were fairly prosperous. Major Ridge ran a large farm, held a half-interest in a trading post, and operated a ferry. His house was an impressive two-story structure with eight rooms, four fireplaces, and two verandas, surrounded by large oaks and sycamores. There were barns and stables near the house, as well as slave cabins. The farm comprised 280 acres, where Ridge grew various crops including cotton, wheat, and tobacco, raised livestock, and tended extensive orchards. By the time John Rollin Ridge was born, his grandfather was a wealthy man.

2

Boyhood at Running Waters

At the time of Rollin's birth, John and Sarah had moved from Ridge's Ferry to a spot six miles northeast. By this time the new father was deriving an income from his law practice and from his half-interest in the ferry at New Echota. He had also realized a couple of thousand dollars in fees from his negotiation of the Creek treaty. On the banks of the Oostanaula, Ridge raised a house befitting a man of his position. The main two-story section measured fifty-one feet by nineteen; a one-story addition was thirty-one feet by twenty. The house, as Rollin remembered it, stood "on a high hill, crowned with a fine grove of oak and hickory, a large clear spring at the foot of the hill, and an extensive farm stretching away down into the valley, with a fine orchard on the left."[1] The farm eventually consisted of 419 acres and included appropriate outbuildings and living quarters for John Ridge's eighteen slaves. The younger Ridge grew much the same crops and fruit trees as his father and raised livestock. The spring Rollin mentions furnished the name of the place, Running Waters.

It was here at Running Waters that John Rollin Ridge was born on March 19, 1827. He spent his first years in these pleasant surroundings, showered with attention by the family, especially his mother and grand-mother. The tranquility of this existence was disturbed, however, by the increasing tension between the Cherokees and the whites, especially the Georgians, who coveted the Cherokee lands. The sight of prosperous plantations like the Ridges' doubtless exacerbated the whites' hunger for expansion. Rollin grew up hearing about these problems, since his parents' and grandparents' homes were important centers of resistance to the whites' demands. When his family became convinced that re-moval was inevitable, their house became the headquarters for the Ridge faction of the Cherokees, the Treaty party. As a child he overheard dis-cussions on policy and debates on strategy among the leaders of his people. Rollin was thus exposed to the excitement and tensions of poli-tics at an early age. Hearing his father and grandfather, both respected orators and political negotiators, arguing forcefully with other national leaders made a deep impression on young Rollin. The influence of the early years became apparent as he grew older; from his teens onward he loved a political fight and threw himself into each new one with passion. More important, though, the debates and discussions instilled in him a respect for the effective use of language and the arts of argument and persuasion. He worked hard to improve his own facility with the En-glish language. Later he would use these skills with great effectiveness in his literary, journalistic, and political pursuits.

Rollin's mind and personality were not nourished only by his ob-servations of the adults around him. The Ridge family's commitment to education was by this time well established. John and Sarah Ridge were determined to provide the best education they could for their eldest son and the rest of the children. In his description of his boyhood home, Rollin remembers that on a hill some two hundred yards from the main house "stood the schoolhouse, built at my father's expense, for the use of a Missionary, Miss Sophia Sawyer, who made her home with our family and taught my father's children and all who chose to come to her for instruction."[2] The school was built in 1834, when Rollin was seven.

Sophia Sawyer was another of the competent, strong-willed women who influenced John Rollin Ridge. Along with his mother and grandmother, Sawyer gave his early life direction. Whereas Susanna and Sarah were sources of love and security, Miss Sophia's contribution was discipline and formal instruction. The teacher was born at Fitchburg, Massachusetts, on May 4, 1792. She grew up in extreme poverty and seemed destined at first to share the lot of her poor parents, but she proved to be an intelligent young woman who was determined to break out of her situation. Her unusual qualities attracted the attention of a Dr. Payson, who took her into his home as a domestic servant. Payson provided her with enough education to qualify her for a place in the Female School at Byfield, Massachusetts, an institution run by Rev. Joseph Emerson, which was well regarded in the region. She helped pay her way at the school by continuing her household duties at the Payson home and, when the occasion arose, by teaching.[3]

In 1823 Sawyer, now just over thirty, was sent by the ABCFM to Brainerd to take over the instruction of female students. Her outspoken personality often rankled her more staid colleagues, but she soon became very popular with the Cherokees. At one point she was assigned to Haweis, one of the schools established by an ABCFM expansion. Haweis was directed by John C. Ellsworth and situated not far from where the Ridges lived.[4] By 1829 she had set up a school in the courthouse at New Echota, the Cherokee Nation's capital. In March 1832 Sawyer was to display the courageous nature that endeared her to the Cherokees. Among her twenty pupils at New Echota were two boys, sons of black slaves owned by the Indians, named Peter and Sam. The Cherokees, unlike most of their white slaveholding counterparts, saw nothing wrong with educating black children. The Georgia legislature disagreed and had recently passed a law making it a crime to teach a black child to read. The penalty was a fine of not less than $1,000 nor more than $5,000, with an added stipulation that the guilty teacher would be jailed until the fine was paid. Obviously, most teachers at the time would have been hard pressed to raise such a sum. Sawyer had been warned in an anonymous letter that she was violating the statute, but she chose to ignore the warning as well as the law. In the middle of March her school received a visit from a company of the Georgia Guard. When the sergeant in charge questioned her concerning the black students, Sawyer replied that she was teaching them and that the Cherokees were too civilized to pass laws against it. The Georgians argued that she was violating state law, to which Sawyer replied that she was teaching in the Cherokee Nation, where Georgia law had no force, at least until the Supreme Court ruled otherwise. The leader of the Guard then threatened to arrest her if she continued to break Georgia law but promised her protection if she desisted. The country was lost to the Cherokees anyway, he reasoned. But Sawyer stood her ground, and the Guard, daunted by either her logic or her determination, left without completing the mission.[5]

By 1833 the school was prospering in spite of harassment by the Georgians. Sawyer had thirty students, including John Rollin Ridge and his cousin Charles C. Watie. Ridge was apparently a model student; he made good academic progress and attended school every day.[6] But in spite of her obvious devotion to her students, Sawyer was not well liked by her fellow missionaries, and that caused her some difficulties. Samuel A. Worcester, especially, did not get along with her. The two wrote complaining letters about each other to the board, and Worcester later recommended that she not be allowed to remove to the West with the Cherokees. She was well thought of, however, in the Ridge-Boudinot family. Her relations with Sarah Bird Northrup Ridge and Harriet Gold Boudinot were marked by cordiality and mutual respect. The high regard in which she was held by the Ridge family was demonstrated in 1834. By that time conditions in the Cherokee Nation had deteriorated, especially at New Echota. In the courthouse where her school was held alcohol was being sold to the Indians, even the children. White intruders ran rampant in the area, and the safety of her students was in question. By December 27, 1834, the school at New Echota had closed. Sophia Sawyer, who had been "shut out" from "laboring with missionaries" owing to the bad feelings between them, had been living with Elias Boudinot's family for some ten months.[7] During this time she had made a lasting impression on the Boudinots and their relatives the Ridges.

In fact, in summer 1834 Sarah Ridge had asked Sawyer to move her school to Running Waters, where the children would be safe. Harriet Gold Boudinot wrote to the ABCFM in support of such a move. She pledged that the parents would build the schoolhouse and provide for Miss Sawyer's support, thus diminishing rather than increasing the board's expenses.[8] Although the offer was attractive in many ways, the teacher was reluctant, mainly because she did not know John Ridge well enough. In a letter to David Greene, secretary of the ABCFM, she said that though Ridge was a gentleman and had used his influence in the Nation to support her school, "He has not religion." This lack made her unsure about the strength of his commitment to the new school. Harriet and Sarah allayed her fears, however, and she determined to move the school to Running Waters for a one-year trial.[9] Miss Sawyer moved to the Ridge home in December 1834. She used their front room as a classroom until the new school was built, and she boarded with the family. Her other pupils were welcomed at the new school on the banks of the Oostanaula.

The new school contrasted with the old one in New Echota. According to Mary Fields, one of the students at Running Waters, the building was "cool and pleasant, the trees are thick all around it. It has a smooth plank floor and a large fire place, and five glass windows." Mary's letter to David Greene is one of a series by Sawyer's students, designed to report on their progress. She went on to report that she, Rollin, Betsey Adair, and Eleanor Boudinot were studying arithmetic, geography, geometry, and United States history. At the bottom of the page is a sample of Rollin's handwriting. The inscription says, "John Rollin Ridge aged eight years."[10]

Sawyer had very definite ideas on educating the Indians, which probably did not help her popularity with the other missionaries. Sawyer did not believe in boarding schools, because she had observed that when Indian students returned to their communities they were regarded as half aliens, often even by members of their own families. In self-defense, the returned students were liable to reject all they had learned in an attempt to fit in better.[11] She also thought it important to supplement the missionaries' standard fare of Bible study with what she called "Profane History." "This will enlarge their views, lead them to see the use of geography, and give them subjects for thought and conversation." [12] Though this belief did not endear her to her colleagues in the Cherokee missions, it certainly kindled a lifelong interest in history in young Rollin. The curriculum at Running Waters included reading, writing, and arithmetic, of course, but they were supplemented with geometry, Bible history, and the study of the solar system. Older students were taught English literature, French, and higher mathematics. Sawyer subscribed to *Purley's Magazine* and sometimes was able to get *Youth's Companion* for the children. In addition, she had John Ridge bring back books from his frequent trips to the East. Many of these titles were purchased with Rollin in mind. [13] Until nearly the time of removal, Rollin was under the wing of this intelligent, forthright woman who brooked no nonsense from her male colleagues, white intruders, or the Georgia Guard, let alone her pupils. She demanded discipline and hard work and was supported in this by John and Sarah Ridge. The lesson was not lost on Rollin. Later, in the West, he was to come under her tutelage again.

As time went on, however, the situation in the Cherokee Nation worsened. The plantation and school at Running Waters were not immune to the problems, especially since the Ridges had come to believe in the futility of Cherokee resistance to removal. Sometimes strangers lurked at the edge of the woods bordering the Ridge farm, terrifying everyone. Adding to the tension, some parents withdrew their children from Sawyer's school in protest after the Ridges' new position on the removal question became known. [14] Their counsel to the people from about 1832 on was to make the best bargain they could and move west. The change from a belief in total resistance to a policy of giving in to the whites' demands came about for several reasons. First of all, Andrew Jackson had been elected president in 1828. The implications of this election were profound for American Indians east of the Mississippi, especially for those in the South. In his first annual message to Congress, delivered on December 8, 1829, Jackson had announced that he intended to push for legislation that would remove all Indians to the West. So it seemed that all the negotiations and memorials to Congress were futile and that no protection was forthcoming from the federal government, despite all the treaties. Second, gold had been discovered in the southeastern quadrant of the Cherokee Nation, increasing the whites' clamor for Indian land. Even though the value of the strike was greatly overestimated by both Indians and whites, it raised the stakes in the conflict. Third, in December 1827 the Georgia legislature extended its authority over Cherokee lands, to take effect in June 1830. Responding to Jackson's attitude and to the wishes of many of its most vocal citizens, the body passed legislation extending its laws to the Cherokee Nation and annexing large sections of Indian land. These actions released a flood of intruders, often violent men who moved into the Nation and forcibly evicted people from their homes and farms. In addition, meetings of the Cherokee general council and other gatherings were forbidden by Georgia law.

At first the Cherokees were united in their response. The Ridges informed General John Coffee of the situation at a meeting at John Ross's farm, hoping to convince the United States Army to act on the Cherokees' behalf against the intruders. Coffee, however, said that in his opinion it was the principal chief's duty to oust the intruders. Ross chose Major Ridge to move against the Georgians. Ridge, decked out in a horned buffalo headdress, led a force of thirty warriors against a settlement of intruders at Beaver Dam and Cedar Creek, who occupied buildings left by Cherokees who had gone west. The Indians allowed the whites to leave the area, then set fire to the buildings. This action, instead of improving the situation, exacerbated it. The Georgians considered the foray proof that the Cherokees were a savage race and far from civilized. Pressure became greater than ever for the Cherokees to move west; in addition to the outcries from Georgia, the federal government urged them to leave.

In response to this pressure, John Ridge and two others were sent to Washington to meet with Secretary of War John Henry Eaton. Eaton's views on Indians were well known; he had made a widely reported remark, for example, that Indians could no more be educated than wild turkeys. Not surprisingly, the Cherokees found little support in official

Washington, despite John Ridge's memorial to Congress outlining the intrusions and depredations against the Cherokee Nation. Some members of Congress, including Henry Clay, Theodore Frelinghuysen, and Edward Everett, supported the Cherokee position, but they were in the minority. The delegation returned to the Nation and made its report. Indian leaders, including John Ross and Major Ridge, agreed that the best policy was to resist the pressure to emigrate and to continue the political fight. Major Ridge and Ross spent the next months traveling to various settlements and urging the people to maintain the status quo as best they could. Ridge and Ross also ordered officials in the Nation to enforce Cherokee laws and ignore those of Georgia.

The Georgia legislature continued to press its case. Early in 1831 it passed a law making it illegal for any white person to remain in the Cherokee Nation after March 1, 1831, without taking an oath of allegiance to the state and receiving a permit from the governor. After defying this law, missionaries Samuel A. Worcester and Elizur Butler, among others, were arrested and tried. Worcester and Butler refused to give in and were eventually sentenced by the Georgia Supreme Court to four years' hard labor. The conviction was appealed to the United States Supreme Court. In the meantime, John Ridge was sent to Washington in November 1831 to offer arguments against Cherokee removal, but again the Jackson administration refused to listen. When Ridge presented a list of crimes committed against his people by white intruders, the new secretary of war, Lewis Cass, replied that if conditions were indeed so bad in the Cherokee Nation, the Indians should move west, out of reach. Disgusted, Ridge sought support from people in the northern cities of Philadelphia, New York, New Haven, and Boston. He and Boudinot, now editor of the *Cherokee Phoenix*, spoke to groups in the North, hoping to excite public opinion against Jackson's removal policy and raise money to publish the *Phoenix*. While on their tour, the two cousins got word of the Supreme Court's 1832 decision in the case of *Worcester and Butler vs. Georgia:* the Georgia law was held to be unconstitutional.

The jubilation the Cherokees and their supporters felt as news of the decision spread was short-lived, however. When Andrew Jackson heard of the Court's action, he reportedly remarked, "John Marshall has made his decision; let him enforce it if he can." [15] In spring 1832 John Ridge requested an audience with Jackson to ascertain the president's position in the matter and was told that the federal government would not act against Georgia. It was probably at this point that Ridge saw the futility of further resistance to removal. This realization was reinforced as white supporters urged Ridge to convince his people to abandon their cause, make the best deal they could, and remove to the West. With no more legal recourse, the state and federal governments against them, and support from friends crumbling, the Cherokees were in a precarious position. But John Ross and a majority of the Cherokees were still firmly against removal and the cession of any more land.

By the summer of 1832 John Ridge, Major Ridge, Elias Boudinot, and a number of others were convinced of the need to remove. They began a campaign to convince the people to abandon hope that they would be able to remain on their land. John Ross and his followers argued the opposite position, however, and publicly questioned the patriotism of the protreaty faction. The Ridge party held a council at Running Waters in November 1834 at which the delegates prepared a memorial to Congress announcing their conviction that removal to the West was the only course left to the Cherokees. After Edward Everett introduced the memorial in the House and Henry Clay read it in the Senate, it became clear that the government would have to treat with the Ridge faction, since Ross and his followers had been carrying out a series of stalling tactics, hoping to outlast the Jackson administration. In spring 1835 John F. Schermerhorn, appointed to treat with the Cherokees, and John Ridge reached a tentative agreement. This pact, to be sent to the Cherokee Nation for ratification, provided that the Cherokees would exchange their lands in the East for 13,800,000 acres in the West, plus a payment of $4,500,000 and an annuity to support a school fund in the Nation. On December 29, 1835, twenty members of the Ridge party, including John Ridge, Major Ridge, and Elias Boudinot, signed the treaty in Boudinot's house at New Echota. Upon adding his mark to the other signatures, Major Ridge reportedly said, "I have signed my death warrant." [16]

After the treaty was ratified, preparations were begun for the great trek west. The family was split into two groups. The older Ridges would remove first, in the winter of 1836–37, taking Rollin's sister Clarinda with them. John and his family planned to follow later. Major and Susanna Ridge decided to accept transportation from the government. They traveled mostly by water from Ross's landing, present-day Chattanooga, to Van Buren, Arkansas. Starting out in flatboats, the party of 466 Cherokees transferred to the steamer *Knoxville*, under the command of George Washington Harris, later to achieve fame as a writer. The steamer took them to Decatur, Alabama, and there they boarded railway cars for Tuscumbia, Alabama, where they were met by the steamboat *Newark* towing two large keelboats. The *Newark* took them to Paducah, Kentucky, down the Ohio to the Mississippi, and down the Mississippi to the mouth of the Arkansas. They proceeded up the Arkansas to Little Rock, where they were obliged to switch to the shallower-draft steamer *Revenue*, which took them to Van Buren. After debarking, Major Ridge's party traveled overland up the military road that generally followed the border between Arkansas and what was to become Indian Territory. They arrived at their destination, Honey Creek, in the northeastern corner of the Cherokee Nation very near present-day Southwest City, Missouri, in late March or early April 1837. Here they began to carve a farm out of the wilderness. The Ridges had brought with them eighteen black slaves, whom they put to work clearing and plowing the land.

The family at Running Waters was also making preparations for the journey west. John Ridge spent his time settling family business affairs and, as president of the National Council, those of other Cherokee settlers. He reported to Sarah's sister in November 1836 that he was doing very well in liquidating the family's assets. Major Ridge's ferry and farm were sold for $22,000. The place at Running Waters was valued at $6,700, and the crops and livestock at $1,745. A ferry in Alabama and "other improvements" owned by John Ridge he expected to sell for about $14,000. In addition, he was being paid $6 a day for his work on the council and still had $2,500 coming for his part in the Creek negotiations. Ridge kept thirteen horses, valued at $100 each, two wagons, and two carriages for the trek west.[17] By the time they left, the Ridges had enough money for a good start in the new land.

John Ridge was thinking hard about the future of his people during this period. In a letter to David Greene in May 1837, he reiterated his often-expressed faith in education and revealed how that process might eventually shape the destiny of his people:

> What is the great instrument in the hands of God to promote civilization and Christianity in the world? It is Education! And if the North American Indians are lifted up from their ignorance and degeneration, the light of letters must shed their bright beams over the western region assigned them for their future habitations. From this light, their hopes must be rekindled and once rekindled the work will be commenced and not stopped until the Indians are received and formed into a community, and that community be adopted as a state into the Union of these U. States.[18]

He then praised the work of Greene's ABCFM missionaries and proposed that they continue their work with the Cherokees in the West. Specifically, he asked that William Chamberlain and Sophia Sawyer be allowed to accompany the Indians.

Sophia Sawyer had completed her last term at her school in 1836. Before her departure, she sent two letters to David Greene concerning her situation.[19] In the first she said that Ridge and Boudinot were engaged in a political struggle but that she knew the issue was settled and that the Cherokees must remove. Her plan in the face of such a move was to send her school's books and supplies west with the Ridges while she herself traveled to the East. Sawyer planned to stay in New York City with a friend until Ridge and Boudinot sent for her. She reasoned that even if she could not join the Cherokees in their new home, her school materials would be there for a replacement teacher to use. The second letter related her readiness to leave for New York; she planned first to travel to Charleston and from there to make her passage north on a ship. This letter also contains a handwriting sample from Rollin. The text is as follows:

> Waft, waft, ye winds, his story,
> And you, ye water, roll,

Till, like a sea of glory,
It spreads from pole to pole;
Till o'er our ransom'd nature,
The Lamb for sinners slain;
Redeemer, King, Creator,
In bliss returns to reign.

John Rollin Ridge aged nine years.

During that summer she left for New York, after promising the Ridges she would return and accompany them to their new home.

In the autumn after her departure, Rollin and the other children were sent to William Potter's school at Creek Path, Alabama, where they remained until the migration began. Meanwhile, John Ridge planned his move. He sent his employee William Childers on ahead with most of his slaves and horses. Three blacks were kept behind: Maria, the cook; Henry, the carriage driver; and Mary, who tended the children. Three horses were also retained, two to pull the carriage and Rollin's pony, Dick, which he refused to leave behind.[20] When all was ready, the party left Running Waters at the end of September 1837 and traveled to Creek Path. Accompanying the Ridges was the family of Elias Boudinot. By this time, Harriet Gold Boudinot had died and Boudinot had married Delight Sargent, a white woman who had come to the Cherokee Nation as a missionary some time before. Filling out the party were the William Lassley family and Polly Gilbreath, who was invited along by the Ridges.

They traveled north from Creek Path into Tennessee to Nashville, and Ridge and Boudinot took a side trip to the Hermitage, Andrew Jackson's home, which is near that city. After their visit with the former president, they continued their journey. Thurman Wilkins surmises that the Ridge-Boudinot group followed the route recommended by the superintendent of emigration, thereby traveling north through Kentucky to the Ohio River.[21] They crossed the river at Berry's Ferry to Golconda, Illinois, where they began to traverse the bottom of that state. As they neared the Mississippi River the land became increasingly marshy, and their passage was difficult. Most likely the party was ferried over the river to Cape Girardeau, Missouri, and continued west, reaching the rises of the Ozark plateau. Travel through this region of hills, ridges, and valleys was difficult but beautiful; the trees were ablaze with autumn colors, and game abounded. For Rollin, especially, the trek must have been exciting. Always a lover of nature, he was to discover terrain, plants, and animals different from those he had known in Georgia. The party did not travel on Sundays, and it is easy to imagine the ten-year-old Rollin astride his pony spending the warm fall Sabbath days exploring his new surroundings. The whole journey was, for Rollin, "a zestful voyage of discovery among new flora and fauna."[22] After crossing the Ozarks, the Ridge-Boudinot party reached Honey Creek in late November 1837.

Before they left Georgia, the Ridges had made arrangements for Sophia Sawyer to join them in the West, where she was to continue the children's education. Boudinot and Ridge had planned to meet her in New York City to discuss plans for her trip, but they were unable to make connections.[23] John Ridge wrote to her in the summer of 1837 and sent $150 for traveling expenses. The plan was for her to meet the Ridges at Creek Path or later at Nashville. She failed to do so, for a number of reasons. First, she was trying to arrange for publication of a book she was writing, "Lights and Shades of Indian Character in Thirteen Years' Residence among the Cherokees." She had met with potential publishers in New York, Philadelphia, and Washington. The book was important to her, and she wanted to make certain it would be published before she left for Honey Creek. At the time she was to depart, too, she had opened a school in Newark in which she taught young black women. She was no doubt reluctant to leave this work unfinished. Also, her best friend in the Cherokee Nation, Harriet Gold Boudinot, was now dead, and her husband had remarried. Harriet's presence in the western Cherokee Nation would have attracted her, but now she had one reason fewer to join the Ridges.[24] Finally, though, her loyalty and her promise to John Ridge made her pack up and leave for the West. In autumn 1837 Sawyer traveled by ship to New Orleans, where she boarded the steamboat *Little Rock*. The steamboat took her up the Mississippi and Arkansas rivers to New Dwight Mission, where she disembarked in December to find a party from Honey Creek waiting to escort her to the new Ridge farm.

The family was thriving in the new land. A house had been raised, along with appropriate outbuildings, and a farm had been cleared. John Ridge was determined to make the best of his new opportunity. He and his father entered into partnership and built a store, so as to set up trade with the Cherokee settlers arriving from Georgia. Ridge was concerned that the resettlement of the Nation go as peacefully as possible. In a letter dated January 16, 1838, he wrote to the United States commissioner Col. John Kennedy concerning emigrants who had left Georgia without receiving payments due them under the New Echota treaty. He mentioned that he had power of attorney for at least one of the emigrants, noting that he was eager to provide services to the new settlers in order to ensure the smoothest transition possible. In the same letter, he described his arrival at Honey Creek and his assessment of the new land. The letter was sent from Flint District, south of the Ridge landholdings.

> I arrived in this Nation on Honey Creek on the waters of the Grand [or Neosho] River in the latter part of November last and found my father and mother and all my friends there in good health. My friends who settled near the river Arkansas where springs are scarce have suffered with sickness and a number have died. In this District, Flint, is a fine region of country abounding in springs and water and the people are thickly settled and enjoying all the comforts of life. There is more sign of civilization and wealth than among the white people adjoining the Nation—But not withstanding all this, I like my part of the Nation much better—the country there is best adapted for agriculture and water privileges. It is superior to any country I ever saw in the U.S. Missouri, or that part which went to the Cherokees is populating very fast and in a few years it will be the garden spot of the U. States.[25]

Ridge mentioned Missouri, since his farm was on the Missouri–Cherokee Nation border. He went on to say that many of the newcomers were settling in Flint district, where they were being charged exorbitant prices for land by the Old Settlers, Cherokees already living in the area. He urged the government to "deliver" the emigrants farther north near Honey Creek, where the land was cheaper and richer. Like a one-man chamber of commerce, Ridge was trying to encourage settlement near his business operation for the benefit of both the emigrants and the Ridge store. At this point he had high hopes for an easy transition, since everything seemed to be working out according to plan. He closed his letter to Kennedy by saying, "Perfect friendship and contentedness prevail all over this land." This picture of Elysian quiet was soon to be shattered by the influx of Cherokees who had traveled the Trail of Tears.

Once Sophia Sawyer had arrived and gotten settled, the school was reopened for Rollin and the other children. At first classes were held in the house, but later the Ridges constructed a two-story building. The first floor was used as a school, and the upstairs provided living quarters for Sawyer and some female students. The teacher reported that the pupils at Honey Creek were so disparate in their levels of learning that she had to teach each one individually. However, she seemed to be happy there. With Sawyer in charge of the school and household and his brother-in-law George W. Paschal and his father minding the store, John Ridge was free to embark on a business trip. Most of the removed Cherokees had yet to arrive, but when they did, the Ridges knew, they would need provisions and supplies. In March, John and Sarah Ridge traveled to New Orleans, Pittsburgh, and New York to buy stock for the store. They also visited Sarah's family in South Lee, Massachusetts. Ridge became ill at South Lee and had to remain there when Sarah left for Honey Creek in the summer of 1838. He was to follow in September if his health improved. While in the East, John Ridge was disturbed by reports circulated by John Ross and John Howard Payne that the New Echota treaty and the subsequent removal from Georgia were the cause of all the Cherokees' troubles. Ridge wrote to eastern newspapers stating that removal was the only chance for the Cherokees to survive as a nation and that he believed the people would prosper in their new homeland. The bitter contention between the two factions at this point was manifested in a propaganda war; before long, the warfare was to become deadly.

Back together at Honey Creek in autumn 1838, the Ridge family continued to improve the farm and to trade with the settlers. The store was stocked with all the goods found in a typical general store, and its proprietors did a brisk trade. Payment was not always in cash, however, since many of the emigrants arrived without any funds. All the Cherokees were due to collect a per capita payment under the terms of the treaty, so the Ridges extended credit to everyone who needed it.[26] Most of these accounts, totaling $9,000 or $10,000, were never collected, but at the time, optimism reigned. The farm prospered, the store was busy, and the school was well attended. Miss Sophia had twenty-two students, including the Ridge children and Cherokee and black children from the surrounding area. Rollin, now eleven, spent much of his spare time astride his pony exploring the countryside. Always a bright student, he made progress in his studies and was often called upon to tutor younger or slower children. The enclave at Honey Creek was thus a busy and peaceful place until the main body of Cherokees began to arrive from Georgia.

The forced removal of the Cherokees known as the Trail of Tears is well documented. The number of emigrants who voluntarily moved to the West as the Ridges had done was disappointingly small to the federal officials in charge of the operation. Accordingly, they began to remove forcibly the Cherokee families who remained, beginning on June 6, 1838. The exodus continued during the summer and fall, and the first group to arrive in the Cherokee Nation got there in January 1839. For the next three months various parties straggled in, the last group arriving on March 25. From start to finish, it is estimated that four thousand Cherokees died, a fifth of the Nation. Many, victims of "the shock of the roundup, the tedium of the detention camps, and the miseries of the march," were women, children, and the aged.[27] John Ross's wife, Quatie, was among those who perished. Obviously, the resentment of those who had suffered and watched loved ones die had turned into a bitterness too deep to describe by the time they reached Indian Territory. This bitterness was not directed at the federal authorities responsible for the removal policy, nor at the individual officers and soldiers who had participated in the operation. It was aimed, rather, at those who had signed the treaty. As Dr. Elizur Butler, the missionary who had accompanied the Indians on their trek, put it, "*All* the suffering and *all* the difficulties of the Cherokee people [were] charge[d] to the account of Messrs. Ridge and Boudinot."[28] Finding the prosperous and happy settlement at Honey Creek no doubt added to their bitterness.

The two parties were to clash almost at once. When the Ridge party arrived, they had accepted the government in place, that of the Old Settler Cherokees. The newly arrived Ross faction, however, brought its own system of laws from the East and were resolved to put it into force. The already tense situation began to heat up. In May 1839 Sophia Sawyer wrote, "The critical situation of the nation I cannot communicate. It is such a time of excitement and I am always getting into trouble." Her troubles stemmed from her outspoken personality and her loyalty to the Ridges, whom she defended, especially to the missionaries who sided with the Ross party.[29] A series of political maneuvers took place, until John Ross suggested a council of all three parties to resolve the issue. The council was held, but for a number of reasons it did not reach an agreement. When the meeting was dissolved, a number of the Ross party men blamed the Ridges and Boudinot for its failure. This group held a secret meeting and decided that the signers of the treaty were to be assassinated. The justification for this decision was a provision of Cherokee law—one John Ridge helped frame in 1829—that anyone involved in the sale of Cherokee land without the sanction of the people would be put to death. The group assigned the executioners by drawing lots and then proceeded to lay plans.

Three execution squads set out on June 22, 1839, to carry out their missions. One group of twenty-five men approached John Ridge's house at dawn and surrounded it. Three men forced their way into the house and found Ridge in bed. They attempted to shoot him there, but a pistol misfired. The three then dragged the struggling Ridge through the house and out into the yard. The whole family by this time was aroused, including Rollin, who gives this account of what happened next:

Two men held him by the arms and others by the body, while
another stabbed him with a dirk twenty-nine times. My mother
rushed out to the door, but they pushed her back with their
guns into the house, and prevented her egress until their act
was finished.[30]

After severing his jugular vein, they threw Ridge into the air and let his
bleeding body crash to the earth. Then the men marched over their victim, stamping on him as they passed in single file.[31] Still Ridge was not
dead. Rollin continues his recollection of the incident, after the assassins
had left:

My mother ran out to him. He raised himself on his elbow and
tried to speak, but the blood flowed into his mouth and prevented him. In a few moments more he died, without speaking
that last word which he wished to say. Then succeeded a scene
of agony the sight of which might make one regret that the
human race had ever been created. It has darkened my mind
with an eternal shadow.[32]

Rollin goes on to describe his father's body, wrapped in a winding sheet
through which blood was oozing and dripping onto the floor:

By his side say my mother, with hands clasped, and in speech-
less agony—she had given him her heart in the days of her
youth and beauty, left the home of her parents, and followed
the husband of her choice to a wild and distant land. And bend-
ing over him was his own afflicted mother, with her long, white
hair flung loose over her shoulders and bosom, crying to the
Great Spirit to sustain her in that dreadful hour. And in addition to all these, the wife, the mother, and the little children,
who scarcely knew their loss, were the dark faces of those who
had been the murdered man's friends, and, possibly, some who
had been privy to the assassination, who had come to smile
over the scene.

John Rollin Ridge was to carry that image in his mind for the rest of his life.

But the bloodshed and violence did not end at Honey Creek. A second group of about thirty men approached Park Hill, the site of Samuel Worcester's mission, early in the morning. They hid in the woods near where Elias Boudinot was building a house. When Boudinot emerged from Worcester's house to talk to the men working on the new building, four of the band came out of the woods and asked for medicine for their sick relatives. As Boudinot was about to comply, one of the Cherokees stabbed him in the back. The victim fell to the ground, where another assassin split his skull with a tomahawk. Before the carpenters could come to Boudinot's rescue he was dead, and the killers had escaped.

Meanwhile a third party ambushed Major Ridge as he traveled down to Van Buren to see one of his slaves who was ill. The men lay in wait along the Line Road, a military track that ran along the Arkansas–Cherokee Nation boundary. About ten in the morning, Major Ridge and a young slave forded a creek along whose banks the several gunmen were hidden. They all fired at once, and Ridge was killed instantly. The slave rode away and carried the news to Dutch Mills, a nearby community. Stand Watie, Boudinot's brother, had also been a target, but he escaped when warned by a friendly Choctaw. Thus in one day the leaders of the Treaty party were eliminated by members of the Ross faction. The violent acts did little to settle the differences between the parties but instead increased the friction, since the avengers now became the targets of revenge. And nowhere was the desire for revenge greater than in the heart of twelve-year-old John Rollin Ridge.

3

The Arkansas Years

After the murder of Major Ridge and John Ridge, the family remained on the farm at Honey Creek for nearly a week, living in fear. In a letter to Secretary of War John C. Spencer, Sarah Ridge says that they expected "every night our sufferings would be terminated by assassination from the murderers of my husband."[1] To escape the threat of violence, the family moved to Fayetteville, Arkansas, some fifty miles away.

There was nothing to do but leave the farm with its livestock and produce. Sarah later recalled with some bitterness, "The Indians considered my property as public plunder and immediately commenced their depredations on whatever they could find. They destroyed or stole my poultry, killed my cattle and hogs, and not satisfied with camping by my fields and eating just what they wanted, they turned their horses into the fields, evidently designing to destroy all the corn in their power."[2]

The Ridge family, along with Sophia Sawyer, arrived in Fayetteville on July 1, 1839. A few months after their flight to Arkansas, Sophia Sawyer wrote her first report to Rev. David Greene, secretary of the American Board of Commissioners for Foreign Missions, in which she related the circumstances of the last days at Honey Creek:

October 11, 1839

Very Dear Friend,

I cannot address you, in these times of trial, in the cold business language of Sir: when no other human being will feel with us as you & I will in the relation you sustain toward me. I thank you for the letter of August which I received a few days since. In that you express uncertainty respecting our situation & offer your sympathy in several possible cases. For this we thank you & truly rejoice with you in one fact, that with Eternal Rectitude, all is safety & comfort.

You have possibly learned from other pens much that has transpired in this family. I left the Nation with Mrs. Ridge, the children & a part of the servants a few days after the murder of her husband. Mrs. Ridge was sustained under the overwhelming affliction, & had not an influence been exerted, by interested persons, to have her leave the nation, urging as reasons that herself & children were in danger, I should have succeeded in keeping the family & school together. This I did for several days after the Ridges' death: but when I saw her sinking under the weight of sorrow—fearful apprehensions & undecided anxieties—I consented to leave for this town as the nearest place of safety and accomodation. Here I have been since, doing, as it respects vigorous effort, what I could for her children & those associated with them.

The last favor I sought of Mr. Ridge was his influence to prevent any among 36 of my pupils attending a *show,* which I knew would exert a bad moral influence, this he granted solely to gratify me two days before his death, & not a pupil was absent except for sickness during the scene which was passing at the store. My wants and wishes were consulted before he left for New York, & that evening before he was killed I saw & received the globe and books, & the last words he spoke to me amidst the crowd of business & people were to enquire if the books &c were such as I wished.

We returned to the dwelling house. The girls & myself took an early supper, & went to our house beyond the shrieks of the murdered, which, before the dawn, were to fill with unutterable woe the peaceful dwelling that we left at evening.[3]

In December, Rollin wrote to David Greene and described the family's situation:

We came to Fayetteville on account of my father's death. When he was killed my mother was so distressed that some of us were fearful that she would not live under it. She heard so much about the nation while she was there, which distressed her that she was obliged to come away. Since we have been here mama went to the nation to see my cousins and aunt before they started to the east. [Ridge is referring to Delight Sargent and the Boudinot children.] When she came back, she fell sick, and was not able to walk about the room. Two Physicians attended on her, and she is now getting better. I think she will soon be well. I do not know much about the nation, but I think it is in a confused state. Gen. Arbuckle the commander at Fort Gibson is trying to take the murderers, but I do not think he will make out because it neeeds a more energetic man than he is to perform it.[4]

Although he professes to know little about Cherokee affairs, in fact Rollin kept abreast of the latest news from the continuing clash between the Ross and Ridge factions and held very strong opinions on most issues. Rollin then goes on to describe the school Sophia Sawyer had set up in Fayetteville:

Miss Sawyer has a school in this town. She has about thirty scholars, the most of whom are boys. My sister, brothers, and myself are going to her school. I have gone through Ancient Geography and the Ancient History of Greece. I am now going over Modern Geography again, and I am studying Arithmetic

and deffinitions [*sic*] and we have paid some attention to grammar. I am learning to play on the flute. My sister studies Modern Geography, Arithmetic, and deffinitions.

Ridge describes his music teacher, a Mr. Rittig, from "the higher
class in Germany," and Rittig's wife, a painter and art teacher from the
same class in Switzerland. It is not known whose assessment of social
status this is, Rollin's, Sawyer's, or the Rittigs'. Young Ridge continues
his narrative by telling Greene about Fayetteville, a place where "the
people sometimes fight with knives and pistols, and some men have
been killed here, but the people do not seem to mind it much." He then
goes on to describe the countryside and the many types of animals that
inhabit the mountains and plateaus of the area.

By this time, Sarah, Suzanna, and the children had moved into a
house at the corner of Locust and Center, having purchased all of block
18, lots 1, 2, 3, and 4.[5] John Ridge had died without a will and left behind a large estate, "consisting of Slaves, Stock and other personal property."[6] The estate was not settled until 1847, however, partly because of
the unsettled state of Cherokee affairs. Some of the estate consisted of
money awarded the Ridge family by article 6 of the treaty of 1846. The
part of this award that was to go to Sarah Ridge and her children was
challenged by George W. Paschal and his wife, the former Sally Ridge,
sister of John Ridge, which further delayed the settling of the estate. The
situation complicated the family's finances during Rollin's teen years,
and funds were often short. After a financially secure childhood, Rollin
spent much of the rest of his life working for and dreaming about a
revival of the Ridge family's prosperity.

Rollin's years in Arkansas were important ones. It was here that he
received most of his formal education, studying under Sophia Sawyer
and later Cephas Washburn. He lived in Washington and Benton counties in Arkansas, whose western borders abutted the Cherokee Nation.
From this vantage point, Rollin was able to view the turmoil within the
Nation and on its borders during the early 1840s. The strife among the
Cherokee factions did much to shape young Ridge's political views as

well as to increase his bitterness against members of the Ross party. Both
were important factors in his later life. His Arkansas border years were
important from other standpoints too: it was in Fayetteville that he met
his wife, Elizabeth Wilson, and it was in Arkansas that he began to write
and publish his prose and poetry.

Soon after her arrival in Fayetteville, Sophia Sawyer decided to
found a school, which later became the Fayetteville Female Seminary,
one of the most respected institutions of learning in the early history
of Arkansas. Carolyn Thomas Foreman offers an account of the school
reprinted from an old scrapbook:

> She began teaching in a small log hut in this town, and there
> were those of our citizens who will remember as they passed
> the school that it presented a marked difference from other
> schools over the country at that early date, but the energy and
> perseverance of Miss Sawyer soon raised it from its obscurity
> and it rose steadily and successfully until it took its rank at the
> head of all female institutions in Arkansas. Viewing the whole
> course of Miss Sawyer's life we cannot withhold admiration for
> her marked characteristics of zeal, energy . . . in the cause of
> education."[7]

In January 1841 Rollin left Sawyer's school along with his brothers
Aeneas and Herman to enroll in a male academy opened by a Mr. Scull,
an Episcopalian minister. His brother Andrew Jackson and his sister
Susan remained with Miss Sawyer. Rollin's relationship with Sophia was
not severed completely, however, In a January 4, 1842, letter to David
Greene, she reports from Van Buren, Arkansas, that she has traveled
there on a short vacation accompanied by Rollin.[8]

In the fall of 1843, Sarah Ridge had decided to send her son Rollin
to the East to continue his education. He enrolled at Great Barrington Academy in Great Barrington, Massachusetts, where he stayed until
1845.[9] The school was begun in 1842 by an association of citizens of the
town and placed under the supervision of James Sedgwick.[10]

While at Great Barrington, Rollin wrote to his uncle Stand Watie in

1844 expressing his ideas on the current state of Cherokee affairs. The letter also reveals Ridge's physical condition and his scholarly activities at the school. (The original letter contains several holes, so a few words are left out. In some sections it is possible to conjecture about what is missing; in these cases words have been supplied, followed by a question mark.) He has this to say on the subject of revenge:

> I heard some time since that you had killed James Foreman, but did not know it to be true until I recd a paper from Arkansas [the *Intelligencer*] stating all the circumstances of his death. You cannot imagine what feelings of pleasure it gave me when I heard of the death of him who was the murderer of my venerable and beloved Grandfather. Although I have always been taught never to harbour feelings of revenge it is impossible for me to control them and it always [missing section] and will give me pleasure to hear of the death of the [murderers?] of my relations. If there is no law in a Nation to [missing section] those who take the lives of their fellow men it [is impos?]sible to have justice done . . . unless it is [missing section] ties of kindred blood to the slain.[11]

This is the first indication we have of the firmly established thirst for revenge that John Rollin Ridge felt toward the assassins, and he made similar statements for the rest of his life. The youngster then goes on to comment on the reaction in the East to the Cherokee situation. His report is similar to the one he sent from Missouri seven years later:

> Every [section missing] have seen in this country feel and say that the treaty [men?] have been basely and meanly treated and that in the death of the treaty men the Cherokees lost their best friends. Everywhere I go I have the sympathy of all as soon as I am known as the son of Jno. Ridge. The people here are all friendly to the Indians and feel for their woes.

His hatred for John Ross, whom he always blamed for his father's, grandfather's, and uncle's deaths, comes through in another passage:

I have read a great deal in the papers about the frauds among the Cherokees and have always thought that the money has been in the hands of Ross. I am glad to hear that it is so well known that the money has been drawn by Ross because his character will perhaps be hereafter understood. I fear though very much that when he comes back to the Nation his good tales will influence the people more than their own judgment. I have been anxious for your safety since the death of James Foreman, the Ross party being so strong. I hope you will not be taken by that party for neither law nor justice would save you from the death they so unjustly wish you to die.

Young Rollin Ridge here is writing about two of his favorite subjects: politics and money. It is fair to say that he was passionate about both. For a boy of fifteen several hundred miles from home, he was remarkably well informed about political happenings in the Cherokee Nation. And money, or more precisely the lack thereof, was a major concern after the death of his father left the family's affairs in disarray.

In the letter's final paragraph, Ridge describes his life at school:

You have heard from Ma [section missing] all about my situation here, which is certainly pleasant [section missing] -perous. For a few days since we have had pretty cool [weather?] and I have begun to wonder how I shall stand the [winter?]. I feel now very homesick and I know that [if I ever?] get home again I shall want to stay there. I have had a very bad cold for about a week and am just now getting well. I left school on account of that cold but have now commenced again and am doing well with my studies. I declaim and read composition every Saturday and I like it very much. I receive the praise of the teacher for my progress in Latin, but I do not improve as fast as I wish to. I intend to and do persevere for there is nothing like it.

Apparently Rollin's stay at the Massachusetts school had the support of his mother's family in the East. Indeed, it was no accident that

Sarah Ridge sent her son to Great Barrington Academy, for it was only twelve miles from South Lee, Massachusetts, where her parents lived. Doubtless Mr. and Mrs. Northrup had a hand in choosing that particular school. The proximity of his grandparents was a major factor in the decision, but there were others. Cornwall, the site of his father's old school and the former home of Rollin's mother, lies only thirty miles south of Great Barrington. The landscape in the area probably was a factor too. The low mountains, secluded valleys, and numerous clear streams of the region are very similar to those in northwestern Arkansas and northeastern Oklahoma and, for that matter, to those in the old Cherokee Nation in Georgia.

In Arkansas, Cephas Washburn was teaching at a school in Mount Comfort, near Fayetteville, when Rollin returned from Great Barrington.[12] The missionary-teacher had come to Arkansas from the Cherokee Nation in the East twenty-odd years earlier. In November 1819 Washburn had set out for the West from Brainerd Mission in the Cherokee Nation, with his brother-in-law Alfred Finney. Earlier, a number of Cherokees had left their lands in the Cherokee Nation and emigrated to Arkansas for a variety of reasons, the chief one being the federal government's policy of encouraging removal. Washburn's assignment was to set up a mission among the Cherokee settlers in the West and to provide for their religious and educational needs. His efforts were part of the expansion of missions to the Indians of the Southeast by the American Board of Commissioners for Foreign Missions, which was outlined in chapter 1. Specifically, Washburn's assignment resulted from a request for a mission in the West that a chief of the Arkansas Cherokees, Tolunskee or Tollontiskee, made while on a visit to Brainerd Mission to see the treasurer of the ABCFM, Jeremiah Evarts. By January 1820 Washburn and Finney reached Elliot Mission in Mississippi. After a brief stay they traveled on to Vicksburg, then up the Mississippi and Arkansas rivers to Arkansas Post. They then continued up the Arkansas River to Little Rock, Cadron, and Dardanelle before landing near present-day Russellville in Pope County, Arkansas. In August Washburn and Finney attended a council of Cherokees who lived in the area. After explaining that they had come to Arkansas because of Tolunskee's request, the two men outlined their plans. The Indians reportedly approved of the establishment of the mission and gave the missionaries leave to choose a location for it. Washburn and Finney then erected Dwight Mission four miles north of the Arkansas River on the west side of Illinois Creek.[13] Washburn established a school at Dwight Mission (named for Timothy Dwight, president of Yale University) and remained there until 1828, when he moved west to New Dwight Mission in Indian Territory. After the Cherokee removal to Indian Territory, Dwight Mission School was continued as a school for white children. By 1835 Washburn had settled in the area of Fayetteville, Arkansas, where he continued his religious activities and taught in various schools.

Washburn began teaching at Mount Comfort in the old church there about 1842 with Robert Mecklin, who later founded Ozark Institute.[14] Washburn's curriculum there seemed to follow the general lines of the earlier school at Dwight Mission, providing a mix of academic and practical training. It was here at Mount Comfort that Rollin received much of his education in classical languages and literature. At this same time, Washburn was planning to expand his Mount Comfort school by establishing the Far West Seminary, which was supposed to be the first college-level institution in Arkansas.[15] The plans made for the seminary provide insight into Washburn's educational philosophy and practice and thus give an idea of the kind of training John Rollin Ridge received while under Washburn's tutelage.

Washburn, along with George W. Paschal, Alfred W. Arrington, Robert W. Mecklin, and Isaac Strain sat on a committee of the proposed institution's Board of Visitors and Trustees that was appointed to "prepare an Address, setting forth the claims of 'The Far West Seminary,' to the citizens of Arkansas, and the liberal philanthropists everywhere.[16] The address had been adopted at a board meeting held November 20, 1843, and was subsequently published as a report entitled "To the Public" in the Little Rock *Arkansas Gazette*. It begins by establishing some general principles:

1. The Bible is to be the standard of morals and Religion.

2. The Institution is never, in all future time, to possess a sectarian character in Religion, or a party character in politics.

3. No person will be allowed to hold the office of President or Professor, who does not maintain a good moral and christian character, though it is not required that they be of any particular christian sect.

4. The great distinctive principles of civil and religious liberty, on which depends the durability of our Republican Institutions, shall be carefully inculcated.

5. In addition to the usual degrees for Academic attainments, an honorary premium shall be conferred upon such students as shall have attended scientifically to Agriculture or the Mechanic Arts, and shall have acquired a practical knowledge of Agriculture or some one of the Mechanic Arts.[17]

The statements on religious liberty and nonsectarianism seem a bit odd, since they are followed later in the report by a warning against the dangers of Roman Catholic education, described as "dangerous strides of Popish and Jesuitical influence." The seminary founders commented on their specific problem:

We are particularly zealous for the success of the project [the Far West Seminary], because a Catholic priest has just come into the country for the purpose of building a Catholic College and establishing a Catholic colony. We are afraid he will impose with the pomp, and ceremonies of his church on the too credulous minds of the ignorant population and we want our Seminary to be a counteracting influence on the intellect of the young and growing generation.

The intention to teach agriculture and "the Mechanic Arts" in addition to the regular academic subjects was in keeping with the curriculum taught in many mission-related schools. The emphasis on vocational training continues in Indian education to the present day.

The practical emphasis did not overshadow academics in the minds of the seminary's founders, however, The report goes on to point out the importance of the traditional liberal arts:

> The civil, social, and moral prosperity of every country depends, in a great measure, upon the intellectual standard of those who pursue the liberal professions. In a Republican Government, where the equality of man is acknowledged—and where the art of War is regarded as one of the evils of the want of perfect civilization, the only road opened to a laudable ambition, lies in the path of letters, attainments of literature, or the acquisitions of science. Our physicians, our lawyers, our theologians, our editors, and our teachers, should be men of liberal education.

John Rollin Ridge came under the influence of such thinking during his adolescence and early manhood. It is not surprising, then, that he pursued a liberal education—the study of Latin and Greek, English literature, and later the law—in a frontier town in the Ozark Mountains. Nor is it surprising, given this influence and this education, that later in life he demonstrated a love of literature and spoke out for what he regarded as democratic ideals.

Washburn and his colleagues saw the necessity and even urgency of establishing an institution of higher learning in that remote area:

> In countries where the means of public or private instruction—of education, through the instrumentality of schools or self-culture, are placed within the reach of every ambitious youth, ardently desiring the lights of science or the pleasures of literature, the patrons of learning may pause and discuss the most appropriate means of promoting the great ends of diffusing universal intelligence. But the situation of those who appeal to the liberality of a generous public in behalf of the "FAR WEST SEMINARY," is altogether different. While we pause, and coldly calculate the merits of this or that plan, our youth

mentally perish. They grow up without the general diffusion of that knowledge which endears the institutions of their country to their minds, and prepares them for the spontaneous defence of the valuable inheritance of civil liberty—that liberty transmitted to them by a glorious and immortal ancestry. But place the means of a liberal and enlightened education within reach of the youths of our country, and the same bold spirit which has caused the hardy pioneers of our western borders to forsake the ease and indulgence of more refined society, and brook the hardships and difficulties of a new settlement, will induce their children to master and overcome every obstacle which conceals truth beneath the most difficult and abstruse science.[18]

To the seminary's founders, then, the very preservation of the republic depended on education, especially "a liberal and enlightened" one. Education, furthermore, was to be provided not just for the white sons and daughters of "the hardy pioneers," but for the children of the Indians, including those settlers who had come west from Tennessee and Georgia:

We regard it as not among the least interesting features of our college effort, that its location is in the vicinity of the Indian country. It is a most interesting fact, that the tribes immediately contiguous to our State, are making most laudable efforts for the diffusion of education among themselves; and they will no doubt be liberal patrons of literary institutions, located so near to them as to afford the facilities of a classical education to their sons. The uniting the youth of both races, the white and the red, in the same pursuits, and in the same seminaries, must have the happiest influence.[19]

This avowed belief by Washburn and his colleagues in equal educational opportunity for Indians and whites enabled John Rollin Ridge and others to attain a level of learning not afforded children in Indian schools in the decades to follow. Washburn, of course, had long been familiar with Indian education in both theory and practice. It is appropriate, then, that the Far West report, which he played a major role in preparing, contains a statement on his philosophy of Indian education. This statement may in fact be seen as a précis of the assimilationist ideas espoused by many of those involved in Indian schools at the time:

> It is now an universally admitted fact, that the Indian cannot be preserved in his savage state. He should not be if he could. His pursuits of the forest and the chase must be exchanged for the mantle of civilization. His manners, his customs, his superstitions and his language, must be exchanged for the pursuits of industry, the habits of the white man, and the faith of the christian. And as they can never become independent Governments they must of course be mingled with the mighty power of the United States. Within thirty years the Indian line has receded a thousand miles. Neglect their moral culture half a century longer, and the last of their warriors would find a grave on the shores of the Pacific. Our brethren in the eastern country have thrown them on our western borders. While many of them are partially civilized, yet many more retain their savage habits. The safety of our people demands their civilization.[20]

Although the latter part of the statement suggests less than purely altruistic motives for educating Indian youth, Rollin Ridge, by all accounts, received an excellent education at Mount Comfort under Cephas Washburn. Ridge studied there until 1845.

The Far West Seminary, chartered by the Arkansas legislature on November 30, 1844, never got a chance to operate in the new building being erected for it on donated land. The building was destroyed by fire on February 27, 1845, after which Washburn sold his interest in the school to Robert Mecklin.[21] Mecklin went on to establish Ozark Institute at the Far West site.[22]

In 1845 or 1846 Rollin began his study of the law at Fayetteville, but as always since the assassination of his father, grandfather, and uncle, his mind was very much on Cherokee affairs and on revenge. On April 14,

1846, he wrote to Stand Watie, who was in Washington trying to negotiate a settlement between the Ross faction and the Treaty party of Cherokees:

> Dear Cousin Stand:
>
> A number of weeks have passed since you left for Washington, and as I know from the papers that you have arrived at that city, I wish to write to you and request all the information you have on hand with regard to Cherokee interests.
>
> No very important transactions have happened since your departure, except the killing of five or six Indians of the Ross party, including Old Ta-ka-to-ka, by Tom Starr and his confederates. Caleb Duncan was way-laid, a short time ago, by several of the Wards who snapped a pistol three times at them; when about to be surrounded, he wheeled his horse and escaped by flight.
>
> I have been in town here ever since you left pursuing the study of Law and will remain for a considerable while, so when you write, as I hope you will do immediately, please direct to this place. One thing in particular I wish to know, and that is, when (if ever) John Ross designs to return, and by what rout [*sic*] he will probably come. A great degree of interest is manifested here concerning him and I desire to be acquainted with his movements on our particular account, which, when summed up and determined, will satisfy me.[23]

A few days later Rollin wrote Watie another letter in which he continues to reveal his own state of mind as well as convey news of events on the Cherokee border:

> Dear Cousin Stand:
>
> I wrote you only a few days ago, and told you all that I desired to say, except of an article which I wish extremely that you would get for me, that is a Bowie knife. I would like one not very large, nor very small, but rather small than large. You

would oblige me very much by doing so. I would ask Paschal
but I know he would not be willing to do me that much favor.
I heard from your family a short time since and they were all
well. I saw a man this morning from Boonsboro who had seen
Tom Starr and Sam'l McDaniels they were in fine health and
spirits. Those fellows, especially Tom Starr, are talked of frequently and with wonderment about here. He is considered a
second Rinaldo Rinaldini.[24] Robberies, Housetrimmings, and
all sorts of romantic deeds are attributed to this fellow, and the
white people in town and around say they had rather meet the
devil himself than Tom Starr!

> I must reiterate my request for you to write soon and often.
> Your sincere friend and Cousin
> John R. Ridge[25]

The situation among the Cherokees after the 1839 assassinations
was often desperate; at times virtual civil war was waged between the
followers of John Ross and the proremoval group, also known as the
Ridge-Watie-Boudinot faction or the Treaty party. The latter were often
allied with the Old Settlers, those who had emigrated to Arkansas and
the Cherokee Nation before removal, against the larger Ross faction.
Many in the Treaty party were forced, like Rollin's family, to leave their
homes in Indian Territory and move to Arkansas or elsewhere. Elias
Boudinot's family, for example, moved to the East because of fears similar to those expressed by Sarah Ridge in her letter to the secretary of
war. The hostilities, often complicated by the actions of the army or
the government, continued until 1846, when a compromise was reached
among the three Cherokee groups and a treaty was signed.

Immediately after the assassinations in the summer of 1839, the
leaders of the two factions, Stand Watie, brother of Elias Boudinot
and nephew of John Ridge, and John Ross, the man who allegedly
ordered the murders, surrounded themselves with armed men for protection. Watie, as the only remaining prominent member of the Treaty
party, feared further assassination attempts. Ross was warned by his

followers that Watie might attempt a reprisal. Eventually, five hundred men were gathered to protect John Ross.[26] General Matthew Arbuckle, United States military commander for the region, invited Ross and the leaders of the other faction to his headquarters at Fort Gibson. Ross refused to come, saying that for his own safety he could not travel without his guards and that the movement of such a large group of armed men would incite further violence. He suggested that Arbuckle and the other Cherokee leaders attend a meeting at his home. His invitation was turned down.

Earlier, Ross had called a meeting of all Cherokees to be held at the Illinois Camp Ground on July 1, 1839. Watie and his followers as well as most of the Old Settlers refused to attend, but the convention was held anyway. One of the first items of business was a declaration of amnesty for all crimes committed since the Ross faction arrived in the West. This action effectively granted pardons to the men who had killed Boudinot and the Ridges. At the same time, the convention declared all signers of the Treaty of New Echota to be outlaws, including the men already murdered (or "executed," according to most followers of Ross). However, an offer of amnesty was extended to the "outlaws" if they would appear before the convention and admit their guilt. Naturally most of the signers refused, including Watie and John A. Bell, who explained their position in a letter to the *Arkansas Gazette*. The two men probably spoke for most of the Treaty party when they wrote that they would rather die than accept Ross's terms for amnesty.[27]

The convention went on to adopt an Act of Union and a constitution for the entire Nation that generally followed the proposals Ross had made previously for the government of the Cherokees. Meanwhile the Old Settler Chief John Brown called a meeting of his group and the Treaty people for July 22, 1839. Ross attempted to send copies of the act and constitution to this convention, but the messenger was turned away. Still another meeting was held by the anti-Ross forces at Price's Prairie on August 21. Here it was decided to send Stand Watie and John Bell to Washington to seek the federal government's aid in punishing the assassins and protecting members of the anti-Ross group. Eventually General

Arbuckle, acting on a request by the commissioner of Indian affairs, dispatched troops to identify and arrest the assassins. The troops, guided through the nation by Treaty party Cherokees, only contributed to the general tension, and no arrests were made. Even though Arbuckle had a list of the accused—James Foreman, two men named Springston, James and Jefferson Hair, and Bird Doublehead—these men were protected by Ross's guard and were never apprehended.[28]

In January 1840 Watie, Bell, and William Rogers, a member of the Old Settlers group, declared to Secretary of War Joel Poinsett in Washington that the Cherokee parties could no longer live together in peace. They proposed that the Cherokee Nation be divided, with the Ross faction occupying one area and the Old Settlers and Treaty party another. Each would be politically autonomous. Meanwhile, back in the Cherokee Nation, Arbuckle was continuing his efforts to mediate between the two groups. He was largely unsuccessful, since each group was reluctant to give in to the other. In April, however, the commissioner of Indian affairs T. Hartley Crawford informed Arbuckle of the proposal to divide the Nation's land and annuities. When Arbuckle put this prospect to the negotiators, he began to get concessions from both sides. On June 26, 1840, an Act of Union was signed, and all the Cherokees agreed to accept the constitution of September 6, 1839.[29]

Despite these political agreements, the bitterness in the Cherokee Nation continued for many years. What one writer has called "a Corsican vendetta" developed between the Ross and Ridge factions,[30] and the violence continued. Watie himself was involved, and in 1842 he killed James Foreman, one of Ross's followers who had bragged about ambushing Major Ridge. Watie was tried for murder in Arkansas, where the event took place, but was acquitted on grounds of self-defense.[31] In 1845 the Nation was particularly violent. James Starr was killed by a mob, and Stand Watie's brother Thomas was killed in his bed by a group of men. Starr's son Tom, mentioned by Rollin in his 1846 letters to Watie, wreaked his revenge on the Ross faction while Watie gathered his forces at Old Fort Wayne on the Illinois River. Here Watie collected guns and ammunition and vowed revenge for his brother's death. Arbuckle dispatched troops to the fort, but since Watie remained in a defensive position, the army took no action. Many people sympathetic to the pro-removal cause joined Watie at Old Fort Wayne, and others left their homes in the Cherokee Nation for Arkansas and other areas. Whites in Arkansas urged the government to take action to end the violence as the situation continued to worsen.

In January 1846 the group at Old Fort Wayne, renamed Fort Watie by this time, resolved to send a delegation to Washington, again urging division of the Nation. In March Watie and five others left for the capital, where John Ross was already conferring with government officials. During the winter and spring of 1846 the violence continued, with frequent raids and killings carried out by both sides. A letter from Watie's wife to her brother describes the situation:

I have nothing worth much to say the police [of the Ross faction] have taken David Nightkiller and run Eli Raper off and several others. I have not heard what they have done with david and them but there is no doubt but what they will either whip or hang him. Several have run over the line for reffuge. Walter Ridge has just come in from honey creek. he says John Watie has collected his men to gether again and is now building a fort at hiliard Rogers place. I wonder what they will do next I expect they all be scalped before long. I have not heard of the Starr boys in some time but I rather think that Joseph Raper has gone to flint to joine them but this is only a thought of my owne that boy that they whipped for steeling is dead. I have not seen the last cherokee advocate but I have heard people say that it implicated Joseph Lynch and James Clem Thompson in the burning of Megs house but you know that wont do they hung Wheeler Faught for having a hand in killing Stand Dority they say he made a long confession but I do not know what it was.[32]

Finally President James K. Polk introduced a bill into the House of Representatives that provided for the division of the Cherokee Nation.

Although the bill was eventually defeated, the furor it caused led to an investigation into Cherokee affairs by a government commission. This group drew up a treaty that was signed by Watie, Ross, and representatives of the Old Settlers. The Cherokee treaty of 1846 was approved by the United States Senate on August 8 and ratified by the president on August 17. One of its provisions was that $5,000 was to be paid to Major Ridge's heirs and $10,000 to the heirs of John Ridge and Elias Boudinot.

The extent and nature of John Rollin Ridge's participation in the events leading up to the treaty are not easy to determine because we lack hard evidence. David Farmer and Rennard Strickland report that "Ridge remembered his teenage years as a time of hard riding back and forth across the Cherokee-Arkansas border, participating in the skirmishes and guerrilla warfare of the continuing Ross-Ridge vendetta." They go on to say, however, "How much of this actually occurred and how much Ridge only dreamed we do not know." Franklin Walker, another of Ridge's biographers, says that "he returned to Indian Territory and allied himself with James Starr, who was leading a guerrilla war against the Ross faction."[33] In the autobiographical account published in the posthumous volume of his poems, the section covering the years 1845 and 1846 has been omitted and the following editorial comment inserted, presumably by Elizabeth Ridge: "Here follows a history of Cherokee affairs, embracing the years 1845 and '46, and Mr. Ridge's connection therewith, which we think proper to omit."[34]

Although it is uncertain whether Rollin participated in the skirmishes between the Cherokee factions in any active way, it is clear that he used his language skills to further the Ridge party's cause. By August 1846 he had left Fayetteville and was once more living at Honey Creek. In a letter to the *Arkansas Gazette* dated August 6, 1846, he takes to task the Ross government in the Cherokee Nation, calling it a "perfect military despotism" rather than a "civil association" or a "municipal organization." His studies had him thinking about the legal implications of the division between the Cherokee factions. He attacks Ross's authority, saying he was not elected by all members of the Nation:

They [the Ridge party, after the deaths of the Ridges and
Boudinot] wished for a regular election, and so I believe would
the majority of the nation, had they not been cowed down
into silence and submission by the intimidation of Ross and
his brethren in blood. What was the consequence that followed
the expression of this wish? The formation of bands to go over
the country and murder every individual who entertained an
opinion different from that of John Ross, and his now growing faction! . . . No man who has not lived in this nation can
appreciate the cruelty of some acts which have been committed
under the direction of this bloodthirsty establishment. . . . It
is in vain to talk of the arts and sciences flourishing among us;
they are confined to the few, and under this state of things will
always remain so. It is in vain to talk of schools, or of any other
civil institution, when the whole country is under the law of
the sword, and that wielded by the relentless hand of one man.

Whatever his role in the hostilities of 1845–46, it is difficult to
overestimate the impact on young Ridge of the events in the Cherokee
Nation and in western Arkansas during his formative years, events in
which his family was directly involved. The trauma that must have been
inflicted by witnessing the brutal murder of his father would itself have
instilled a sense of revenge in the boy. But the prolonged struggle between his family and friends and their enemies doubtless fueled the smol-
dering fire and explains his request for a Bowie knife, his half-formulated
plan to ambush John Ross, and his exuberance over the terrorist acts of
Tom Starr.

With the Cherokee treaty of 1846 enacted, however, Rollin's prospects seemed brighter. Because of the promise of his share of the pro-
ceeds from the treaty, he was able to purchase a farm at the family
settlement at Honey Creek. His financial future seemed more secure,
too, since his father's estate was finally being settled in the courts. At
age nineteen Rollin was a confident young man. "I look forward to the
future with hope and pride," he wrote to Stand Watie in 1846. At this

time, too, he had his eye on "a prettily shaped girl, of about 16 or 17 years, who is very friendly and gives me a quantity of enjoyment in her company."[35] The girl may have been Elizabeth Wilson, Rollin's future wife, although about this time he also was attracted to a daughter of Cephas Washburn, according to Mabel Washbourne Anderson.[36] But Ridge always had an eye for the ladies, so he may have admired both.

Just as his prospects seemed brightest, another thundercloud loomed. On November 28, 1846, John Rollin Ridge wrote to William Medill, commissioner of Indian affairs, on behalf of his mother, Sarah, and his brothers and sisters, Clarinda, Susan, Herman, Aeneas, Andrew Jackson, and Flora. The letter asked for the payment of funds provided for in the 1846 treaty and expressed concern about possible attempts to defraud the Ridges:

> Believing that justice is aimed at by your Gov in all its con-
> cerns with us: and knowing too that efforts will most probably
> be made by persons this side the Mississippi River to defraud
> us even of this donation, under specious pretences, we have
> concluded to protest against the payment of the above Five
> Thousand Dollars to any individual whatever, except ourselves,
> or an attorney, who is fully and carefully furnished with all the
> powers of attorney as required by the law of Congress on that
> subject—not, that we would intimate a disobedience to that
> law by an officer of the U.S. Government knowingly; but there
> exist various methods by which a dishonest individual might
> very easily evade both law and justice in regard to the rights of
> a widow and orphans.[37]

The "dishonest individual" Ridge referred to was George W. Paschal, a lawyer married to Sally Ridge, Rollin's aunt. Paschal wrote to Medill on May 18, 1847, asking that a guardianship be set up for all the Ridge children, including Rollin, who had not yet reached his majority. On May 27 Josiah Woodward Washbourne, attorney for the Ridge heirs, husband of Susan Ridge and son of Cephas Washburn (the son changed the spelling of the name), wrote to the commissioner on behalf of the family, asking for their share of the treaty money. He also asked to be notified of Paschal's "demands" of the government and informed Medill of Paschal's maneuvers back in Arkansas:

> *Judge* G. W. Paschal has sued the heirs of John Ridge for every-thing they have on earth on the grounds that Mrs. Sarah B. N. Ridge "being a white lady and having no 'clan' her children are not the heirs of their father, but that himself and his wife are, because the latter was John Ridge's sister. He is now gone, I understand, to procure the whole of the $10,000 allowed by Treaty to the Ridges and will no doubt set before you much *false* evidence of his rights. I most solemnly declare him to be a swindler and a scoundrel in his attempts thus to defraud the heirs of John Ridge.[38]

Rollin doubtless was still confident about his future in spite of recent complications, because in May 1847 he and Elizabeth Wilson were married in the Cherokee Nation. Rollin and "Lizzie," a white woman from Fayetteville, Arkansas, settled down on their new farm. In June Washbourne again wrote to Medill, reiterating the Ridge heirs' claims and providing further documentation. His letter alludes to an enclosure written by Rollin and adds Washbourne's own comments on Ridge's situation:

> Document, marked "Letter I" is a letter from John Rollin Ridge requesting that his portion of money be paid to him at once as but a few months will intervene ere he be of age. His letter bears evidence to all, that if not "of age," Mr. Ridge has come to years when he can manage for himself. He has finished his education, has lately married, bought him a farm in this state (to be paid out of this money) and he is subject to procure money by paying the highest rates of interest.[39]

The treaty money was tied up for some years, but at least John Ridge's personal estate had finally been settled on May 21, 1847. It was entered in chancery court in Benton County, Arkansas, in May 1845.

Rollin's share consisted of two slaves, Simon and Grigg, "and also ten dollars in hogs, one yoke of oxen, four cows, one colt and wagon & etc."[40] Elizabeth and Rollin settled down at Honey Creek, and their only child, Alice, was born there in 1848. Little is known about their life for the next two years except that Rollin began to write for area newspapers; several of his poems, published under the pen name Yellowbird, appeared in Arkansas and Texas newspapers at this time, as did some articles on Cherokee politics and history. In a piece published in the Clarksville, Texas, *Northern Standard*, he proposed that the Cherokees be admitted to the Union as a separate state.

Poetry written around this time included love poems and conventional pieces dealing with nature. Examples are "An October Morn" and "To a Mockingbird Singing in a Tree," both imitative of the romantic style then in vogue. But it is clear that he also was thinking about the fate of the Indian peoples in the ever-changing modern world. In a poem dated July 18, 1847, he seems to say that the old Indian cultures, however noble and appealing, are gone forever. In their place have risen the modern cities of the progressive white society. This untitled poem, which begins "Far in a lonely wood I wandered once," does not appear in the 1868 edition of his poems. It describes the thoughts of a solitary walker in the woods who happens upon an Indian grave. He remembers

> That many years ago a noble race
> Had roamed these forest-wilds among and made
> These mountain-fastnesses rebound to shouts
> Of liberty untamed and happiness
> That knew no bounds.
>
> (Lines 16–20)

Though such an existence is attractive, it is no longer possible in the modern world:

> A thousand cities
> Stand, where once thy nation's wigwam stood,

And numerous palaces of giant strength
Are floating down the streams where long ago
Thy bark was gliding. All is changed.

(Lines 49–53)

The poem closes with a wish for eternal peace for the dead warrior.

The ideas expressed in both the poetry and the prose Ridge wrote during this period seem to follow closely those held by his late father. John Ridge had advocated that the Cherokees leave their old ways and adapt to the dominant white society. He had insisted that the Indians provide an "English" education for their children, and he predicted that someday an Indian state would be admitted to the Union. These opinions were shared by the younger Ridge, who seemed determined to live the life of a successful planter and stockman. He emulated his white neighbors even to using black slaves on his farm. For Rollin and Lizzie, settled in the verdant, rolling countryside along Honey Creek, the future looked bright.

Then in 1849 an event took place that was to shatter the young couple's dreams. During an argument, Rollin killed a neighbor, a pro-Ross man named David Kell. The incident, as reported by area newspapers, took place when Ridge confronted Kell at the man's farm and asked if he had seen Ridge's missing stallion. Kell reportedly replied, "What, do you mean that gelding over there?" and gestured toward Ridge's horse, still bleeding, which was standing nearby. An argument ensued during which Kell advanced threateningly toward Ridge. After warning the larger man to keep away, Ridge drew his pistol and killed him.[41] Fearing that he would not receive a fair trial in the Cherokee Nation, which was controlled politically by Ross and his followers, Ridge fled over the Missouri line, just a couple of miles from his farm. Later it was reported that the Ross faction had encouraged Kell to provoke a fight with young Ridge in order to have an excuse to kill him.[42]

Shortly afterward he traveled to nearby Springfield, Missouri, and from there he wrote Stand Watie a letter that explains his plight and reveals his state of mind:

Dear Cousin:

Your letter of June 25th I have just received. I was rejoiced
to get it, as I had received letters from every other quarter and
I was more particularly anxious to hear from *you* than from any
one else. My mother and the family are very desirous that I
should leave the nation forever, and have nothing more to do
with it—so that information from them with regard to affairs
in the Cherokee country wouldn't do me much good, because
they would represent impossibilities to return, and dangers
thickening every time I might happen to mention the name of
the Cherokee Nation. But from you I would expect (of course)
the true state of the case. There is a deep-seated principle of
revenge in me which will never be satisfied until it reaches its
object. It is my firm determination to do all that I can to bring
it about. Whenever you say the word, I am there. Whatever ad-
vice I receive from you, therefore, will always presuppose that
I have not left the nation forever, and be given in view of that
object. I believe you understand me fully on that point.

I have talked with a great many persons out here on Cherokee matters, and carefully drawn the distinction between the
two parties; the feeling here is that of indignation against the
Ross party. They would be glad to have every one of them mas-
sacred. I have been out a few days in the country on a visit,
by invitation, to an old fellow's named Weaver. Yesterday there
was a "reaping" which took place in the neighborhood and I
attended. While I was there a good many common Hoosiers
gathered round me and wished me to enlighten them somewhat
about the differences in the nation. I gave them a statement of
what Ross had done; described the murders of '39 and with all
the aggravations of the act (such as killing the best and truest
friend of the Nation, etc., etc.) described the events which took
place previous to your collecting your men at Fort Wayne, etc.
They all listened with intense interest and when I went into
particulars, how young men were dragged out into the yard

and murdered while their mothers were crying over them and begging the inhuman assassins to have mercy, and how husbands were taken out of their sick beds and butchered to death in the presence of their distracted wives, several of the rough old fellows spoke out.

"The whole Cherokee Nation can't take you out of here."

I *had* thought there was a feeling of apathy existing toward the Cherokees, but I find it is the very reverse. The whites out here, and I have seen a great many, say, if [the] Government would only hint to them to go in, they'd slaughter "that damned Ross set" like beeves.

This man Weaver, who is quite a rich old fellow, owning some fine blooded horses and young colts besides a good many breeding mares and who lives about twelve miles from town, is very anxious to induce me to raise a company of some twenty-five or thirty white men to go and kill John Ross. He says it can be easily done and he will furnish the horses to escape on. I thought I would mention the fact to you as I wish, since I am out in the States, to keep you informed of whatever is said and thought with respect to matters which concern you and me. If you think it best to undertake such a thing, I will try it, and I have no doubt it can succeed. Other persons have urged me to undertake the same thing, that is, white persons out here. I have, however, held back my sentiments on the subject, not knowing but what you might have something better in view.

I'd like it well, if we could finish matters pretty shortly. But patience may be necessary. One thing you may rest assured of, the whites are with us.

I was out at Osage (as you understand). I went for the purpose of getting some funds if I could raise them, but I could not. My mother is not able to do anything for me. My only dependence is my Grandmother. I told Lizzie, as I was starting back to this place, to go down and see her and get her to let me have my share of the property now, because now is the time that I need it more than I ever will again in my opinion. Lizzie writes me that Grandma says she must have a letter expressing what I intend to do. I must therefore write her a letter and get you to mail it to her, or cousin Elizabeth, one. It is not worth while to be so very particular about waiting for everything to go in due process of law, dividing the property and so on, just let Grandma say how many negroes she will give me, and send them on to me by Lizzie or someone else. You see I haven't time to wait so long. I need money or what can be converted into money right away. I might sell the negroes or I might hire them out as it suited. I would like very well to take the trip out to the East as you recommend, but I don't have the wherewith at the present. I will board out in the country at Weaver's until I can get money. He is a man of great respectability out here. I have Simon hired here in town for only three dollars a week.

P.S. I suppose I need apprehend no danger from the U.S. Marshall.

J. R. R.[43]

Watie rejected Rollin's hotheaded scheme to invade the Cherokee Nation with twenty-five or so white men in search of Ross. It is clear that most of the family, including Watie, knew that Rollin's temper and desire for revenge would lead him into further trouble if he returned to the Nation. This is probably why Watie suggested that Ridge move east. It is clear, too, that the family's financial problems had not completely disappeared and that they were not about to use what money they possessed to finance Rollin's dreams of revenge.

Ridge left Missouri in late summer of 1849 and returned to Osage Prairie, Arkansas (present-day Bentonville), where his mother and the rest of the family now lived. At this time Watie suggested to Rollin that he arrange to stand trial for the murder of Kell and plead self-defense, as he himself had successfully done in the Foreman incident. Ridge knew that a trial meant paying legal fees, however, and he was still short of cash. In fact, he had earlier mortgaged Grigg, one of his slaves, to Watie to raise funds.[44] In a letter to Watie, Rollin tells of his attempts to borrow money for a trial from his family's estate:

> Osage Prairie, Arks.
> Septr. 20th, 1849

Dear Cousin,

   I was happy to receive the word which you sent me the other day respecting my prospects in the Nation. I was greatly in hopes that I would walk triumphantly out of my difficulty. With high expectations I showed your letter to my mother, to Susan, Herman, Enas, Andrew, and Flora! They hesitated about agreeing to your proposition because they had been looking to the money, which you have in your hands, for the payment of considerable debts which are hanging over the estate and threatening every day to crush it. If the estate was free, they would agree immediately. Finally, my mother approved of the arrangement, and Enas consented to it heartily, as well as Andrew and Flora, but Herman was unwilling and Susan very much opposed to it, because she has a great aversion to the Nation any how and besides must hear what Woodward [her husband, J. W. Washbourne] says about it. It would surprise me if he would agree to it on any consideration. To induce *all* to agree with me, I offered to pay back to each one what they had let me have, as soon as I could sell property sufficient. But this they wouldn't agree to. Now you have the state of the case and I must candidly confess I don't know what to do. I am afraid this is the only opportunity that presents itself under present circumstances. I know it is money that will take me out, and nothing but money, but it is impossible for me to raise it unless your proposition could succeed. . . . God only knows what I am to do, for I don't. . . .

> From your Cousin
> John R. Ridge[45]

John Rollin Ridge never did stand trial for killing David Kell. By spring 1850 Ridge had signed on to travel overland to the goldfields of California. One of the company's supporters was John F. Wheeler, a Fort Smith editor and a relative of the Ridge-Boudinot family. To finance the journey, Rollin mortgaged Simon, one of the slaves he had inherited, to Stand Watie for $533 in a complicated financial maneuver. In a letter to Watie in which he discusses the transaction, Rollin expresses some hesitancy in leaving but concludes that it would be "very difficult for me now to recede from my original purpose, on account of having arranged my matters to that end, and having made promises, which I can scarcely disregard." He makes it clear, though, that he intends to return as soon as possible. He closes the letter by saying, "I will be back in this vicinity. So soon as I can get back conveniently."[46]

He left for the goldfields of California on April 18, 1850, leaving his wife and daughter to follow later. He never returned to the Cherokee Nation or to Arkansas.

4

The Plains and
the Goldfields

When John Rollin Ridge decided to leave Arkansas for the California goldfields, he was not the first to do so. As early as spring 1849, Captain Lewis Evans organized a large party that traveled overland to California from Fayetteville. Nor was Ridge the only Cherokee; many young men from the Nation were attracted by the lure of easy riches and set out to become miners. Among them was Ridge's relative John A. Watie, brother of Stand Watie. John left for California about the same time as Rollin, but he took the southern, or Sonoran route. A second of Stand Watie's brothers, Charles, took the northern route that Ridge followed, and later he stayed with the Ridges in 1856 when they lived in Sacramento. Another Cherokee, Edward W. Bushyhead, had a career surprisingly similar to Ridge's. Bushyhead, a member of the Ross faction, traveled across the plains to Placerville, El Dorado County, California, which was to be Ridge's first stop in California. A year later he moved to Tuolumne County, to the south. He mined there for two years before prospecting in Calaveras County. In that area Bushyhead supplemented his income from the mines by doing printing. In 1868 he moved to San Diego, where he started the San Diego *Union*.[1] Other Cherokees caught the gold fever as well; some remained in California, others eventually returned to the Nation or to Arkansas.

The mines doubtless appealed to Ridge for a number of reasons. He was chronically in economic straits, to the point that he had to mortgage one of the slaves his father had left him. Then, too, his family—if not he himself—worried about the danger of his situation. They believed that members of the Ross party were out to harm him and that the encounter with David Kell was a direct manifestation of that intent, and they thought other encounters were sure to follow. Sarah Ridge was especially outspoken about the imminent danger she saw for her firstborn son. Finally, Rollin was highly motivated to become a "success," a respected and prominent citizen. As the oldest son of the Ridge family and heir to his father and grandfather, he felt a responsibility to restore his family to eminence among the Cherokees. California must have seemed like a great opportunity to solve his problems. Through intelligence and hard work he could amass a fortune in a relatively short time, thus solving his financial difficulties. And his leaving the area would allow the heat generated by the Kell affair to dissipate, at least temporarily allaying his family's fears for his safety. Finally, the promise of riches in California gave him hope that he would be able to return to Arkansas and elevate his family to its former position.

With these factors in mind, Rollin formulated his plan. He and his brother Aeneas, accompanied by a slave named Wacooli, would join one of the wagon trains being organized for the trip to California. Once there, the three of them would engage in mining, save their money, and amass a fortune. Later they could return home and set themselves up in whatever enterprise seemed suitable. Elizabeth would remain in Arkansas with the family until Rollin returned. If the plan took longer than expected, Rollin could always send for her to join him.

Accordingly, the three left Fayetteville, Arkansas, on April 13, 1850, with the wagon train of Major Elias Rector of Fort Smith and Colonel Matthew Leeper of Fayetteville. The group traveled to Fort Scott, Kansas, followed the Santa Fe Trail to Fort Laramie, Wyoming, and westward over the Emigrant Trail to South Pass, Salt Lake City, then went on to Placerville, California, one of the new towns that had sprung up in the goldfields. The earliest known report of the wagon train's travels is a letter from Mark L. Evans, written on June 26, 1850, from Pacific Springs, Wyoming, which gives an idea of the problems the emigrants encountered. Water and fuel were scarce, and money was being extorted by unscrupulous ferrymen and traders along the trail. The travelers were not lonely, however. Evans estimates that some five thousand wagons were ahead of the Rector-Leeper train. He comments on the status of the train in his letter: "Many are throwing away their wagons and are packing. I have never seen before in no place such destruction of property. The most I see is wagons, carriages, harness, axes, cooking stoves, mining tools, log chains and horse shoes and everything that is not essentially necessary." [2] Evans says that Rollin and Aeneas Ridge are among those preparing to pack. He reports that most of the emigrants have suffered diarrhea near the Platte River and predicts more hardships. And he says that many travelers have exhausted their provisions and probably will suffer in the extreme.

The story of the journey is picked up where Evans leaves off in a letter John Rollin Ridge wrote to his mother from Yuba City, California. The letter, dated October 4, 1850, was published in the Fort Smith *Herald* on January 24 and 31, 1851; it had been furnished by Ridge's brother-in-law, J. Woodward Washbourne. The account begins with Rollin, Aeneas, and Wacooli at Deer Creek, a tributary of the North Platte, where they have decided to abandon the wagon and pack their belongings on their animals. The letter's opening demonstrates Ridge's disappointment with what they have found in the Golden State:

> Dear Mother: It is with pleasure that I sit down to relieve what
> I know must be your great anxiety to hear from your wander-
> ing children torn as they are from you, and cast, as they so well
> can feel each morning that they rise and each night that they
> lay down, on a strange and distant land. Believe me, it is no
> ordinary thing to come to California, as the thousands that sigh
> here in the midst of all its wealth can testify. [3]

Ridge then writes about the decision to abandon the wagon. He says that 150 miles out of Fort Laramie the grass began to give out, and they feared for their animals. Following the example of thousands of other emigrants, they determined to lighten their load, jettisoning all but the essentials. This policy extended even to their own clothing. They threw away everything but an extra pair of trousers and underwear each and their overcoats. Also discarded was all the meat they had, except enough, in their estimation, to last until Salt Lake City. Their estimate, it turned out, was wrong. They also saved their flour, a coffeepot, a mill, and a frying pan.

From this point on they traveled lighter, but the journey became no easier. Ridge gives an idea of the hardships:

> After traveling over wide sand plains, traversed here and there by steep mountains all day at times to relieve our wearied beasts, having walked many hours, fatigued, worn out; nearly dead, we reached our "camping place," tug away with our tired hands and legs in "fixing" the horses, in fetching water and wood, both of which we would frequently be compelled to walk after a mile or more, (owing to the non-proximity of the grass) then at last to sit down, faint and hungry to strong fat meat that tasted like rust, and a piece of bread that made the stomach retch at every swallow, was anything but comfortable! Yet appetite was so strong the stomach, though it loathed, still called for more.[4]

In spite of the difficulties of travel, the three pressed on the two hundred miles to Salt Lake City, besieged by clouds of dust, "mountain fever," and back pain that seemed to enter their marrow. Ridge reports that they encouraged each other and cheerfully shared their tasks; Wacooli was called upon to do what the others did and no more.

When they reached Sublette's cutoff, which avoids Salt Lake, they continued straight on into the city, intending to rest themselves and their animals and replenish their supplies. Their first task was to find a range where their horses and mules could graze. This they did after some difficulty. With the stock taken care of, the men set out to find food for themselves other than the fried bread and bacon eaten on the trail. They found milk, light bread, butter, and cheese, all of which, Ridge says, made them fall in love with the place. The love affair was short-lived, however; after a few days of resting and eating wholesome food, the travelers prepared to lay in supplies for the rest of the journey.

All they had left was a few pounds of flour, so they set about looking for more flour and some cured bacon. They found there was no bacon in the whole area save what the emigrants themselves brought in. The alternative to bacon was cured beef, but there was none to be had. They solved the problem by buying fresh beef and curing it themselves. The "Mormon Guide," a booklet the Mormons sold to the emigrants, estimated that it would take twenty-five or thirty days to travel to Sacramento, so they cured some 90 pounds of beef. They completed the major part of their store by purchasing 150 pounds of flour.

At this point Ridge was beginning to worry about money. The journey was costing more than they had reckoned, and they had been forced to discard a wagon, equipment, and clothing, all of which would eventually have to be replaced. All along the trail there had been unanticipated expenses. Ridge gives an accounting: "Our expenses had all along the road been very heavy: 25 cents at every bridge over a mud-hole; $5 per wagon over the different rivers we ferried—where we always found white men ready, and if necessary, backed by the Indians; and $250 for a pack mule or horse—when we had no wagon."[5] Things were not much better when they reached Salt Lake City. When he sold a pony, he got only $35 for it. Shoeing their animals cost $4 a head, and the Mormons even charged toll on the forty-four miles of road to the city. The beef had cost 12½¢ a pound, and the flour twice that much. Rollin says that as he rode out of the city, he felt "shelled" of his money. The three left Salt Lake about July 15, 1850, with certain expectations: "Now comes the tug of war. We expect to reach Sacramento in 25 days. We expect to eat dried beef, which is very good; sleep without a tent, which is not good; to cross a desert, which is worse, but we expect not much more hardship."[6]

For the first 150 miles after Salt Lake City, the traveling was relatively easy; they found grass and water plentiful and the weather agreeable. After that point they were crossing the desert. The weather turned extremely hot, and the grass gave out altogether. At some points they were forced to stop traveling at midday, spread their blankets over the sagebrush, and try to find shelter from the sun underneath. Even then the heat from the parched earth seemed to broil their bodies. The water found along the way was nearly always brackish; sometimes it proved potable, but at other times they could not drink it at all and often went without for a day or two. The effects of the heat and dehydration on the men and their animals slowed the party down considerably.

When they were still fifty miles from the head of the Humboldt River in northeastern Nevada, they ran into mineral dust four or five inches deep. This dust, according to Ridge, consisted of "saleratus [a carbonate of potash], saltpeter, sulphur, and whatnot." The powdery substance rose in clouds that limited visibility and made breathing difficult. It caused sores in the nose, ears, and throat and even made Ridge's hands break out. When they reached the river, they realized they were still several hundred miles from their destination and provisions were running low, so they rationed their remaining supplies. They tried hunting, but game was scarce. Hearing that supplies were being sold cheaply on the other side of the desert, they determined to get there as quickly as possible. They struggled down the three hundred miles or so of the Humboldt, traveling through alkaline dust that also found its way into the water. Ridge blamed the alkaline water for a series of ailments suffered by the men and animals, including weakness in the joints and general fatigue.

It had become impossible to keep clean, and by this time they had given up trying. Ridge reports that their heads looked like mops that had been used to scrub floors from time immemorial. A comb was useless, since it was impossible to draw it downward. Each of them looked as if he had been rolling around in the dirt, determined to get as filthy as he could. They realized that were they to come riding back into Fayetteville in this state, astride their bony mounts, they would cause hilarity among the townspeople. Small boys would follow them, hooting and taunting. Of course the trio were not the only ludicrous-looking people on the trail. Ridge confesses to breaking into laughter at some of the sights:

> I have seen packers pass us on the road whose appearance was so exhilerating that I leaned back in my saddle and nearly killed myself with laughter! But when some poor ragged devil, who started with a most meagre outfit under the expectation that it was only necessary to reach California to be a rich man—came riding along on his gaunt old steer which was fully able to run a race with a snail, drubbing the poor old beast at every step to get him along, I confess my mirth was such that gods and men might have envied me!

He ends the passage by giving this assessment of himself and all who had set out on the trail to the goldfields: "Poor Humanity! to what miserable passes will it put itself for money." [7]

They reached the "Meadows" at the bottom of the Humboldt, a prairie covered with long grass. Here they found other emigrants gathering the grass to carry along as fodder on the trek across the desert lying between them and the Salmon Trout River. The party set about harvesting its share, an amount they determined would last them through the arid wastes. The work was hard, since they had to carry the cut grass through many of the sloughs of the river that traversed the prairie. After bundling and loading the grass, they set out at sundown to cross the Humboldt Sink, where the river disappears underground, and the desert. When they had traveled about an hour, they came upon a slough too deep to cross. Their detour around the water took them all night, and when sunrise came they looked out onto the desert. To make matters worse, they were forced to feed the newly harvested grass to their stock after their all-night trek. The water in the slough was not fit to drink, so they could not replenish their supply. Nonetheless the desert had to be crossed. They set out to travel forty-five miles through deep sand in the heat of the day, without water or fodder.

After about thirteen miles the party met some wagons traveling eastward, coming from the Salmon Trout River, now known as the Truckee. The cargo was barrels of water that the teamsters were selling for a dollar a gallon. Although Ridge was appalled at having to pay that price, he had little choice. They were able to purchase enough water for the rest of the journey and counted themselves lucky that they had money to pay for it. Other travelers with no cash were turned away by the unscrupulous water merchants even when they begged for a drink. The trek continued across the sand, which was strewn with the carcasses of horses and other animals. The stench of rotting flesh filled the air.

At about 2 A.M. Ridge and his party got through the desert and sighted the Salmon Trout River shimmering in the moonlight. In addition to its promise of free fresh water, the river was lined with trading posts where they could buy provisions. But Ridge's money was used up. He had had to sell a pony to finance their stay at Salt Lake City; now he was faced with selling off more stock to pay for the provisions they would need for the last leg of the journey over the Sierra Nevada. Though he had been assured that horses and mules fetched a high price, his animals brought offers of only $10 to $40. "At the same time they asked me two dollars a pound for hard bread and crackers, and a dollar and a half for a pound of flour." Ridge was perplexed, he says. "I felt strange all over! I scratched my head several times! Indeed I was considerably addled."[8] By this time Rollin was getting used to being cheated by opportunistic and unscrupulous men all along the trail. But his choice was to take what was offered or starve, so he and his brother conferred and decided to sell Aeneas's small mule, for which they received fifteen pounds of flour and $8 that they spent on meat. They also sold one of Ridge's mules for $11. When he got to California, Ridge found out that the traders were buying stock cheap from emigrants who were short of cash and later selling them for up to ten times the purchase price.

After leaving the Truckee River, they traveled to Carson's Valley in western Nevada. From there they struck out across the Sierra Nevada. Because of the steep and treacherous trails, they were forced to walk, leading their pack animals. The going was tedious, but the scenery was beautiful. Provisions again gave out—Ridge's underestimation of the supplies needed followed him across half the continent—and they were forced to spend more of their precious cash on exorbitantly priced food. After a week, the three ended their eighty-mile trek across the mountains when they arrived at Placerville, California, then known as Hangtown.

Placerville was a bustling mining town at the western foot of the Sierra Nevada. It was here that the Ridges intended to set up a mining operation. Their first act was to acquire some cash to buy provisions, food for themselves and hay for the animals. Ridge sold his best mule for $45, so they were able to make do for a few days as they rested from the long journey. They began to look around and inquire about mining prospects in the district. The situation was not encouraging, since "thousands were already digging in the town itself and at every little hole for six miles, up and down the creek. There was not a solitary place to dig. Every claim was taken up."[9] Ridge discovered drawbacks to mining besides the shortage of claims; he saw that digging for gold was extremely hard work, and he learned that very few miners ever "struck it rich" in any real sense.

The mining process used in the district at that time is called "placer" mining. Placers are deposits of sand or gravel that contain gold or other minerals, often found in ravines on hills, mountainsides, or riverbanks. Accessibility was often a major problem because of the heavy equipment needed at the mining site. Once they located a promising placer and had the equipment in place, the miners had to dig out the material and shovel it into a large, heavy box called a gold washer. Water from sluices was then used to "wash" the sand and gravel away from the heavier metal. The sluices, of course, were part of the equipment and had to be erected each time a new site was mined. Often they were several hundred feet long. After the placer was dug out and washed, the miners had to dismantle the equipment, load it on mules, and start "prospecting" for a likely site to begin again. Sometimes their efforts were rewarded, sometimes not; it was usually necessary, however, to dig out the entire placer before they could determine whether it contained gold. The sheer physical labor, coupled with the many opportunities for disappointment, made placer mining a disheartening occupation for many gold seekers.

The disappointments were widespread and frequent. Ridge reports on what newcomers to the mines could expect: "There is an immense sight of gold in the bowels of the earth. But it is hard to get at and to get it in large quantities depends entirely upon luck. There is no certainty in it, any more than in a game of cards. At all the diggings $5 or at least $4 a day is got out by almost every miner. This is in reality a great yield, but it don't make the fortune of the miner because his expenses swallow it up."[10] Compounding the problem, the cost of living at the mines was high. Supplies and equipment had to be shipped in, adding to the cost; and the people who dealt in goods and services at the mining sites had little competition and thus could charge whatever the market would bear. In this situation, the best a miner could reasonably expect was to break even after expenses were paid. The tales of huge fortunes extracted from the mines were greatly exaggerated too, Ridge soon found out. He was told that no one had ever made $50,000 by digging in California. A very few had made as much as $20,000, but most made only enough to break even or to finance the journey back home. Ridge estimates that one in a thousand had made what could be called a "fortune."

They tried their luck with some other people from Arkansas and Missouri who had traveled to the goldfields along the divide between the Cottonwood and Trinity rivers. "Fine gold there," Ridge recalled later in a newspaper column. "So fine we couldn't see it." Next they tried mining on Whiskey Creek in Shasta County but had little success. Ridge reprinted a reminiscence about his days there from the *Shasta Courier*, which said it had published several of Yellow Bird's poems, including "Mount Shasta." It also reported that it remembered Ridge's involvement in "a bar-skrimmage or two in these parts." Rollin's response to this jibe was to say that in reality he always left before the fight began. He published a description of life in the mining camps in the New Orleans *True Delta*:

> Two or three months have placed me on the list of acknowledged miners, by giving me the miner's experience, with its sweet and bitter fruits. I am fully acquainted with the nature

and uses of the pick, the shovel, and the cradle; and I believe I could guess, nine times out of ten, the weight of each article, so often have I made myself the substitute of a mule, in scaling precipices and descending hillsides with them on my back! I have been initiated into the mysteries of the miner's home. I have seen him with his long beard, and sometimes very long face, seated in his lowly tent, and dissipated the clouds of care with clouds of tobacco. I have feasted with him on the de-licious "slap jacks," and the heavenly slices of pickled pork—(just a little too salt). I have spread my blankets side by side with him in the mother dirt, and "laid me down to pleasant dreams," wherein the little sparkling "pile" I had gathered when awake, grew mountain-like in my sleep. In truth, I have had opportunities of viewing human nature in many of its phases.[11]

The last sentence makes it seem he was as interested in mining for the pure experience it offered as for the "pile" he might accumulate. There is no doubt that at this time he was thinking seriously about some sort of writing career.

After Whiskey Creek, they mined the area next to the Bald Hills. It was here that Ridge spent his final day mining. After working all day in the rain and snow, knee deep in mud, he had panned fifty cents worth of dust. At that point, he says, he put down his pick and shovel and walked away from mining.

Although Rollin was disappointed with the prospects for mining in California, he still recognized opportunity when he saw it. "Never-theless," he says after enumerating the difficulties miners face, "so many thousands a-digging puts an immense amount of gold dust into circula-tion, and if one can get into any business about towns, or on the rivers, it will come to him like magic."[12] After selling their remaining mules for $75 each, the three men decided to travel to Sacramento, the capital city and keystone of the gold mining region. There Ridge searched for em-ployment in some business that would bring some of the great quantity of gold dust in circulation into his own pockets.

His arrival in Sacramento on August 25, 1850, was chronicled by "Old Block"—Alonzo Delano, a California writer of some note during the period. "His dress, too, was unique and added much to his personal beauty," Old Block says sarcastically as he begins his description of Ridge's appearance. He then goes on:

> He was crowned with an old weather-beaten hat, filled with holes, from which locks of his black hair protruded, as if to keep it from falling from its elevated position; he wore a faded red flannel shirt, which buckled around his waist with a leathern belt, from which was suspended a murderous-looking butcher-knife; his nether limbs were encased in a soiled, greasy pair of leathern unmentionables; while, to cap the climax of his *outre* appearance a pair of glistening patent-leather shoes covered his feet.[13]

His appearance must have somewhat hindered his chances of success in job seeking. He made inquiries all over town but had no success. According to Delano, he was determined to take whatever job was open:

> He was willing to do anything that was honest; never having been brought up to stealing, he could not do that, and even to this day he has not improved in that respect, with all the luminous examples that have been set before him—indeed, he never held office under the Government, which may in some way account for his obtuseness.[14]

Although plenty of dishonest opportunities probably existed in that boomtown atmosphere, legitimate work was hard to come by because there was a surplus of labor. Many of the emigrants who had come over the plains found themselves flat broke upon arrival; mining required some investment capital, so these people were forced to turn to whatever occupations were available. Block reports that the "general error of emigrants of the period" was that "there was no use in overloading the pocket with coin when going to the very fountain of gold itself."[15]

Ridge continued to seek work until "some wag, for the sake of a little sly fun, directed him to the original, noble-hearted, whole-souled, but eccentric Colonel Grant." Joseph Grant was the local agent for the New Orleans *True Delta*, which Delano calls "one of the best Atlantic papers which has been sent to California." [16] In this capacity Grant made orations on the street praising the newspaper and other goods he had for sale. Ridge approached the colorful figure and asked for employment. Grant looked over the handsome but strangely attired figure before him, then asked Ridge what he could do. "Almost anything that is honest," the young man replied. When Grant asked if he could write, Rollin answered that he had done some writing back home. He was then instructed to write a piece for the *True Delta* and bring it back the next day to be judged.

According to Delano, Ridge spent his last dime on writing materials and sat down under a tree to write an article on crossing the plains. The next day the article was presented to Grant at the City Hotel. The agent, with "the air of a Caesar," began to read the piece out loud to passersby. After a few lines Grant realized that he was reading a competently written article, so he asked if Ridge had really written it, then said, "This is an excellent and valuable article—I cannot pay you what it is really worth. It is the best thing I have read upon the subject, and deserves more than my means will permit me to pay; but for this and all equal to it, I will give you eight dollars an article. I shall be glad to secure you as a correspondent for the *True Delta*." [17] Ridge took the job as correspondent and later became the "traveling agent" for the newspaper, which was published in New Orleans, shipped in by steamer, and widely circulated in the goldfields.

As correspondent and traveling agent for the newspaper, Ridge, along with Aeneas and Wacooli, traveled by whale boat up the Sacramento River to the mouth of the Las Plumas or Feather River, then up that stream to Yuba City and its sister community, Marysville. It was from here that Ridge wrote his first letter home. After a few days Aeneas and Wacooli found employment as teamsters, for the shipping companies that supplied the mining camps were doing a brisk business. The two received excellent wages and after a while were able to save enough money to finance their travel back to Arkansas. But Rollin had decided to stay on working for Joseph Grant, evidently thinking he had found the business that would get him his share of the gold dust.

The base of operations for Grant and his young assistant was the True Delta Depot in the Tehama Block, on the corner of Front and J streets in Sacramento. From here Grant held forth with his sidewalk speeches advertising his wares and services. Besides selling the *True Delta*, the firm exchanged coin for gold dust "in large or small sums at highest rates" and also sold books and periodicals. A new shipment of books received in March 1851 included titles by Ned Buntline, Alexander Dumas, and Charles Dickens.[18] While Grant manned the main store, Ridge was sent out into other parts of the city and to the outlying districts to sell the *True Delta* as well as other periodicals and books. One of his venues was the horse market in Sacramento, one of the liveliest places in the city, according to a local newspaper: "But horses, mules, oxen and cows, are not the only articles offered for sale at the stock market. Col. Ridge, the travelling agent of True Delta, made his debut there yesterday with a large amount of choice literature, which he disseminated at satisfactory prices."[19] Ridge's new title was doubtless conferred upon him by his employer and benefactor. He probably was effective as a traveling agent; his personality has always been described as outgoing and energetic, and he seemed to get along with most people. His appearance had also improved—by this time he had exchanged his dilapidated clothing for the attire of a businessman. In his new clothes he was an imposing figure, a handsome man with a "splendid physique and a noble bearing." One of his editors described Ridge, with his jet black hair and large dark eyes, as "the handsomest man I ever saw."[20]

His work as traveling agent took him back to the Yuba City–Marysville area. He lived for a while in Yuba City but later joined the exodus of citizens who moved across the river anticipating a great boom for Marysville. The two cities had been rivals from 1849 until early 1851, when the "stampede" took place, which considerably reduced Yuba City's population. Ridge published a poem, "Yuba City Dedicate," in the Marysville *Herald*, commemorating the event and celebrating the town's remaining citizens. The poem lists the town's beauties and says it has a bright future because of its fine children. He singles out one, the "fairest child" of the city, alluding to Caroline, the daughter of Captain Harvey Fairchild, one of the area's leading citizens.[21]

That Ridge was well enough acquainted with people of Fairchild's caliber to know his daughter by name, and that he was getting his work published in the local paper, seems to show he was making important contacts. An earlier poem, "The Harp of Broken Strings," had appeared in the *Herald* on December 24, 1850. By this time it appeared that Ridge's writing career held promise. Through the contacts he was making as a purveyor of periodical literature, opportunities were opening up for him. He began to look on the burgeoning literary market in California as an apt place for a writer of his talent and promise.

5

Romantic Poet

By 1851 Ridge was writing seriously and attempting to have his work published in publications that circulated more widely than local newspapers. He began writing for the *Golden Era* in its first year of publication. The *Golden Era* was begun in San Francisco in 1852 by Rollin M. Daggett and J. Macdonough Foard. The literary journal's circulation and fame went far beyond that city, however. It was popular with farmers and miners all over California, and Horace Greeley called it "the most remarkable paper."[1] Its content ranged from novels, short stories, and poems to jokes, local gossip, and rumors. Besides Ridge, other writers contributing to its pages during the 1850s include Bret Harte, Mark Twain, Joaquin Miller, Charles Warren Stoddard, Orpheus Carr, and "Old Block" Delano. In the *Golden Era*, Ridge used the pen name "Yellow Bird," as he had done earlier in Arkansas. This is a literal translation of his Cherokee name, Chees-quat-a-law-ny.

Ridge published in other California periodicals as well. His poetry appeared in *Alta California*, a popular newspaper, *Hesperian*, and *Hutchings's California Magazine*. *Hesperian*, which featured a cover depicting three robed maidens reaching for the golden apple of literature while the dragon of ignorance lurked nearby, was founded in 1858 as a women's magazine and featured fashions as well as literature. *Hutchings's California Magazine* was founded two years earlier by J. M. Hutchings, an Englishman who wanted to spread the word about the natural splendors of the West. He published essays on various aspects of the area's wonders and printed lithographs of spectacular scenery, such as Yosemite Valley.[2]

Ridge's poetry during this period and in his last years at Honey Creek is clearly in the romantic vein that was so popular in the middle of the nineteenth century in both Britain and America. Further, much of his writing during this tempestuous time is autobiographical and intensely personal; from it we can draw some conclusions about how he saw himself and his situation in this time of "exile." Further, the poems are helpful in understanding the man's temperament.

A poem addressed to his wife was written on his trek across the plains to California. "To Lizzie" gives us some insight into the early years of their marriage, especially Elizabeth's influence on her husband's mercurial tendencies. The poem shows that Ridge recognized, valued, and missed her calming influence. It also expresses Ridge's image of himself as a Cain figure, a defiant exile who is cursed with dark thoughts:

> A wanderer from my distant home,
> From those who blest me with their love,
> With boundless plains beneath my feet,
> And foreign skies my head above;
> I look around me sternly here,
> And smother feelings strong and deep,
> While o'er my brow are gathering dark
> The thoughts that from my spirit leap.
>
> (Lines 1–8)[3]

But his wife can give peace to his tortured mind, he says, and bring out his positive qualities:

> O lovely one, that pines for me!
> How well she soothed each maddened thought,

And from the ruins of my soul
A fair and beauteous fabric wrought!
                              (Lines 21–24)

Ridge's self-image is revealed in another poem that is perhaps a romanticized version of his and Lizzie's courtship. "The Stolen White Girl" tells of a "wild half-breed" (line 1) who takes a beautiful white girl captive, not by means of the usual weapons and bonds, but by his own attractiveness. The poem predicts for the couple a future full of happiness far "down in the depths of the forest" (line 9). Each of the pair is described; first the woman:

The contrast between them is pleasing and rare;
Her sweet eye of blue, and her soft silken hair,
Her beautiful waist, and her bosom of white
That heaves to the touch with a sense of delight;

The following stanza takes a look at the "wild half-breed":

His form more majestic and darker his brow,
Where the sun has imparted its liveliest glow—
An eye that grows brighter with passion's true fire,
As he looks on his loved one with earnest desire.
                              (Lines 17–24)

If the poem does present the self-portrait it seems to, Ridge saw himself as a romantic hero—a dashing, passionate adventurer. Other poems, however, depict a darker side.

A work dated August 16, 1847, "The Robber's Song to His Mistress," depicts a tortured soul who is wracked with guilt over his deeds. The poem may reflect Ridge's ambivalent position: his often-stated desire for revenge for his father and grandfather's assassination pitted against the desire for a happy and peaceful marriage. This short poem was not published in the posthumous 1868 edition.

In "The Harp of Broken Strings," several themes emerge, the chief one being isolation. Written shortly after Ridge's arrival in California, the poem depicts an exile, "a stranger in a stranger land," as he announces in the first line. He is downhearted, saying "present joy is not for me" (line 6), and the future is no less bleak: "no hope its promise brings" (line 5). The persona recognizes his own psychic instability when he says he takes a sort of perverse delight in his misery.

Part of the pain of his isolation is caused by separation from his loved one. In his imagination he sees her:

> The beauteous one before me stands
> Pure spirit in her downcast eyes,
> And like twin doves her folded hands.
>   (Lines 33–35)

But she is changed, he sees, by the pangs of separation. The "bloom has left her cheek forever" (line 45), and her face is "o'errun with tears" (line 48). The situation does not promise to improve, and he broods upon his "ruined fortunes" (line 53). His pain is intense.

The power of poetic imagination is invoked throughout. His imagination can conjure up his loved one and also delivers him some "delight," even though it is the perverse variety. But included too is the threat of losing this power, since his harp bears broken strings, implying the loss of youth, potential, and opportunity, strengthened by his sense of "ruined fortunes" and "shattered feelings" (line 9).

The poem is clearly driven by the circumstances of the writer's life. Written "by Sacramento's stream" (line 28), probably in 1850 or 1851, the poem depicts Ridge's near despair over his situation. By this time he had realized that the promise of instant fortune in the goldfields was empty. He found himself adrift in an alien environment, estranged from family and friends, with little money and few prospects. Most of all, he was separated from Elizabeth, his wife of only a few years, and understandably concerned for the future of their relationship. While one may regret the strong streak of self-pity and self-centeredness in the poem, the extreme nature of Ridge's personal dilemma should be taken into account; also, this expression of his feelings probably had some therapeutic value for him.

"The Still Small Voice" is another poem written in Ridge's romantic period, in which he assesses his situation. Here he comments on the twin forces of fate and history that he believes govern his life. The persona asserts that wherever he goes, whatever he does, he hears a voice within him saying, "Too late! too late! the doom is set, the die is cast." This line appears as a refrain at the end of each stanza, and the word "past" is repeated at the end of the second-to-last line. Whatever he does, the persona believes, has been ordained in the past. His present and future are ruled by his own history. Applied to Ridge's own life, this theory is correct. His preoccupation with revenge, his ambition to become a "successful" man, his chronic financial instability, all had their genesis in two key events in Ridge's past: the assassination of John and Major Ridge and the related killing of David Kell. In this poem, as in "The Harp of Broken Strings," the persona seems to relish his despondency and the hopelessness of his situation; perhaps like a Byronic hero he considers that he is being given special attention by Fate:

> A raven-thought is darkly set
> Upon my brow—where shades are met
> Of grief, of pain, of toil, and care—
> The raven-thought of stern despair!
>
> (Lines 33–36)

But Ridge wrote of another inner voice too, a more positive one, in a poem composed on March 28, 1851, and published in the Marysville *Herald*. This work also bore the title the "Still, Small, Voice." Here, however, the message is one of cheer, and even though the speaker of the poem insists he is "doomed" (line 36) and "ruined" (line 27), the voice supplies the only solace he receives in his troubles:

> Then let my brow grow sadder yet,
> And mountain-high still rise regret;
> Enough for me the voice that cheers
> The woes of these my darker years.
>
> (Lines 37–40)

These autobiographical poems seem to give us some idea what John Rollin Ridge thought of himself at a time he certainly regarded as a turning point in his life. His future was uncertain and, to some degree at least, his self-confidence had been shaken. But he was a proud, determined man. He saw himself as an intense person who hated and loved deeply, like most heroes of literature and myth. He admitted that his passions sometimes led to reckless behavior, but his temperament could most times be calmed through his wife's influence. Probably dating from the Kell affair, he saw his life as controlled by forces outside himself, by history and fate. His concept of the romantic adventurer proved to have a dark side, and by the time he got to California he saw himself as a Cain figure, an exile who was prevented from taking his rightful place as an important leader of his people like his father and grandfather. These poems also reveal an exaggerated sense of self-importance, and the last two works, especially, demonstrate a large capacity for self-pity.

The largest group of poems written in Ridge's early manhood are love poetry. For the most part they are conventional in language, imagery, and structure; most read like the love poetry of his own and earlier times. For example, "A Cherokee Love Song" and "Song—Sweet Indian Maid" are traditional invitational poems in which the speaker urges his love to escape with him into a bower of bliss. "Song—Sweet Indian Maid" was published in *Hutchings's California Magazine*[4] but did not appear in the 1868 edition. Here an Indian maiden is asked to accompany the speaker on a journey on the river to an island he knows of, "Where all alone and undisturbed, / We'll talk and love as we may please" (lines 27–28). In "A Cherokee Love Song," another young maiden is invited to take a canoe trip to an out-of-the-way river isle, but this time she is a white girl. Nature is no less friendly, though, and as the persona is quick to point out, smiles on the couple. With nature's approval gained, he offers other arguments:

Oh, look to heaven, how pure it seems,
No cloud to dim, no blot, no stain,
And say—if we refuse to love,

Ought we to hope or smile again?
That island green, with roses gemmed,
Let's seek it, love—how sweet a spot?
Then let the hours of night speed on,
We live to love—it matters not!
                              (Lines 25–32)

Traditionally, love verse makes use of elaborate conceits and indulges in exaggeration; Ridge's work is no exception. An example can be found in his "To A*****," another conventional love lyric published in the April 15, 1851, edition of the Marysville *Herald*, which noted that it had appeared previously in the *Daily Union*. The poem's speaker promises that for A's love he would forfeit "a monarch's crown" (line 5); the sun, moon, and stars (lines 9–10); half the days of his life (line 15); and other valuables. "Lines on a Humming Bird Seen at a Lady's Window" also contains such conceits. A hummingbird sees a lady at her window and mistakes her mouth for a flower: "That ripe, red mouth he takes / For rarer flower than ever yet was quaffed" (lines 9–10). The persona identifies with the bird as a worshiper of the young lady when he says, "But, rainbow wing'ed bird, / Thou'rt not alone from those sweet lips debarred" (lines 15–16). The bird, though, has the advantage, because it can bring a smile to the woman's lips, an accomplishment that has so far eluded the man. The bird has it over the man in another way, too— it is able to escape the "enchantress" (line 28).

The man is again held in thrall by a beautiful enchantress in "Of Her I Love." His description echoes the sonneteers of the English Renaissance as he writes of "coral-hued lips" (line 5) with the texture of roses (line 7) that enclose teeth like pearls (line 6). Her bosoms are more white than the breast of a swan (stanza 3), and her form is "angel-like" (line 14). At first glance the persona knows he has been taken prisoner by love.

Other poems continue in this vein. In "Do I Love Thee?" the object of his love is the most sublime vision of his imagination. By the fifth stanza, the persona has worked himself into such a froth that he proclaims he ranks "disease among his friends" because she appears to him in dreams brought on by fever (line 30). This is certainly an original conceit, if a bizarre one.

Whereas most of Ridge's love lyrics are written in a highly conventional mode featuring smitten young men yearning for the affection of young women with overblown charms, two are strikingly different. "The Forgiven Dead" and "False but Beautiful" are ballads that portray the dismal side of the male-female relationship. In "The Forgiven Dead" the persona tells of his former love, who left him for another man who offered her riches. The woman, "pain-haunted / That truth she forsook for gold" (lines 13–14), has pined away on her expensive bed and finally died. Now, the persona says, all his anger has disappeared, and he is able to forgive her. After her death, he says that even though she had given herself to another physically, he realizes that she really belonged to him:

> To strew her tomb with roses,
> Pure-white, as virgins' tombs should be,
> I had not thought: but Fate disposes—
> Her *soul* was virgin unto *me*.
>
> (Lines 21–24)

In "False but Beautiful" the speaker tells of his lamialike lover, who has great physical beauty but an evil, poisonous soul. "Dark as a demon's dream is one I love— / —in soul," he says in the opening lines, "but oh, how beautiful in form!" Even though he recognizes the danger, he finds her irresistible in a perverse way:

> To wander in that wilderness of wiles
> And blissful blandishments—it is to thrill
> With subtle poison, and to feel the will
> Grow weak in that which all the veins doth fill.
>
> (Lines 11–14)

She is a "sorceress" (line 15) with a glance that fascinates him; he is like a bird that "Hangs trembling on the serpent's doomful eye" (line 22).

Ridge's love poems for the most part use traditional language, imagery, conceits and exaggeration, and structure. Some are clearly written to his wife; the objects of some others are uncertain. But for all their conventionality, the love lyrics reinforce the conception of Ridge as a passionate, emotional man.

Much of the poetry written in this period uses poetic conventions common in the works of English and American romantic poets of the early nineteenth century, poets that Ridge read at school. Themes and structures often imitate earlier writers, especially in those pieces that may be called "nature" poems. The nature poems attempt to recreate the poet's personal experiences with the natural environment, which often have mystical or transcendental qualities. In addition, imagination is nearly always the force that makes the experience possible.

"A Night Scene" is a good example. The poem is a romantic ode reminiscent of those by John Keats. It follows the same three-part structure as "Ode to a Nightingale" and other odes and contains some rather standard romantic metaphors, found throughout the poetry of Wordsworth, Shelley, and Byron.

As the poem opens, the persona waits for that Wordsworthian "impulse from the vernal wood":

> I sit
> And muse alone—the time and the place are fit—
> And summon spirits from the blue profound,
> That answer me and through my vision flit.
> (Lines 7–10)

At this point his vision has not yet come, but in the next stanza it appears in the guise of a maiden, "a beauteous being" "with hair night-hued, and brow and bosom white" (lines 11–12). She seems to float in the soft light and shadows of evening, and for the moment all is still. Then he hears a heavenly sound whose "tones are filling up the air, / That brings them, with the star-light blended now, / And wavelet murmurings from below" (lines 21–23). The maiden's voice and harp are making this nightingale song, and the music lures him to her. He knows there is an abyss between them, yet still he reaches out for that momentary glimpse, that fleeting perception of immortality: "But o'er that gulf my spirit loves to lean," he says (line 30). With his "spirit bride" (line 35) he senses a connection with the divine, if only in promise; but as with the Keatsian communion with the bird, the tryst is futile and it is not long before he is called back, forlorn, to his "sole self." The poem ends on a plaintive note:

> Fair words, like ripples o'er the watery deep
> When breezes softly o'er the surface play,
> In circles one by one ye stretch away,
> Till, lost to human vision's wildest sweep
> Our souls are left to darkness and dismay.
>
> (Lines 36–40)

Ridge's poem is clearly built on the model of Keats's ode. It opens with the persona outside the vision, isolated in his own humanity, but clearly reaching beyond himself. The second part of the tripartite form is the possession, the interconnection, or the communion with the object of the poem. But this union is transitory and doomed to failure, and the subject is called back to the isolation of self, at which point he contemplates the vision, the process, and the experience.

It is important to recognize that here too Ridge's diction and imagery are typically romantic. Obvious examples are his use of the "watery deep" to convey the vast immutability of eternity and the reference in the same extended metaphor to the breezes that play over the sea, changing the configuration of its surface. The wind brings to mind the "intellectual breeze" that plays on the aeolian harp, an image pervasive in English romantic poetry. The form the vision takes is important, too: it recalls the ghostly maidens of many romantic poems, such as "La Belle Dame sans Merci," "Alastor," and "Endymion."

"The Singing Spirit" is another poem that seems close to Keats's nightingale ode. Again, at the beginning of the poem the persona is in a pastoral setting, wandering with, if not a drowsy numbness, at least a feeling of sadness and melancholy. But then he hears the healing

melody, the spirit song that triggers his mystical vision. He mistakes it
first for the voice of a water sprite and then for the sound of "some
lonely singing bird" (line 4). His response to the song is twofold. First
the music helps him chase away the spirit of sadness; the shadows then
leave his "sobered, pensive brow" (line 9), and his soul is refreshed as
his melancholy is magically lifted.

Then the second response comes. He stands there, the song thrill-
ing him "Along my being's inmost strings" (line 22). He listens until
the music takes on new tones that seem to warn of death. The hint of
death does not terrify him, however; it is more the "easeful Death" of
Keats that he has intimations of, and the persona here seems more than
half in love with it:

> And yet there was no dread—I thought how meet
> 'Neath such a dirge to sink and die!
> While viewless o'er was heard that harp, how sweet
> To close the dim and fading eye!
>
> (Lines 25–28)

The song continues rich and deep for a time, and he compares its
sound to "the feeling of the soul / When might thoughts our natures
sweep" (lines 31–32). But the singing spirit ceases before long, like the
nightingale, and the persona returns homeward, sad because he hears it
no longer. The poem closes, like Keats's, with his contemplation of the
experience.

In Ridge's "Remembrance of a Summer's Night" we see another
variation on the romantic experience, a Shelleyan treatment of the
coming together of the mortal and the infinite. In what seems to be
an argument for an epistemology based on mystical and transcendental
experience, Ridge closely follows Wordsworth and Shelley.

The poem opens with a familiar setting: the persona, with his book
of ancient lore, sits in the midst of a beautiful sylvan scene and muses,
oblivious to the "holy spell" (line 10) being woven around him like
the approach of the "awful shadow of some unseen Power" in Shelley's
"Hymn to Intellectual Beauty." With the fall of night, though, he gazes

on the darkened sky, on the moon and stars, where "wing'd imagination roams" (line 25). Soon he seems to rise, to "mingle with the mighty dead" (line 40), and is transported into space, into the realm of the eternal. Here he is certain that the wisdom of the universe has been opened to him:

> Upon that mighty page unrolled
> I read, bright syllabled in blazing sphere
> What science hath but feebly told
> In all the wisdom of her garnered years.
> (Lines 49–52)

Knowledge and wisdom can be attained by feeding one's mind with a "wise passiveness," as Wordsworth says in "Expostulation and Reply." Ridge's epistemology also seems to embrace the idea of the visionary experience in Shelley's "Hymn to Intellectual Beauty." The voice in that poem, like Ridge's persona, seeks commerce with ghosts and "high talk with the departed dead" before the transcendent moment, that feeling of intense certainty that both poets see as central to the romantic experience. Ridge's attainment of wisdom is also reminiscent of the mystical instant in Shelley's "Alastor" when

> meaning on his vacant mind
> Flashed like strong inspiration and he saw
> The thrilling secrets of the birth of time.
> (Lines 126–28)

"Mount Shasta," the best known of Ridge's poems, is also in the romantic vein. Specifically, it closely follows Shelley's "Mont Blanc" in theme, natural description, diction, and even meter. Both poems are written in blank verse with indiscriminate rhyme. The diction in many cases is strikingly similar. For example, Ridge's "vast Reflector in / The dome of heaven" (lines 44–45) resembles Shelley's "infinite dome / Of Heaven" (lines 141–42). Shasta as a "monarch mountain" (line 35) and "Imperial midst the lesser heights" (line 2) compares with Mont Blanc towering above "Its subject mountains" (line 62). The American poem, like the English, deals with the perception of eternity in the face of the all-consuming flux of time. The mountain peaks in both cases symbolize the ultimate reality that stands behind and occasionally intrudes into this transient and mortal world. Mount Shasta is seen as "the great material symbol of eternal / Things!" (lines 56–57) in much the same way as the Alpine pinnacle is depicted as the immutable in a changing universe.

"To a Star Seen at Twilight," another of Ridge's nature poems, is important for its presentation of his public persona and for its assertions about the power and role of the artist. The poem's structure is three part. In the first section, lines 1–16, the persona describes a solitary star in the twilight sky, "companionless in light," peerless and aloof. Separate from earth, the star is part of another reality; it seems to have an eternity and immutability not found in mortal realms. After the persona describes the star, he begins to meditate on the similarity between his own spirit and the distant object. Both are isolated, distant from the rest of their kind. But there the similarity ends. The spirit of the persona, anchored by his own mortality, cannot match the pureness and nobility of the star. Although his spirit can soar, can partake of the transcendental experience, it cannot sustain the vision, cannot as yet enter the eternal world permanently as the star has done.

It is at this point that Ridge makes a statement about his own poetic vision and, by implication, the ability of all poets. He wishes all people could "in their bosoms drink / Thy loveliness and light like me" (lines 31–32). Poets are special and are able to make their mystical perceptions visible to common people. The poet's role, for Ridge, is to use his special power to translate his own experiences, transcendental and otherwise, for his readers. The poet is to recreate, as far as possible, his own special insights into the universe surrounding us all. Thus Ridge establishes himself as one of the seers, one of the priests of nature. In the third section the persona exults in the star's isolation: "Thou are the throne / Of thy own spirit, star! . . .'Tis great to be alone!" (lines 38–39, 50).

"To a Mocking Bird Singing in a Tree" also treats nature in the romantic vein. The speaker hears the song and identifies the bird as a "Poet," albeit a "Sarcastic" one (line 2). He wishes he might duplicate the notes he hears, sounds that show the bird is happy and "free from pain" (line 18). This ability would enable him to rise above the trials of this world. But he would not rob the bird of its song, even for such a reward.

Here the poet raises a point about artistic inspiration. He asks if birds, like people, look to heaven for their songs. There are echoes here, too, of the belief that poets and other artists can see beyond this world, can glimpse the ideal, the eternal, whose image they then pass on to other people through the work of art. Poets, in Browning's phrase, lend out their minds.

Finally Ridge takes the idealistic stance that thought never dies and but remains in the sphere of pure Idea. If this is true, he asks, should not the bird's song, like that of Browning's Abt Vogler, remain forever in the ineffable mind of the universe? The final lines of the poem express the wish that the listener might be present when those ideal notes are sounded again.

For all his idealistic writing on nature, Ridge also portrays the darker side of his romanticism. His "A Scene along the Rio de Las Plumas" is an inversion of his usual nature poem. Here the persona describes a walk along the banks of the Feather River near Marysville and Yuba City, California. Now, instead of depicting the nature universe as a nurturing source of inspiration, the traveler finds the world along the river hostile and menacing. As his journey continues, the hostility grows more intense. Nonetheless, nature provides inspiration here, though the images conjured up are hardly those of "The 'Singing Spirit,'" "A Night Scene," or "Mount Shasta." He describes a slimy, oozy place where "birds of sullen flight," little resembling his mockingbird, "Pierce darkness with their screams" (lines 6–7). The traveler sees creatures rising from the bottom of the swamp and watches predatory birds. What seems at first to be a spirit hovering over the scene turns out to be not a "heavenly sprite" (line 24) but a more mundane crane, who "makes his vulgar dish / Of creeping things and fish" (lines 30–31). In contrast to the nightingales and skylarks, the immortal birds of romantic literature, Ridge's owl, which "looks like a druid priest" (line 36), is in reality much less, apt to "Not higher thought inspire / Than lowest wants require" (lines 37–38), since the bird's attention is on its next meal. A pair of flaming eyes startle the persona, and in his mind images of "Dante's damned abode" (line 48).

As the wanderer travels deeper into the swamp, nature's hostility becomes more acute. Nightshade and other poisonous plants grow in his path, and he sees tarantulas, centipedes, and scorpions lurking in the undergrowth. Finally he is forced to retreat from an attack by stinging insects.

"Humboldt River," too, depicts a harsher nature than is found in the more idealistic poems. A note on the poem's title reads, "For three hundred miles its banks are one continuous burying ground. Emigrants to California died on its shore by thousands." Here Ridge describes a nature that is hostile not only to mortal humans, but to their spirits as well. As the spirits of the dead emigrants guard their remains, natural forces are at work to dissipate them:

> For the elements aye are in league,
> With a patience unknowing fatigue,
> To scatter mortality's mould,
> And sweep from the graves what they hold!
>
> (Lines 27–30)

At night the situation is worse, for then the plants effuse gaseous vapors formed when their roots penetrate the graves. Night travelers, the poem says, face an atmosphere thus poisoned, and they themselves take on the aspect of death. Ridge finishes by comparing the Humboldt to the Styx. "Humboldt River" reminds one of the dark and brooding side of William Cullen Bryant's poetry. Ridge probably read Bryant's works at Great Barrington, where the older poet had lived for a number of years. The California poem's pseudoscientific aspects evoke works like Bryant's "Thanatopsis."

Similar to "Humboldt River" is a companion piece, "The Humboldt Desert," published in an 1866 anthology, *Poetry of the Pacific*,[5] but not included in the 1868 *Poems*. The bleak landscape depicted in this poem is forever at odds with the travelers who attempt to cross it. The trail across the desert is "parched and dreary" (line 17), lined with "the bones that bleaching lie / Where fell the wearied beast o'er driven" (lines 29–30). Ridge compares the pioneer's trek across the desert to the Christian pilgrim's journey through life. For each, he predicts, there will be rest "When camped upon the heavenly River" (line 72).

Other nature poems include "The Rainy Season in California," "A June Morning," and "October Hills." The first of these appeared in 1858 in the California magazine *Hesperian* as well as in the 1868 *Poems*. The magazine version has a note affixed to the title: "Written in a Lonely Cabin in the 'Bald Hills,' Shasta County, at the approach of and during a storm." The poem describes the tempests of the season and predicts more pleasant weather to come. The storms remind the persona of his own bleak situation in the mining camp, but he holds out hope for better times. "October Hills" has a Wordsworthian flavor and celebrates nature's healing of a human psyche under stress. "A June Morning" is an innocuous description of a pleasant outdoor scene.

Ridge's nature poems run the gamut of nineteenth-century romanticism and suggest he was familiar with major British and American romantics such as Byron, Shelley, Keats, Poe, and Bryant. Nature generally is congenial to human beings, rejuvenating both mind and spirit. It is also a source of poetic inspiration. Much of Ridge's nature poetry shares with that of other romantic writers the quest for ideality, often expressed as a spiritual figure that can be momentarily approached but not fully obtained. The true artist, however, continues the quest even though the goal is not attainable in this world; the artist then translates the experience of the quest for his audience, individuals who do not share his powers of perception. Found in Ridge's nature poetry, too, is the evil aspect of the quest. In nature is found not only the ideal, the pure and divine, but also the base and sordid. Nature can evoke hell and death as well as heaven and the eternal.

During this phase of his career, Ridge was having some success in publishing his poetic works. For example, "The Woods" was written on May 16, 1853, and published in the Sacramento *Union* on May 27. "Eyes" was printed in the *Daily Evening Herald* at Marysville on August 12, 1853, and on November 8 his famous poem on Mount Shasta was published in the same newspaper. But writing poetry for local and regional periodicals does not often pay well, and Ridge was forced to seek additional employment. His education and legal training helped him get an appointment as deputy clerk, auditor, and recorder for Yuba County at a salary of $135 a month. This, he reported in a letter to Stand Watie, was enough to give him "a pretty decent living and some surplus money." Some of that surplus was to go toward the purchase of 160 acres of government land, on which he planned to build a house as soon as his family could join him.[6] In the meantime, he was living at Tremont House on Second Street in Marysville.[7]

His plans to purchase land and build a new house in anticipation of his family's joining him in California suggest that Ridge had given up his ideas about returning to his people. Yet he reported to Stand Watie in September 1853 that he still yearned to go home:

> If I could have contented myself to remain permanently in the country I could have succeeded in making a fortune, but I have been struggling all the time to make one in a hurry so that I might return to Arkansas, and (I will say it to *you*) to the Cherokee Nation.[8]

Later in the same letter he states, "I intend some day sooner or later to plant my foot in the Cherokee nation and stay there, too, or die." He notes that he broached the subject of a return to his family earlier, with or without his fortune, but was rebuffed:

> I am tormented so by the folks at home whenever I talk of going back to the Nation, and they urge me in their letters so much not to venture to stay even in Arkansas with my family that I am resolved to quiet their fears by providing for my family in this country so as to place them above all want; and then I will be at liberty to follow the bent of my mind which leads me back to my own people and to my own country.

His wish to return was fueled by two related things: his desire to avenge the deaths of his father, grandfather, and uncle and, just as important, his own sense that he too was the target of oppression by the Ross faction. He believed the Kell affair was only the first of actions to be taken against him by Cherokee rivals. He says,

> I had rather die than to surrender my rights. You recollect there is one gap in Cherokee history which needs filling up. Boudinot is dead, John Ridge and Major Ridge are dead, and they are but partially avenged. I don't know how you feel now Stand, but there was a time when that brave heart of yours grew dark over the memory of our wrongs.

At this point he is careful not to call Watie's bravery or loyalty into question, knowing full well that as leader of the Ridge party, Watie holds the key to his return. He says, "But we'll not talk about it because I believe you feel right yet and I admire your prudence in keeping so quiet." He then asks his cousin to let him know "how things stand, what are the prospects of coming safely out of a trial, etc., etc." He seems genuinely interested in returning home and says he would have done so before now had it not been for his mother. "It is only on my mother's account that I have stayed away so long. It was only on her account that I did not go back in '49 or the spring of '50 and risk my trial." Other members of the family apparently had also advised him to remain in California because, he says, every time he mentions the subject of returning all he hears is

> "danger, danger, danger," as though a man had to be governed by his *fears* in place of his reason and his judgment. The Lord deliver me from the advice of women. They never think of anything but the danger—the profits and advantages all go for nothing with them, if there is any risk to run at all!

Rollin's ideas on the subject of a return to Arkansas and the Cherokee Nation can best be described as ambivalent. He did write to Watie in 1855 suggesting that he return to Arkansas to establish an Indian newspaper, and he did make plans with J. W. Washbourne and E. C.

Boudinot in the 1860s to form a partnership with them in the Cherokee country. On the other hand, there were the plans for the new house and the way his poetry and editorials describe California as a golden land of opportunity, an ideal place to carry out one's dreams. He seemed to be tugged in both directions.

In the fall of 1853 Ridge fell ill. His mother reported that he was suffering from "billious fever" which resulted in "ulceration of the bowels."[9] The situation was exacerbated because no family member was there to nurse him and tend to his needs; Aeneas had returned to Arkansas in August 1853. His condition was probably the immediate reason Elizabeth decided to travel to California to join her husband at that time. She and five-year-old Alice were living at Fayetteville, patiently awaiting the right opportunity for a reunion. Rollin's sickness must have been deemed dangerous, since Elizabeth set out alone, leaving Alice in the care of her grandmother, Sarah Ridge. Late in 1854 or early 1855, Alice was reunited with her parents when she traveled to California, apparently with Aeneas and his family. Lizzie left for New York in the company of a Fayetteville merchant and his wife on December 14, 1853. Once in New York, she traveled by ship to Central America, probably Nicaragua, and went overland to the Pacific Ocean. She then sailed to San Francisco, arriving early in 1854.[10] When she met her husband, she learned of his plans for a new literary venture, his story of the notorious California bandit Joaquín Murieta.

1. John Ridge, father
of John Rollin Ridge.
Courtesy of the West-
ern History Collections,
University of Oklahoma
Library.

2. Sarah Bird Northrup Ridge, mother of John Rollin Ridge. Courtesy of the Western History Collections, University of Oklahoma Library.

3. Elias Boudinot, Cherokee leader. Courtesy of the Western History Collections, University of Oklahoma Library.

4. John Rollin Ridge. Courtesy, The Bancroft Library.

5. Elizabeth Wilson Ridge, wife of John Rollin Ridge. Courtesy, The Bancroft Library.

6. John Rollin Ridge with his daughter, Alice. Courtesy of the Western History Collections, University of Oklahoma Library.

7. The Southern delegation of Cherokees, 1866. Members included (from left) John Rollin Ridge, Saladin Watie, Richard Fields, Elias Cornelius Boudinot, and William Penn Adair. Courtesy of the Archives and Manuscripts Division of the Oklahoma Historical Society.

8. John Rollin Ridge in later years. Courtesy of the Western History Collections, University of Oklahoma Library.

6

The Romance of Joaquín Murieta

John Rollin Ridge's *The Life and Adventures of Joaquín Murieta, the Celebrated California Bandit*, was published in 1854. The book was widely read and reviewed and, eventually, frequently plagiarized. Pirated versions appeared as books, were serialized in periodicals, and were translated into foreign languages. Adaptations appeared in verse, and at least one film was made based on Ridge's story. Although many of the versions were produced in the nineteenth century, others have appeared more recently, including Pablo Neruda's 1967 drama *Fulgor y Muerta de Joaquín Murieta*.

More important than the literary imitations, however, is that prominent historians of nineteenth-century California adopted Ridge's tale as an essentially true account of the affair. Ridge himself claims the story is true and important to the early history of the state. In the opening paragraph of the work he says his purpose is "to contribute my mite to those materials out of which the early history of California shall one day be composed" and asserts that Murieta's story "is a part of the most valuable history of the State."[1]

In a way it is. Murieta's story tells of the plight of "foreigners" in the goldfields of the early 1850s, of their unfair treatment by the "Americans," of resistance to the oppression, and of retaliation to the resistance. In California at the time, "Americans" were defined as white people from eastern states and territories who had settled there, but the definition also included white immigrants from Europe. The Irish, Germans, French, and even people from Australia's convict settlements were "Americans" in the goldfields. Others, notably Peruvian, Chilean, Mexican, and Chinese newcomers to the state, were considered "foreigners," even though many of them had arrived in California before the great influx of miners known as the gold rush. Indeed, a large number of "foreign" miners were actually native Californians who had worked on the Mexican ranchos before the discovery of gold. White miners especially resented the foreigners because they believed most of them meant to mine all the gold they could and take it back to their countries rather than contributing to the growth of California as whites did. In formulating this hypothesis, the American miners conveniently overlooked the fact that most of their number had the same idea in mind; those who traveled to California, for the most part, planned to make their fortunes quickly and return home to their families and friends. Nonetheless, the resentment against non-European miners grew from 1849 on.

The problem was exacerbated by the large number of United States Army veterans of the Mexican War who became gold miners. They harbored little love for the people they had recently been fighting and probably made little distinction between Mexicans and Spanish-speaking Chileans or Peruvians. The conquerors also saw little reason to share "American" gold with the conquered, especially when the goldfields were as crowded as Ridge found the area around Placerville in 1850. The veterans' attitudes were bolstered by the actions of General Persifer F. Smith, the military commander of California, who had formerly served in Mexico. Smith, in a letter to the American consul in Panama that was widely published in South American and Mexican newspapers, declared that it was illegal for foreigners to mine for gold on public land in California.[2] His vow to enforce the law spread fear in Latin American countries and encouraged vigilantism against Spanish-speaking miners.

As early as 1849, vigilantes moved against Chileans, Peruvians, and Mexicans who were digging near Sutter's Mill.[3] Violence directed at foreigners in other gold camps was common during the period.

Opposition to foreign miners spread to the state legislature. Its members sent a memorial to Congress in 1849 claiming that "during the year, swarms of foreigners had come, worked in the mines, and extracted thousands of dollars, without contributing anything to the support of the government or people."[4] When no support was forthcoming from Washington, the legislature took action and passed a law that became known as the foreign miners tax. Passed on April 13, 1850, the law provided that all foreigners pay a tax of $20 a month to allow them to mine gold. Collectors were to receive $3 for every tax paid and were empowered to seize the property of those who refused to pay. The legislature estimated that the state treasury would receive as much as $500,000 a month from the tax, but actual revenues were much lower, largely because many collectors simply pocketed the entire $20.

June 1, 1850, was the first day the tax was to be collected, and most people expected trouble. When the collectors moved into the mining camps, however, they found that the Spanish Americans were packing up and leaving the mines. Because the foreigners constituted such a large percentage of the population of the mining towns, up to half in some cases, the impact of their leaving was felt immediately and severely by the businesses that supplied the mines with goods and services. Merchants in Stockton and Sacramento, cities that depended on the mines for business, led the fight to repeal the law. Their voices were heard, and the bill was found unconstitutional by the California Supreme Court. The legislature repealed it on March 14, 1851.[5]

Repeal of the law did not end the animosity between the "Americans" and the "foreigners," however, and the violence continued. Spanish-American miners were insulted and attacked; many were unjustly accused of crimes, given summary trials by the whites, and punished. When they were effectively forced out of the mines by white violence, many Mexicans and others turned to robbery and even murder. They raided the farms and ranches of the area, stealing livestock and other valuables. For a time, open warfare existed between the two groups.

Resentment among the Spanish Americans was fueled by several factors: many of the foreign miners were veterans who had fought on the Mexican side in the recent war; most native Californians believed that the provisions of the Treaty of Guadalupe Hidalgo had not been honored completely by the United States; the large land-grant ranchos were being broken up, leaving most of their dependents destitute and homeless; and the new American California had a distinctive racial bias, especially against Spanish Americans and Orientals. Because of these factors, it is not hard to see why Spanish-speaking Californians turned outlaw and were regarded as patriots by people of similar backgrounds.[6]

Shortly after Ridge arrived in California, the newspapers were full of reports of Mexican banditti stealing livestock, holding up businesses, and waylaying travelers. Some of the bandits organized into large bands and became well known. The leaders of some of these bands have been identified as Solomon Pico, Pio Linares, Silvestrano Chavez, Jesus Castro, and Joaquín Lugo.[7] But many of the accounts identified the leader simply as "Joaquín"; as time went on and Joaquín's stature as a superbandit grew, he was assigned several surnames, including Murieta (or Murrieta or Murietta), Valenzuela, Carrillo, Ocomorenia (spelled by Ridge as O'Comorenia), and Botellier (or Botilleras). It is not known whether all five existed or whether one or more Joaquíns operated using aliases. Ridge's explanation is that there were only two Joaquíns, the other names being aliases. Joaquín Valenzuela was merely the lieutenant of Joaquín Murieta, who, Ridge writes, was the "Rinaldo Rinaldini of California."[8] In any case, Joaquín became the scourge of the state. Such was his prowess that he seemed able to be in two places at once, robbing a saloon in one town as he terrorized miners in another. He robbed both whites and Orientals but refrained from molesting Mexicans or other Spanish Americans. In return he was protected by members of the Spanish-speaking population, who provided him with hideouts and refused to cooperate with the authorities trying to catch him.

Joaquín's career continued for three years, 1851 through 1853.

Newspaper accounts and purported interviews with the bandit provide a sketchy account of his life and the events that led him into banditry.[9] Joaquín Murieta reportedly had fought in the Mexican War as one of the Jurate guerrillas. He moved to Los Angeles in 1849, where he fell in love with Rosita Felix, whose father opposed Murieta's display of affection. The couple consequently eloped and moved to Shaw's Flat, where Joaquín engaged in mining. After a short time, a group of Americans approached him and told him Mexicans were not allowed to mine for gold in that area. When Murieta protested, he was beaten and his wife was insulted. In some versions Rosita was raped in front of her husband. He started mining in another spot but was forced off that claim as well. According to the tradition, he tried gambling for a living, setting up a monte game at Murphy's Flat. But there too he ran into trouble with Americans who tried to run him out of the camp. In a final outrage, Murieta was unjustly accused of stealing by a mob who probably seized upon the first Mexican they could find. He was summarily judged guilty, tied to a tree, and flogged. In one version of the story, Joaquín's half-brother was hanged by the American mob. After this episode Joaquín, who said he had liked Americans until he moved to California, vowed to retaliate. He organized his outlaw band, drawing on desperadoes such as the notorious Manuel García, or Three-Finger Jack, and began his campaign of revenge. It was not long before Joaquín too was well known as a bandit and killer.

As his notoriety spread, so did stories concerning his exploits. George Tinkham supplies the following anecdotes, the first of which appeared in Ridge's *Joaquín Murieta*:

> Joaquín's most daring exploit was at Stockton. Upon a house there was tacked a large poster: $5000 for the body of Joaquín Murieta DEAD OR ALIVE.
>
> While a number of persons were standing reading the poster a Mexican rode up. Dismounting, he wrote beneath, "I will give $10,000 myself.—Joaquín Murietta." With a quick spring he again mounted his horse and swiftly rode away.[10]

Another reported exploit concerns one of Murieta's frequent visits to Marysville about the time Ridge lived there:

> On one occasion he visited Marysville and, entering a saloon, began playing monte. During the play the conversation turned to Joaquín Murietta and his crimes. One of the braggarts at the table exclaimed, "I would give $1,000 for a shot at Murietta." The daring bandit sprung upon the table and shouted, "You cowardly gringo, look, I am Murietta." Before the astonished players could collect their senses, Joaquín jumped from the table, ran to his horse and quickly rode from sight.

Still another story of the bandit's bravery was doubtless heard by Ridge and contributed to his curiosity about Joaquín:

> At a fandango one evening it was reported that Joaquín would be present. Quietly a party was organized to catch him. The would-be detectives entered the room and made inquiry of every one present if they had seen Murietta. One dancer replied to the deputy sheriff, "Yes, I have seen him, but I do not know where he is at present." The next day the deputy was chagrined to learn that he had been conversing with the much sought bandit.

Reports like these circulated and were eagerly picked up by newspapers, as were accounts of all the crimes attributed to Murieta and his band. Citizens of various districts where Joaquín operated, particularly around Mariposa, Tuolumne, and Calaveras counties, were terrified. Enough of them left the area in fear of the bandits that local government and business became alarmed. Petitions were sent to the governor and state legislature demanding protection. Governor John Bigler announced a $1,000 reward for the capture of Joaquín, an amount deemed entirely too small by the citizens of the Mother Lode area, which had been most seriously affected. The petitions continued, and considerable pressure was put on the politicians in Sacramento by constituents and rivals. Finally, in 1853 it was proposed that a group of twenty to twenty-five men be organized to track down and capture or kill Murieta and his band. Several ad hoc posses had set out in pursuit of the bandits over the years, but they had all been spectacularly unsuccessful, adding to Joaquín's reputation for cunning and daring. On May 17, 1853, Governor Bigler signed a bill authorizing the creation of a group to be called the California Rangers, under the leadership of Captain Harry Love. The group would remain in existence for three months, and the rangers would receive $150 each. The men were also eligible for the $1,000 reward.

The call to establish the California Rangers stated that the group's purpose was to capture the robbers under the leadership of the five Joaquíns: Muriati [sic], Carillo, Ocomorenia, Valenzuela, and Botellier.[11] William Secrest reports that the problem of identification was cleared up when Valenzuela was captured at San Luis Obispo. Before he was hanged, Valenzuela, who had been Murieta's lieutenant, testified that Murieta had used the aliases Carillo, Ocomorenia, and Botellier. Newspaper reports of the time used all five names at various times, with widely variant spellings, adding to the confusion. After Ridge's book was published the identity of the bandit chief was widely accepted, though some denied he was ever caught. Ridge's spelling of his surname was accepted as well, though occasionally an extra r or t was added. William Secrest says the correct spelling is probably Murrieta.[12]

Whatever the name of the bandit chieftain, Harry Love was in charge of bringing him—or them—to justice. Love had been nominated in a petition signed by a hundred citizens of Mariposa County. A native Texan, he had been serving as deputy sheriff of Los Angeles County. He had been a scout and messenger in the Mexican War and had fought in the Texas border wars. The newly appointed captain, aided no doubt by his reputation and his six-foot-two frame, easily recruited twenty men at Quartzburgh in Mariposa County. The group included a former army colonel and two medical doctors in addition to some young adventurers.[13] Armed with pistols, rifles, and Bowie knives, the Rangers divided into scouting parties and set out to capture or kill the bandits.

For the next two months the California Rangers traveled around

Mariposa County chasing bandits, recovering stolen livestock, and keeping the peace. In July they headed north tracking a suspected band of Mexican horse thieves as far as Tulare Lake. On July 24, 1853, northwest of the present city of Coalinga, they came upon a group of Mexicans camped on Cantua Creek. William Byrnes, one of Love's lieutenants, reportedly recognized Murieta from when the two had gambled in earlier days. A fight ensued, and four bandits were killed. Among the fallen were Murieta and Three-Finger Jack. Two of the band were captured and others escaped, but the rangers had done their job.

Now they needed to authenticate their victory. They decided to decapitate Murieta and García and preserve their heads in alcohol. García's mutilated hand was included for good measure. Two of the rangers were dispatched to Millerton carrying their grisly cargo in a flour sack; their orders were to find a preservative for the heads and hand. On the way, García's head began to deteriorate rapidly in the summer sun because of bullet wounds, and so it was discarded. When they reached Millerton, they deposited their trophies in a keg of whiskey. Meanwhile, Love and the rest of the rangers took off in unsuccessful pursuit of the escaped members of the band. They joined their comrades in Millerton, where the head and hand were transferred to a large glass jar of spirits. They then brought the jar back to Sacramento after collecting affidavits at Quartzburgh and Stockton stating that the head was indeed Murieta's. They collected their reward and ninety days' pay; later the legislature rewarded them with an extra $5,000. For years afterward, the preserved head was on public display in California and elsewhere. It perished in 1906 during the San Francisco earthquake and fire.

In spite of the affidavits, many people refused to believe it was Murieta who had been killed. Some, including the editor of the San Francisco *Alta California*, stated that the whole affair had been a fraud.[14] The argument went on for a while, but the outlaw depredations had largely stopped, and the legend began to grow.

For a number of reasons, it would have been hard for John Rollin Ridge to resist setting the legend down on paper. First, he lived and traveled in the region where Joaquín and other bandits operated. According to a report, Murieta had a sister in Marysville whom he visited frequently in 1850 and 1851, when Ridge was in the area.[15] It is likely that Ridge heard the stories of Murieta's exploits and read about him in the newspapers, especially when the sensational details of the Love expedition were published. Second, Ridge had already launched his writing career, having had both poetry and prose published in the *True Delta* and in various California periodicals. Here was a ready subject, since by this time he was thoroughly familiar with the background of the disputes between the "Americans" and "foreigners"; he could provide a good sense of the setting from his travels in the area; and he knew people he could model his characters on. As for the plot, it had already been supplied by the bandits, the legislature and governor, and Harry Love's rangers. Ridge knew a good story when he saw it. Another major factor in his decision to write the story was a problem that he had grappled with before and that would haunt him in the future: a shortage of money. With much of California buzzing about Murieta's exploits as reported in often conflicting newspaper accounts, the possibility of offering the whole story to an audience hungry for it must have seemed a financial opportunity too good to pass up. Finally, Joaquín himself must have fascinated Ridge. Here was a man who had tried to live peacefully despite wrongs inflicted on his family and friends. Joaquín's only crime at first was that he did not belong to the faction in power. Driven over the brink by his enemies, he had to react violently. This action forced him into exile, where his intelligence and courage let him revenge himself on his persecutors. He was admired by his own people and feared by his enemies. In many ways Joaquín's early history was much like that of the writer who was to immortalize him; his later career had to appeal to Ridge's deep thirst for revenge. More important, in Joaquín Ridge had found a kindred soul, with the same personality and motivation. Telling his story was natural.

Ridge finished his *Life and Adventures of Joaquín Murieta* in late spring 1854. The copyright was applied for on June 3. Curiously, though the copyright listed the names of both Ridge and Charles Lindley, there is no evidence that Lindley assisted Ridge at all. No subsequent claim to authorship by Lindley has ever been found.[16] The book was published on August 3, 1854, by William B. Cooke and Company, Booksellers and Stationers, of San Francisco. It apparently was widely sold around the state. References to it appear in mining district towns such as Sonora and Weaverville,[17] and an advertisement for it ran in the San Francisco *Daily Placer Times and Transcript*.[18] *The Life and Adventures of Joaquín Murieta, the Celebrated California Bandit* was ninety pages long. It was bound with yellow paper covers and contained two lithographs, one representing Joaquín and another Harry Love. The title page identified the author as "Yellow Bird."[19]

Ridge's book was reviewed by the San Francisco *Daily California Chronicle* on August 7, 1854. The review emphasizes the controversy over Joaquín Murieta, and it, along with the author's published reply, probably helped sales considerably. The *Chronicle* identifies Ridge as "a cross breed of the Cherokees." His style is "respectable, and is an argument favorable to Indian capacity." The reviewer adds, "It might be said also that the fancy of the author is undoubtedly equal to the style of his writing." This comment is interesting because it raises the issue whether Ridge was writing fiction or history. The question was to be debated until the present.

The *Chronicle* review goes on to say that there is little to commend the book for and that the reviewer has no taste for tales of horror. The *Life and Adventures of Joaquín Murieta* is full of atrocities and gratuitous violence, the reviewer says, then adds, "It leaves Jack Sheppard to the rear, and makes the sins of Bluebeard appear mere peccadillos." But the part of the review Ridge most took offense to was the following:

> The book may serve as very amusing reading for Joaquín Murieta, should he get hold of it, for notwithstanding all which has been said and published to the contrary, we have little faith in his reported death at the hands of Love's party. The whole affair savors much of gammon, and the head which was exhibited might as well have been claimed as belonging to Lopez as Joaquín.[20]

This statement expresses an opinion shared by many Californians that the real Joaquín was never captured. Reports said he had escaped Love's rangers and had either adopted the life of a peaceful California rancher or returned in triumph to Sonora. In any event, the reviewer's words challenged Ridge's public claim of his story's authenticity, which he deemed important to the book's sales. For this reason he felt it necessary to respond to the *Chronicle* review.

He did so in a letter published in the *Daily Placer Times and Transcript* in San Francisco. The letter, sent August 21 from Marysville, was later reprinted.[21] In it Ridge recounts the *Chronicle* reviewer's contention that Joaquín is not dead. To this he retorts, "Prove it!" He then invites the reviewer to duplicate his own research, to travel over the state as he did, consult the files of different newspapers that have published authenticated accounts of Joaquín, and converse with those who knew the bandit personally. Ridge thus reveals his own research methods. He goes on to say that the governor, the legislature, and the Chinese merchants of San Francisco were convinced enough of Joaquín's death to pay Love and his men handsome rewards. He then promises, "In the next edition of my work, I shall prove that he is dead beyond all hope of resurrection."

That Ridge was contemplating a second edition a little over three weeks after the first appeared is puzzling. It may be that the copies printed had sold much more quickly than anticipated, making a second edition necessary. Ridge reported a press run of seven thousand to Stand Watie, but this number seems high, especially since only three copies still exist. That he was thinking about a second edition seems clear, however. He gives an account of his life of Joaquín to Stand Watie in a letter sent from Marysville on October 9, 1854. As in many of his letters to his cousin, he says he needs money and is beset by circumstances beyond his control. After commenting on the whereabouts of Watie's brother Charles, Ridge reports on the fortunes of his book.

> For my own part, I am struggling along with adversity as well as
> I may. I expected to have made a great deal of money off of my

book, my life of Joaquín Murieta (a copy of which I have sent
you) and my publishers, after selling 7,000 copies and putting
the money in their pockets, fled bursted up *tee totally* smashed,
and left me, with a hundred others, to whistle for our money!
Undaunted by this streak of back luck, I have sent the work on
to the Atlantic States for a new edition, and when that is sold
out I will have a few thousand dollars at my command. There is
not so much danger of one of those heavy eastern houses failing
as these mushroom California concerns at San Francisco.[22]

There are two problems with this account. First, there is no record
or subsequent mention of negotiations to publish a second edition with
an eastern firm. Second, the William Cooke Company did not go out
of business as Ridge asserts. No record has ever been found of the company's bankruptcy. Further, the San Francisco city directory for 1855
lists Cooke as doing business half a block from where he had been a
year before.[23] If he fled, he did not go far. Ridge was doubtless trying
to put the best face on his affairs. Much of the rest of the letter in-
volves an attempt to get Watie to finance an Indian-oriented newspaper
that Ridge would edit, and projecting financial success as a writer might
help in this endeavor. In any case, a second edition was not immediately
forthcoming.

The San Francisco *California Police Gazette* printed in ten weekly
installments "The Life of Joaquín Murieta, Brigand Chief of California" in 1859. This version, obviously pirated from Ridge's account, was
published from September 3 to November 5. Three weeks after the
serialization, a seventy-one-page pamphlet of the pirated version appeared, illustrated by the noted California artist Charles C. Nahl.[24] This
account is based on Ridge's text, but the sequence of events is altered
and its language is sometimes garbled.[25] Although some of the facts
have been changed, the *Police Gazette* version obviously follows Ridge's
account closely. The biggest variant is the omission of Rosita as Murieta's
wife and the substitution of two mistresses, Carmela and Clarita. Ridge
was quick to complain about the obvious plagiarism in the pages of

the Marysville *Daily National Democrat*, which he was editing by that time.[26] His complaints got him nowhere, however, and the *Police Gazette* account became very popular. It was used in many of the versions that followed.

The edition of Yellow Bird's book that appeared in 1871 was dubbed the third, perhaps a sarcastic reference to the obviously pirated *Police Gazette* version. Although the publishers claimed that before his death Ridge had "prepared a revised edition of his story of Joaquín Murieta, to which he had added much new and heretofore unpublished material," this claim has never been authenticated. Ridge, assuming he did work on the 1871 edition, comments on the plagiarism in the Author's Preface: "A spurious edition has been foisted upon unsuspecting publishers and by them circulated, to the infringement of the author's copyright and the damage of his literary credit—the spurious work, with its crude interpolations, fictitious additions, and imperfectly designed distortions of the author's phraseology, being by many persons confounded with the original performance."[27]

The 1871 edition does include some new material, including more description of the scene in which Murieta is flogged and an account of a raid at Mono Lake. In addition, it carries the Author's Preface mentioned above, supposedly written by Ridge before his death.[28] Ridge, of course, may have worked on a revised edition as early as 1854; we know he at least contemplated such a work. Ironically, the posthumous *Joaquín Murieta* was much better received than the original.

Remi Nadeau reports that the pirated *Police Gazette* version was the basis for the many subsequent Joaquín stories. Even before Ridge's "third" edition, a New York publisher came out with an adventure yarn, "Joaquín (the Claude Duval of California); or the Marauder of the Mines," in 1865. Claude Duval was a celebrated English highwayman in the seventeenth century. Joseph E. Badger, Jr., published his Joaquín story in Beadle's Dime Library in 1881; Joaquín novels were subsequently published in France and Spain. The Spanish translation was published in Santiago, Chile, and its hero is not Mexican but Chilean. Other versions included a biography by El Professor Acigar, published in Barcelona, and one by Ireneo Paz in Mexico City. By this time the tale had become greatly embellished, according to Nadeau. Whereas the *Police Gazette* edition was 71 pages long, Paz manages to extend Joaquín's life and adventures to 281 pages. As many as a dozen other versions of the story appeared in the twentieth century, including *The Robin Hood of El Dorado*, by Walter Noble Burns. Burns, a popular writer of westerns, accepted many of the additions to the story by earlier writers.[29]

The Joaquín legend extended to genres other than fiction. Cincinnatus Hiner Miller wrote a long poem called "Californian" and published it in his *Songs of the Sierras*.[30] The poem is original in the sense that though its main character is Joaquín, it depicts a wounded Joaquín fleeing his enemies and describes his eventual death. Later Miller greatly condensed "Californian" and published it as "Joaquin Murietta." At the end of the truncated version, the poet adds this note:

> The third poem in my first London book, if I remember—you see I never kept my books about me, nor indeed any books now, and have for present use only a copy that has been many times revised and cut down—was called "California," [*sic*] but it was called "Joaquin" in the Oregon book. And it was from this that I was, in derision, called "Joaquin." I kept the name and the poem too, till both were at least respected. But my brother, who had better judgment and finer taste than I, thought it too wild and bloody; and so by degrees it has been allowed to almost entirely disappear, except this fragment, although a small book of itself, to begin with.[31]

Miller kept the name Joaquin, however, and today he is known as one of the premier nineteenth-century western writers.

The story did not escape the attention of the dramatists either. In 1858 a five-act play by Charles E. B. Howe reenacted the legend. Other dramatic presentations were to follow, including a pageant in 1927 by B. Ignacio Ortega, a romantic comedy by Charles D. McGettian produced in San Francisco in 1932, and a Chilean production in 1936 by A. Acevedo Hernandez. Pablo Neruda's 1967 play on Murieta is overtly political; it depicts Joaquín as an early victim of Yankee imperialism. In 1936 Hollywood produced a film version of the story starring Warner Baxter. At the same time, the story was serialized in newspapers by western writer Peter B. Kyne, who claimed that his series was based on Burns's earlier novel.

But not only was Ridge's tale picked up by writers of popular literature and poets like Miller and Neruda, important nineteenth-century historians, apparently believing Ridge's claim of authenticity, adopted it as real biography. Hubert Howe Bancroft, in his *History of California*, takes his "facts" from Ridge's 1871 edition, including even the episode in which Joaquín, by writing on the reward poster, offers to increase the price on his head. Theodore H. Hittell, another major historian, adopted Ridge's story as well. For chapter 4 of his *History of California*, "Joaquín Murieta and his Banditti," he extracts his information almost exclusively from the 1871 edition, as his own footnotes readily show.[32] Ridge's story, then, passed not only into the popular imagination, but into the history books as well.

In his introduction to the University of Oklahoma Press edition of Ridge's book (1986), Joseph Henry Jackson concludes that Ridge decided California needed a folk hero and set about creating one. Jackson discounts the authenticity Ridge claims, calling the Joaquín story a "myth." He does say, though, that the basic story was there: Mexicans and other "foreigners" had been mistreated, many of them had turned to crime, one of these had been named Joaquín Murieta, and Captain Love and his men did kill someone they claimed was Joaquín and pickled his head. Jackson goes on, "What form the legend might have taken if left to itself is impossible to determine, for very soon something happened to give it shape. This was the publication of the small, paper-covered book . . . the preposterous, fantastical tale out of which Californians were gradually to construct the folk hero they unconsciously wanted."[33]

Whether Californians were seeking a hero in their heart of hearts is not clear. What is clear is that John Rollin Ridge's *Life and Adventures of Joaquín Murieta* is not pure history, but it is not pure fiction, either. It is more like today's television "docudramas" or the currently fashionable

news novels, productions based loosely on history but liberally sprinkled with embellishments and added emphasis designed to titillate the
audience. There is no doubt that *Joaquín* was meant to be sensational.
That Ridge wanted a best-seller, the equivalent of a box office smash, is
clear from his letter to Stand Watie; he expected to make money from
his book—if not from the first edition, then from a subsequent one.
Money was his prime motivation, and his quest for literary fame was a
close second.

As for the historical part of the tale, it is clear that Ridge gathered
his basic information from newspaper stories of the day. The major episodes in Ridge's book had been reported, reprinted, and rehashed, with
or without the gory details, in the local press. There was no need for
him to invent the story out of whole cloth. The accuracy of the press
accounts is another thing, however. As Angus MacLean points out, "it
seems highly improbable that any one man with a following of twenty
to thirty men could possibly have committed so many atrocities, over so
wide a territory, in so short a time, as the hysteria of the times attributed
to 'Joaquín'; so logic would say that Joaquín Murrieta and his men were
getting the blame for all these crimes even though they were not the
only foxes raiding the chicken coop."[34] Since Ridge relied to a large extent on contemporary newspaper accounts, it is possible and even likely
that some of his facts were not straight, no matter how conscientious he
had been in his research or how dedicated he was to historical accuracy.
Nonetheless, the meat for his literary stew was provided to him.

That *Joaquín*'s author embellished the basic story is beyond doubt.
For example, he includes in his narrative verbatim records of conversations he could never have heard. In one instance Joaquín and his men
come across a party of young American hunters. Although the Americans have not threatened the bandits, Joaquín suspects they have recognized him and feels his only recourse is to kill them to prevent their
reporting his presence in the area. When he tells the hunters what is in
store, one of them, "a young man, originally from the wilds of Arkansas,
not more than eighteen years of age, [advances] in front of his trembling comrades" and bravely addresses the bandit captain. He promises

not to reveal his group's encounter with Joaquín and furthermore vows to shoot any of his companions who attempts to do so. Joaquín, taken with the man's bravery, allows the hunters to leave unharmed. Ridge's comments follow: "I have never learned that the young man, or any of his party, broke their singular compact." If the hunters never broke their silence, it is difficult to understand how Ridge came upon the story, unless he was concealed nearby, close enough to overhear the conversation, and had his pencil and notebook handy. Even if one gives credence to Ridge's claim that he interviewed people acquainted with Murieta, it is difficult to account for the verbatim reports of whole conversations. It is as if Ridge were a Joseph Conrad recording one of Marlowe's incredible feats of memory.

In another episode one of the bandit chasers, a Captain Ellas, rides into Yankee camp and sees a young Mexican, who pulls down his sombrero and lays his hand on his pistol when he sees the American. But Ellas leaves without recognizing Joaquín or, Ridge reports, even knowing the bandit has been in the area. Here again it is difficult to see how the episode was brought to Ridge's attention or, for that matter, was known to anyone outside Joaquín's band. Similar problems in the book suggest the author gave himself a free hand in writing his "history." This artistic license is appropriate to an author who was out to exploit a situation in the news of the day and to present a sensational and profitable tale to an audience eager to hear about a dashing, handsome hero and his forays into romance and danger, all heavily laced with sex and violence. Writers looking for a quick profit have not changed much over the years, nor have their audiences.

One interesting aspect of Ridge's *Joaquín* is the way the author describes his hero. Physically, Joaquín bears a strong resemblance to his biographer, according to photographs and written descriptions of Ridge:

> He was then eighteen years of age, a little over the medium height, slenderly but gracefully built, and active as a young tiger. His complexion was neither very dark or very light, but

clear and brilliant, and his countenance is pronounced to have been, at that time, exceedingly handsome and attractive. His large black eyes, kindling with the enthusiasm of his earnest nature, his firm and well-formed mouth, his well-shaped head from which the long, glossy, black hair hung down over his shoulders, his silvery voice full of generous utterance, and the frank and cordial bearing which distinguished him made him beloved by all with whom he came in contact.[35]

These words could have come from the pen of Sarah Ridge in a description of her eldest son. Joaquín's situation before his troubles with the Americans is also described.

He had built him a comfortable mining residence in which he had domiciled his heart's treasure—a beautiful Sonorian girl, who had followed the young adventurer in all his wanderings with that devotedness of passion which belongs to the dark-eyed damsels of Mexico. It was at this moment of peace and felicity that a blight came over the young man's prospects.

Joaquín and his wife are in a position analogous to that of Elizabeth and Rollin Ridge at Honey Creek before the episode with Kell. It is hard to tell whether Ridge discovered similarities between himself and Joaquín in his research for the book or created Joaquín in his own image and likeness.

In any event, *The Life and Adventures of Joaquín Murieta* made an impact on the popular imagination in several countries. In addition, largely through the efforts of Bancroft and Hittell, it had an influence on California history—the book was judged by Robert Cowan to be one of "the twenty rarest and most important works dealing with the history of California."[36] The respect Ridge yearned for was achieved, but not till six decades after his death. The profit he expected never developed, at least for him.

7

California
Newspaperman

After the disappointment of *Joaquín*, Ridge continued to seek new opportunities in the publishing profession. In the 1854 letter to Stand Watie in which he reports the financial failure of his romance, he also makes a proposition. His idea was to establish a newspaper that would be devoted to Indian affairs, defend Indian rights, and provide Native Americans with a powerful friend. One of its main goals would be to preserve Indian history and the memories of its major figures. He was convinced that through his writing he could make a major contribution to his people, much as John and Major Ridge had contributed politically. He says,

> I want to write the history of the Cherokee Nation as it should be written and not as white men will write it and as they will tell the tale, to screen and justify themselves. All this I can never do unless I get into the proper position to wield influence and make money. Don't you see how much precious time I am wasting in California? Instead of writing for my living here I should be using my pen in behalf of my own people and in

rescuing from oblivion the proud names of our race. Stand, I
assure you this is no idle talk. If ever there was a man on earth
that loved his people and his kindred, I am that man.[1]

But in the same letter, Ridge makes it clear that Indian patriotism is not
his only motive. He says, "I want to preserve the dignity of our family
name; I want the memory of my distinguished relatives to live long after
we have all rotted in our graves." Among the distinguished Rollin no
doubt included Stand Watie. Ridge has determined at this point that the
way to avenge the deaths of his relatives is to make sure that the true
story—as seen by the Ridge-Boudinot-Watie faction—of the Treaty of
New Echota is told.

More important, Ridge demonstrates here that he knows his only
path to success, to money and influence, is by using his mind and his
pen. His determination in this direction never seriously wavered, but he
was a practical man too, one with responsibilities. In 1854 he augmented
the income from his post as Yuba County deputy clerk by working part
time as a special policeman.[2] This was a time when many towns in California hired a town marshal to keep law and order, supplemented with
special police recruited from among the townspeople who were under
the marshal's direction. In the following year Ridge advertised his services as a notary public.[3] Lizzie no doubt encouraged Rollin's quest for
middle-class respectability; in 1854 he became an officer in the Olive
Branch Social Degree, Number 5, of the Sons of Temperance at Marysville.[4] His wife encouraged him, too, to continue the study of law he
had started in Fayetteville during their courtship. Although his heart
and mind were set on a writing career, he agreed to consider the law as a
backup, insurance for independence and financial security. In a letter to
his mother he says,

> I will not practice the law unless I am driven to it. The general
> science of the law I admire—its every day practice I dislike.
> But for the sake of having something upon which to rely in
> case of necessity, I have patiently burned the midnight oil since
> I have been in Marysville. I was determined, that if untoward

circumstances gathered around me, and I was thrown out of employment, I would have some sure thing to depend upon, so that I might stand boldly up and say to the world, "I ask you no favors." I prefer a literary career, but if I cannot place myself in a position as a writer, I will even go into the drudgery of the law.[5]

Although he gave in to Lizzie on the point that the family's security came first, he was still determined to make a career with his pen. Encouraged by Stand Watie's promise to support him in his plan to publish an Indian newspaper in Arkansas, Ridge eloquently described his aspirations for the enterprise and for himself:

If I can establish such a paper, I can bring into its columns not only the fire of my own pen, such as it may be, but the contributions of the leading minds in the different Indian nations. I can bring to its aid and support the Philanthropists of the world. I can so wield its power, as to make it feared and respected. Men, governments, will be *afraid* to trample upon the rights of the defenceless Indian tribes, when there is a power to hold up their deeds to the execration of mankind.[6]

It is no wonder that a man with such noble and lofty aims would disdain a career as a small-town lawyer, settling disputes between miners and merchants and preparing mortgages and deeds. Ridge clearly saw himself in a role that would continue the work of his father and grandfather, men who had tried to further the "great idea of civilizing and improving" the American Indians. He considered himself a crusader, a feared and respected national leader who would bring "all these scattered tribes one by one into the fold of the American Union." But while he sided with those who would assimilate the Indians into white society, he was also determined to tell the true story of white-Indian relations. Ridge wanted to write the history of the Native Americans from the first white contact, "handing down to posterity the great names of Indian history, and doing justice to a deeply wronged and injured people by

impressing upon the records of the country a true and impartial account
of the treatment they have received at the hands of a civilized and Christian race!"[7]

Ridge and others continued to press the idea of an Indian newspaper on Watie for many years. Rollin enlisted the help of Charles E.
Watie, Stand's brother, who had emigrated to the goldfields and for
some time lived with the Ridges. In a letter to his brother in August
1856, Charles writes that he and Rollin have discussed the idea at length
and have concluded that it is the "best thing that can possibly be done"
for the Indians. He asks that Stand reply "immediately" that he will buy
a press to start the enterprise.[8] Ridge never gave up the idea, which per-
sisted into the 1860s, when he interested Elias Cornelius Boudinot, son
of Elias Boudinot, and Ridge's own brother-in-law, J. W. Washbourne,
in the scheme. The Indian newspaper was never published, however,
and so ended Rollin's vision of becoming a leader and champion of his
own people.

In autumn 1855 he had been promised a position on a Sacramento
newspaper by the state printer, General James Allen. Allen was a native
of Pennsylvania who had come to California in 1852. Previously he had
been an editor in Ohio and had fought in the Mexican War. He published or edited several newspapers in Sacramento and Marysville from
the time he arrived in California until his death in 1863. Allen was also
a prominent political figure who was elected mayor of Marysville in the
spring of 1855 and state printer in September of the same year on the
Know-Nothing, or American party, ticket. By autumn 1855 he had become proprietor of the Sacramento *State Tribune*. In January 1856 he
changed the name of the paper to the *California American* and hired
John Rollin Ridge as a writer. This marked the beginning of a long
association between the two men. Although Charles Watie said Rollin
was "one of the editors" of the *California American* in August,[9] his name
does not appear on the masthead of that newspaper as an editor until
January 1857. Allen is identified as editor, while Allen, S. J. May, and
Ridge are "proprietors." It is likely that Ridge did most of the writing
for the paper, however; even though the news stories and editorials are
unsigned, many bear Ridge's stylistic stamp.[10]

The *California American* was clearly an organ for the Know-Nothing party, a nativist organization that rose to prominence in the early 1850s. Originally called the Order of the Star-Spangled Banner, the party was established by Charles B. Allen in New York in 1850. The name Know-Nothing stems from the fact that the organization was a secret one, and when members were questioned about the group, their standard reply was "I know nothing about it." The party's main tenets were that foreigners are unfit for citizenship until they lose all interest in their homeland and that Catholics should be denied citizenship because they are loyal to a foreign power. In many ways the rise of the Know-Nothings was a reaction to the influx of Irish and other immigrants at the time.

The Know-Nothings first organized in California at San Francisco in May 1854.[11] The party held its first nominating convention in Sacramento on August 7, 1855, and adopted its state party platform. This set of principles differed markedly from the more radical national party platform adopted earlier in Philadelphia. The only references to the nativist question were in sections 11 and 3. Section 11 reads, "Eligibility to office, both in the states and nation, should be restricted to persons born on some part of the territory included within the jurisdiction of the United States." Section 3 calls for "a judicious revision" of naturalization laws, without defining "judicious." The usual Know-Nothing anti-Catholic position seems to be rejected by the platform's section 4: "Universal religious toleration."

Several of the American party planks took positions that were to show up in the editorials of the *California American* as well as in newspapers that Ridge subsequently edited. Among these are sections calling for support for the Union against attempts to dissolve or overthrow it; defense of the Constitution; separation of church and state; opposition to fraud and corruption in government; the establishment of a transcontinental railway; legislation in favor of settlers on government land; and the application of the so-called Jeffersonian principle of selecting men for public office: "Is he honest? Is he capable? Will he support the Constitution?" Ridge was to argue forcefully on all these points in the years to come. Although the slavery question had effectively split the national party, the California branch sidestepped it adroitly in section 12:

"The firmest and most enduring opposition to the agitation of all questions of a merely sectional character."[12] Ridge supported this position as well as the closely related principle later espoused by the Democratic-supported Stephen A. Douglas, the right of the citizens of a state or territory to decide whether to allow slavery within its boundaries. This issue, known as popular sovereignty, was one Ridge would editorialize on again and again. The Know-Nothing party went on to elect its entire state ticket on September 5, 1855, including James Allen as state printer.

The *California American* followed the party line faithfully during 1856. Its Democratic rival, the Sacramento *Journal*, lambasted the *American* for its positions and supported "Freedom's Phalanx," a group organized to stop the Know-Nothing movement. Despite the *American*'s best efforts and the party's control of the executive, the state supreme court, and both houses of the legislature, the Know-Nothings accomplished little during their year's tenure in office. They were even unable to get one of their number elected United States senator because of intraparty squabbling. In spite of their campaign stand against corruption and graft in public office, many party members used their positions for private gain; thus the political organization that had sold itself on a reform platform was unable to sustain its momentum.[13]

One of the main political events of 1856 in California was the re-emergence of vigilantism.[14] After the discovery of gold and the subsequent influx of people from around the world, authorities were hard pressed to maintain law and order. Gangs of men defied local governments and police forces and terrorized the citizens almost at will. San Francisco, particularly, suffered violence at the hands of various groups of criminals while its outraged inhabitants stood by helpless. In June 1851 some local citizens organized "the Committee of Vigilance of San Francisco" under the leadership of William T. Coleman. The committee and similar groups in other California towns did much to stem the tide of violence and were for the most part supported by a majority of citizens. After a few years of relative quiet, the situation again came to a head in San Francisco. Hoodlums, often employed by corrupt politicians, harassed people at polling places. Crimes, even murder, went unpunished by complacent local officials, and soon the public and the newspapers were again calling for action. Prominent among the journalists demanding reform was James King of William, editor of the *Daily Evening Bulletin*. King editorialized against those he considered leaders of the criminal element in San Francisco, including the politician and businessman James P. Casey. Casey responded by shooting King down on a city street; he was arrested and locked up in the local jail. Shortly thereafter, several thousand vigilantes broke into the jail and seized Casey and another accused murderer, Charles Corey. The crowd established a drumhead court, which tried the pair and condemned them to death. Even before King's body was buried, Casey and Corey were hanged. The vigilantes were soon joined by others, and a second San Francisco Vigilance Committee was formed, again under Coleman. Soon the committee was able to summon six thousand armed volunteers to its sandbagged headquarters by ringing a large bell.

The response of California's Know-Nothing governor, John Neely Johnson, was to order out the California militia, under General William Tecumseh Sherman, to help state officials enforce the law. Sherman, realizing that his orders included moving against the popular vigilantes, was reluctant to act quickly. The committee had broad popular appeal, partly because many of the state's newspapers rose to its defense. The *California American*, while deploring the necessity of vigilantism, nonetheless supported the San Francisco group despite Governor Johnson's opposition to it. This is a good example of the fragmented state of the Know-Nothings at the time. Far from being a local question, vigilantism was a hot issue all over the state. In Sacramento John Rollin Ridge and other citizens organized a petition drive to urge Johnson to rescind his order mobilizing the militia. The petition's signers took the position that the militia's presence exacerbated the already tense situation and could result in civil war that might "drench the Streets of San Francisco and other cities and towns throughout the State in Blood." [15] The petition was delivered to Johnson in June 1856, but the governor failed to act. Ridge's newspaper and others throughout the state reiterated the position of the petitioners in their editorial pages until the committee, considering its work finished, voluntarily disbanded in August.

By early 1857 it was clear to nearly everyone that the Know-Nothing party in California was badly broken up, and what had been at best a loose coalition began to fall apart. This state of affairs was not lost on John Rollin Ridge, who realized that a newspaper most readers identified with a moribund political party was doomed to fail. Ridge and S. J. May worked out an agreement with John Church, W. C. Chandler, W. K. Tobey, and L. P. Davis—all Sacramento businessmen—to publish a new journal that would supplant the *California American*. Accordingly the group, known as Church and Company, purchased the *American*'s plant from James Allen. On Tuesday morning, February 3, 1857, journalism history was made when the first issue of the *Daily Bee* was published at Sacramento. The newspaper appeared every morning from Tuesday through Sunday. On April 6, when F. S. Thomson joined Church and Company, the *Bee* became an evening paper issued Monday through Saturday.

Ridge immediately made it clear to readers that the newspaper had broken with the Know-Nothings. Although in most respects the *American* and the *Bee* were materially the same, the editor pointed out, the new publication had shed "its past responsibilities and dependence upon party" and would henceforth be independent in politics.[16] In its pages would appear judgments on public issues without regard for partisan politics, for this policy was deemed to be in the best interests of the people. The editor was aware of the "dignity and power" of truly independent publications and pledged to steer "far out of the stormy latitudes of partizan strife." The newspaper's first editorial then goes on to assess the state's Democratic and American parties. Although the Democratic politicians are described as "selfish," Ridge reserves his most forceful language to describe the leaders of the Know-Nothings, as if to underline the newspaper's break with that party. These men posed as reformers, Ridge says, but "they were the most loathesome and political lepers, that ever tainted the atmosphere of the world with their persons." Vowing to keep the tone of the *Bee* dignified, the editor goes on to explain the name of the new publication: "The name of the *Bee* has been adopted, as being different from that of every other paper in the State, and as also being emblematic of the industry which is to prevail in its every department."

Here, then, was a chance for Ridge to assert himself editorially on a variety of issues, subject, certainly, to some restrictions imposed by Church and his associates, but largely free from partisan loyalties. Like most editors then and since, he was not shy about presenting his theories on journalism and the writing profession generally. Calling the "true" editor the "slave of the quill," Ridge says that it is the nature of the profession that the journalist's life is "one of continual toil and his position one of the most difficult on earth. While the lawyer must know about law, the physician about medicine, and the mechanic his craft," the editor, he reasons, must know almost "everything." He must have a "vast fund of general information, for there is not a subject which engages men's minds, in whatever range of science or literature, upon which he is not peremptorily called to write." He makes a distinction here between "true editors" and those "apologies for editors" who pass off articles from other papers as their own, whom he regards as a "disgrace to the profession."[17] He also comments on the vicissitudes an editor must suffer to be true to the profession by saying that opposition, even personal dislike or downright hatred, is to be expected when an editor speaks the truth. Nonetheless, an editor must "utter boldly his honest convictions" and "speak fearlessly . . . regardless of consequences."[18] Never loath to offer his opinions, Ridge followed this policy religiously. And though he expected opposition, he did not keep quiet about it. When his independent political position was attacked by one of the partisan newspapers, he fought back. At least half of the editors of political journals in California, he says, "are nothing more than the sneaking apologists of scoundrels who pay them for the trouble of lying—if you might call that trouble which seems to come to such men by nature."[19] He goes on to say that the partisan newspapers seldom if ever criticize a member of their own party, while politicians in the opposition are fair game. In other pieces he deprecates "literary sneaks," those editors who insinuate that writers on rival papers are untalented, and takes plagiarists to task. He praises the many small mountain newspapers that, he says, barely eke out an existence but stay in business to serve the public. While editor of the *Bee*, Ridge also defended women journalists and writers against attacks by "Atlantic" newspapers. "The lady-writers of America are among the very best of our contributors to the literature of today," he says. It is difficult, however, to determine whether Ridge is speaking from a critical or a chivalrous position, since he bases the value of women writers on the following: "They throw their own peculiar charm over every subject that they touch. They are in the world of letters, as compared to men, the sunny side of the picture—the flowers upon the rugged brows of the mountains—the sweetly singing birds in the wildernesses of thought— the silver sounding rills that help to swell the mighty river pouring ever into the great ocean of mind."[20]

As a poet of at least regional note, Yellow Bird felt qualified to theorize on other literary matters, including popular reading and the nature of poetry. The *Bee*'s editor discusses the reading habits of mid-nineteenth-century Americans and laments that few people read "substantial" books anymore. The public's attention is held by ephemeral publications, "the yellow-covered literature" made possible by efficient print methods. This would be a dire situation, Ridge writes, were it not for the popularity of magazines and newspapers. People generally read for amusement, but literature should instruct as well as delight. Periodicals do both; those publications can present ideas from "substantial" books in a more palatable form through "condensation and a popular, off-hand style." Newspapers and magazines can bring great and lofty ideas to people too busy for scholarship. Ridge correctly assessed the social, political, and economic impact of periodical literature in the nineteenth century.[21]

During his several months' tenure at the *Bee*, Ridge wrote and published poetry. The front page often carried a poem or two while he was editor. Yellow Bird's "Sunday in the Woods" appeared in June, as did his "A June Morning," reprinted from the *Southwest Independent*, a Fayetteville newspaper that Stand Watie was thinking about buying at the time.[22] As he was reading and writing poetry, he was also thinking about it; in an essay published in the *Bee*, he attempts to define it. He begins by saying poetry is not something distinct from real life but is a part of every person to a greater or lesser extent. Its presence was felt long before Homer and is experienced even by the uncivilized. "The speech of the North American warrior or chief in council, is full of metaphor and the essence of poetry," he writes. An example he offers is the death-bed speech of Pushmataha, the Choctaw leader who died while leading a delegation to Washington. He goes on to quote the Choctaw's last words. Poetry stems from every noble sentiment of the human heart, Ridge asserts, and its spirit is constantly around us. He takes a typically romantic position when he says it is up to the "true poet" to find that spirit and give it back to us. Using "his pen, his chisel, or his pencil," the artist gives the rest of us "these pictures of our nobler selves."[23] Yellow Bird was both jealous and proud of the title "poet" and held an almost Shelleyan belief in the power of the pen, especially during the early years of his writing career.

Ridge's belief that literature, including periodical writing, should instruct as well as delight caused him at times to use the *Bee*'s pages to wax philosophical. Of course newspaper readers at the time were used to seeing essays on "character" or "loyalty" or other uplifting subjects next to advertisements for saloons, patent medicines, and false teeth. Although such essays were often reprinted from other publications, Ridge wrote his own, a practice in keeping with his ideas on the role of the writer and the responsibilities of the editor. In one such essay, "The Value of Principle," he castigates many members of California society for their lack of morals and ethics. He takes to task young people who spend much of their time drinking and carousing. The article also attacks older members of society who engage in cutthroat business practices. He especially condemns the banks that have "crushed thousands of honest, hard-working men, with their families."[24] Here we see an early example of a democratic attitude that Ridge was to take for the rest of his life. Although in many ways he viewed himself as an aristocrat, in terms of both lineage and personal talent, he nonetheless proved to be a defender of working people's political and economic rights. Other essays in this same vein dealt with leadership and with conscience.

In addition to these self-improvement pieces, Ridge wrote other essays aimed at educating his readers. His legal training is in evidence when he holds forth on the "science of government" and attempts to explain how the forms of government in ancient Rome and Egypt contributed to the downfall of those empires. His belief in the inexorable march of progress is revealed in various articles on the laying of the first transatlantic cable, the expansion of railroads, and his confidence in the working out of America's Manifest Destiny. He made a major statement on the idea of progress in an essay published in the April 13 issue, "The Present Age." Here he writes, "The thinker of the present age beholds the universal progress of mankind." This process is made possible by advances in communications and transportation: "No sooner has a new fact, theory or event transpired, than it is caught up by the winged god of electricity—more swift than the fabled Mercury of the Ancients—or by the only less rapid messenger of steam, and borne to almost every conceivable quarter of the world." The result is "mutual benefit and improvement" of nations, and the process leads, he is certain, to an age of universal peace. The march of progress is both natural and unstoppable:

> In the same manner that our whole solar system is said to be gradually tending to some distant central point in space, so, to the illumined and prophetic vision of the enlightened reasoner of the present age, are the races of mankind progressing, slowly but surely, toward the grand ultimatum of a common destiny. In the march of events, those races which have an affinity will be brought together; the others will be improved while they last, and afterwards become extinct. But the time is rapidly approaching when the world will be inhabited by a few leading races, speaking each a language not hard to be understood by the other, and having a few well perfected forms of government, either monarchical or republican—the question is yet to be solved as to which form will prevail—while all other distinctive languages, peoples and governments will go down into the gulf of the past.

This myth of progress, along with all its accoutrements—cultural imperialism, colonialism, and inherent racism—was widely accepted in nineteenth-century Britain and America. It is not surprising that one with Ridge's education and background would accept these ideas as truth. Many of the "substantial" books he so revered contained the message of progress. Further, his reading was bolstered by what he was told by missionary teachers and by members of his own family. Sophia Sawyer and Cephas Washburn, after all, had dedicated their lives to the "improvement" of the Indian race. Theirs and other missionaries' reports to supporters in the East stressed the "progress" their followers were making. The major ambition of all the family since Major and Susanna Ridge began farming in earnest was to become as "civilized" as people in white society. And the Ridges carried these ideas beyond the family circle, urging their fellow Cherokees to educate themselves in Euro-American values and methods and to emulate white Americans. Little wonder that John Rollin Ridge espoused the sociohistorical theories encapsulated in his essay in the *Bee*.

Deeply embedded in the philosophy of progress Ridge accepted is the idea that more "civilized" nations or races will extend their hegemony over other "less developed" countries or peoples. Given this theoretical base, it is not hard to explain Ridge's views in the *Bee* on two major issues of the era, Manifest Destiny and filibustering. Ridge's own definition of Manifest Destiny is "the acquisition of territory, through conquest and purchase, by the Government of the United States."[25] He makes a succinct statement concerning American expansionism in a report on the commissioning of the ship *Morning Star*, a craft intended for missionary efforts in Micronesia. After giving an account of the commissioning ceremonies, the editor writes, "Well, all we have to say is, civilize, Christianize, Americanize the Polynesian Islands, and—annex them to the United States."[26] It is not surprising that a person holding this view would support filibustering. Filibustering in the nineteenth century was designed to "free" unprotected territory from foreign control and, often, to bring that territory and its inhabitants under the control of the United States. It was tied to the idea of Manifest Destiny, the doctrine by which the United States sought to expand toward its "natural frontiers."[27] Spurred on by the acquisition of California and

Texas, the filibusters looked south and made incursions into Mexico, Central America, and South America. Although frequently supported by Americans, especially people from the South and West, filibustering was generally opposed by those living in the lands that were the object of the filibusters' aims.

One of the most famous, or notorious, filibusters was William Walker, who at one point controlled a large part of the Nicaraguan army and even declared himself president of that country. Walker and the Americans in his band were ousted by the Nicaraguans in spring 1857 and allowed to return to America. The *Bee*'s editor laments the development and says that had Walker been successful, "Manifest Destiny would soon have embraced the whole of Central America" and gradually absorbed all the country from Nicaragua north to the American border.[28] In another editorial, Ridge defends Henry A. Crabb, a former classmate of Walker's, who had organized an earlier unsuccessful incursion into Nicaragua. In 1857 Crabb and his newly organized Arizona and Gadsden Colonization Company moved into Mexico, ostensibly to aid one of the factions involved in a struggle for power in that country. Crabb's real purpose, though, was to take control of a large part of Sonora.[29] The Sonoran response to Crabb and his armed band was to consider them invaders; in the end, his forces were beaten in battle and he was executed. Ridge defended Crabb against charges that he was "a land pirate and a robber, or at best an unprincipled filibuster." The editor judges that Crabb is a liberator, one who would free the Sonorans from a despotic government.[30] Other editorials argue the right of Americans to help the Sonorans secure independence from Mexico and to annex the Mexican state in the same way Texas became part of the United States. At one point Ridge advocates annexing Sonora with or without Sonoran assent unless the Mexican government can maintain law and order.[31] There is no doubt in Ridge's mind that Manifest Destiny and filibustering efforts will succeed, in spite of temporary setbacks like the failures of Walker and Crabb. He writes, "The progress of Anglo-American acquisition will . . . not be permanently checked. It may be stopped for awhile, but the returning wave will sweep with accumulating force in its destined

track and roll onward." The process is a natural one, dictated by the doctrine of progress: "The glory of a probable success, assimilating more
or less nearly to that which tore from the Mexican galaxy of States the
'lone star' of Texas, and that which all but crowned the first efforts of
Walker in Nicaragua, is sufficient to make ambitious men regardless of
all dangers and press right onward, in the name of Liberty and Progress,
to their object."[32]

It was as editor of the *Daily Bee* that John Rollin Ridge began to
publish anti-Mormon articles. His major objection to the Church of
Jesus Christ of Latter-day Saints seems to have been the attempt by Brigham Young and his followers to establish a Mormon state in Utah. Ridge
argued that a state government controlled by a religious sect violates
the constitutional mandate against an established religion. He considered himself a watchdog protecting the concept of separation of church
and state. In a May 19 editorial, "Political Preachers," Ridge speaks out
against preachers' interjecting political issues into their sermons. He sees
the practice as on the rise and views it as "a positive evil." The biggest
danger to the peace of any nation, he writes, is "to mix up political
questions with religious fanaticism." The result is a sure recipe for revolution or anarchy: "The bloodiest civil contests that have ever destroyed
nations and governments . . . have been those in which religious preju-
dices were arrayed on the side of political issues." He documents his
assertions with examples from European history. Ridge believed that
every religious sect is given the liberty of its beliefs; so, he reasoned,
there is no cause for the clergy to exhort their followers to take political
action. He finishes his essay with typical Ridgean fire: "A minister of the
gospel, therefore, in the United States, who would speak of politics in
the pulpit, and seek to array religion and politics in an alliance together,
is nothing better than a vile incendiary, torch in hand, in the very temple
of our liberties, and deserves to be looked upon as a common enemy,
taken down from the position which he disgraces, and branded with
universal contempt."[33]

Mormonism and Utah Territory held a special fascination for Ridge
and other Californians. The territory was established in 1850 out of the

Mormon region known as Deseret, with Brigham Young appointed by President Fillmore as territorial governor. From the start there was friction between the federal government officials there and the territorial government controlled by the Mormons. The conflict was inevitable, since Utah constituted "a polygamous theocracy within a monogamous and democratic nation."[34] Among the major sources of difficulty were the treatment of the "apostates," those who had decided to leave Mormonism; the practice of polygamy; and the authority of the federal government. Ridge contended that a policy of "secret assassination" was being carried out against the "apostates" by the territorial government, basing this assertion on reports from people who had emigrated from Utah to California. Although Ridge ridiculed the idea of polygamy— he writes that it is difficult for a man to presume to be loved by one woman, let alone seventeen—he did not attack the philosophy of the practice. Rather, he based his objections on certain ramifications. First, he reported that eleven-year-old girls in Utah were taken from their parents and assigned to elders who then provided for their education for the next four years, thus practically ensuring their indoctrination into the system of polygamy. Ridge regarded this custom as virtual slavery and an affront to the family. Second, the editor reported that a wife in a polygamous marriage who was unfaithful to her husband was subject to the death penalty. He offered the example of the young wife of Orson Pratt, who was stoned to death for infidelity in 1852 under a church edict. The incident, he said, directly violated the due process clause of the United States Constitution and thus called for federal intervention.[35] Ridge saw the authority of the federal government being undermined in Utah, too. By 1857 all federal officials except the Indian agent had been expelled from Utah Territory by Brigham Young, including judges who refused to follow the orders of the territorial government. A further problem was the establishment by the Mormon-controlled territorial legislature of courts that superseded the jurisdiction of the United States district courts. Ridge makes the point that though religions are protected from government interference, in this case the Mormons' usurpation of the territorial government and disregard for federal law erased that guarantee. The only recourse was for the federal government to remove Young and his followers from the territorial offices they held.[36] Eventually President Buchanan did send in troops to reestablish federal sovereignty. Ridge was to continue his opposition to the Mormons for all of his career. Though some might regard his anti-Mormonism as a campaign based on personal dislike for the sect, his stance was a popular one in the West in the mid-nineteenth century. Anti-Mormon feeling probably stemmed as much from jealousy over the Saints' economic success as from opposition to their "different" religious ideas.

Land issues centering on the validity of Mexican and Spanish land grants were debated in California from the end of the Mexican War through the rest of the century. At issue were the claims of the owners of vast tracts of land under the prewar grants versus those of American settlers who had emigrated to the West in search of free or cheap land. Many arrived in California and took apparently vacant land as their own. They erected buildings, grew crops, and raised livestock only to be challenged by the holders of grants who said they were "squatting" on private property. Many settlers were, of course, aware of the Spanish and Mexican claims, but they did not see why a few Hispanics—who after all had been defeated in the war—should control land needed by American pioneers. Compounding the issue, other settlers who had gone to neighboring Oregon got free land from the federal government. "Settlerism," as Ridge called it, was a hot issue when he edited the *Bee* and was debated in both Sacramento and Washington.[37] Ridge saw the problem as a class struggle between "aristocrats" and working people, and he responded characteristically. By defending the rights of settlers against land-grant holders, Ridge writes, "we speak for the whole people of the State, for the masses against the aristocratic few who would rob and oppress them." Ridge supported settlerism because it was "the only policy which can save the cultivators of her soil from being mere serfs or tenants-at-will upon the vast possessions of an aristocratic landed proprietary." Ridge supported settlers' political organizations in his newspaper and warned that if settlers' lands or crops were seized, the settlers were prepared to take up arms.[38]

While Ridge was editor, the *Bee* became the official newspaper of Sacramento. In a report to readers, he reveals that the *Bee* organization had obtained the contract for printing from the city government. The former city printer, Ridge reports, had not lived up to the terms of his contracts, and the city had to rely on the *State Journal* and the *Bee* instead of on the official printer's company to get its printing done. The contract helped put the young newspaper on a solid financial footing, but it was not the only factor in the *Bee*'s success. A steadily increasing subscription list and paying advertisers also helped bolster Ridge's claim that "although it has been launched into the sea of newspaper existence only three months, it is at this moment as much a permanent institution as if it had been established for years." The editor credits the company's bold policy of investing in telegraphic news dispatches and modern printing equipment for attracting subscribers and advertisers. This, coupled with the editorial staff's diligent work, resulted, in Ridge's words, in "all that is most desirable in a public print."[39]

It was while he was at the *Bee* that Ridge began writing extensively about American Indians. When he arrived in California in 1850, the plight of the native people of that state was desperate. As in much of the rest of the country, the American Indians in California were regarded as threats and nuisances by the white ranchers, miners, and farmers who flocked to the West in the late 1840s and 1850s. Indians were pushed off their land and often relegated to remote locations not considered valuable by white Americans. Resistance by the Indians brought swift reprisal by the United States Army and armed bands of civilian "volunteers." Persecution of the Indians, moreover, was sanctioned by officials, both state and federal. In 1850, for example, Governor Peter H. Burnett declared total war on the Indians, vowing to press against them until the race was extinct.[40] The next year the legislature passed a law called "Government and Protection of the Indians." Far from protecting the Indians, the law called for their exploitation by making men, women, and children subject to involuntary servitude through various legal means. For example, if an Indian was arrested on charges of drunkenness and could not pay his fine, a white rancher could pay the amount levied by the court and then set the prisoner to work until the debt was paid. The Indian had no voice in setting the terms of this transaction, those details being left to the judge and the rancher.

In these circumstances clashes between the two groups were inevitable. In addition to the repressive actions of government officials, the behavior of private citizens often made Indians resent whites. Contemporary newspaper accounts, for example, cite reports of Indians' being shot for "sport" and of the captivity of Indian women by miners and others in remote areas where few white women lived. These unfortunate women were taken as "wives" by the white men, forced into conjugal relations, and made to perform household duties until the men grew tired of them, moved on, or otherwise abandoned them. Incidents like these, especially in the northern areas, led to reprisals by Indians, which in turn resulted in attacks by white soldiers and civilians. Whole villages—men, women, and children—were sometimes obliterated.[41]

The administration in Washington, taking stock of this chaotic situation in the new state, determined to extend its removal/reservation policy to California Indians as a way of restoring order. Accordingly, a three-person commission was established to treat with the various bands and tribes, the aim being to remove them as far as possible from white population centers and to settle them on reservations. The commissioners signed thirty-five treaties with between 118 and 139 Indians groups (reports vary) during 1852–53. The treaties called for the Indians to cede 75 million acres to the whites and to move onto ten reservations totaling 7.5 million acres.[42] In addition, the federal government promised to provide education and training in farming and ranching as well as tools and implements so the Indians could emulate their white neighbors. Many white Californians, however, reacted negatively when the treaties' terms were announced; the combination of the protesters' political pressure and many senators' reactions to what they considered the high cost of the program resulted in the rejection of the pacts. The upshot was that the Indians were coerced into settling on very small reservations on often marginal lands, where they sometimes could eke out a meager subsistence and sometimes could not. One historian estimates that the California Indian population was reduced from about 100,000 in 1846 to about 50,000 ten years later. By 1870, three years after Ridge's death, poverty, malnutrition, and disease brought that number to 29,000.[43]

In the early 1850s the "Digger" Indians of California were in real danger of extermination. Genocide was seriously contemplated as one way of "dealing with them," as a *Daily Bee* article put it in 1857. The "Diggers" were actually several groups and tribes who were given the common name because of their practice of harvesting wild roots. They were considered by many whites to be inferior not only to white Americans and Europeans, but to other Indians as well. This notion no doubt contributed to some people's belief that their extermination was a real option. Although Ridge agreed that the California Indians were "inferior," he did not subscribe to the view that they should be killed off. Indeed, he thought their almost helpless situation in the face of white expansion into the West made it imperative that the more advanced whites devise a system for the Indians' protection.

Ridge's views on the "inferiority" of the California natives are apparent in many of his writings. In an April 7, 1857, editorial in the *Bee*, he calls them "a peculiar and strange race" unlike the tribes east of the Rockies or in South America. He goes on to praise the other North American Indians for their mental and physical qualities and the Incas for having established "a civilization of their own." On the other hand, he writes, "the Diggers of California, when first discovered by the whites, were so low in the scale of being, that it puzzled the observer to conceive of a condition more nearly illustrating the absolute *primitive* state of mankind." Ridge goes on to describe the Indians' ways of living—a description, he says, that is gleaned from firsthand observations. He characterizes their collective disposition as "peaceable, friendly, and kind-hearted, not brave but timid and yielding" and asserts that these attributes lead to their victimization by whites.

According to Ridge's theory on the subject, "The reason that these Digger Indians of California are indiscriminately slaughtered in this manner, without distinction of age or sex, is that it is easy work to kill

them." Had the California natives acted like Indian groups east of the
Rockies, their rights would have been better respected, he asserts. In
what can only be termed a bizarre reading of the history of the North
American Indians since white contact, he makes the following statement:

> The Indian's rights have been the best respected, since the first
> white settlement of this continent, in those places where he has
> held his ground by bow and gun, tomahawk and scalping knife;
> where he has shown himself a warrior, and ready to mingle his
> blood with the soil upon which he grew, rather than leave it;
> where he has met encroachment upon his rights, or what he
> deemed his rights, by the torch of midnight conflagration and
> the death-menacing war whoop and the death-dealing toma-
> hawk; where he has made it unsafe to lie down at night or to
> get up in the morning or to journey forth by day—*There* has his
> title to land been recognized and there has he been negotiated
> with and there have mutual terms of peace been subscribed to
> and respected.[44]

The "Diggers," though, a "poor, miserable, cowardly race," "permit
themselves to be slaughtered like sheep in a shambles." The implication
seems to be that somehow the victims are to blame, at least in part, for
the actions of their tormentors and murderers.

Though he considers the Diggers primitive, Ridge admits a certain
interest in them, especially individuals. One such individual is depicted
in "A True Sketch of 'Si Bolla,' a Digger Indian," rendered by Yellow Bird
in the *Bee* of June 24, 1857. Si Bolla, in Ridge's account, is the leader
of a band of California Indians, having come by that position naturally
because of his eloquence and other fine qualities. He served as a messenger between mining camps in the hills and was efficient and dependable.
Ridge writes that he was so impressed with the Indian he hired him as a
servant and thus got to know him well. He then recounts how Si Bolla
used his intelligence and speaking ability to free an Indian accused of
stealing, who was about to be hanged. Ridge professes admiration for
the man, which probably stemmed in large part from the surprise he felt

when he discovered that the Indian possessed intelligence, eloquence, and a "feeling heart"—qualities not expected in a lowly Digger.

He expressed similar admiration for a Yolo leader nicknamed "Captain Harry" by the miners. Apparently Harry was well known in Sacramento and environs for his fighting prowess, which he often exercised against an enemy band called Fremont Indians. After one skirmish he was captured and executed, an incident that precipitated an obituary from Ridge in the March 23, 1860, issue of the Marysville *National Democrat*. Accompanying the article was a verse, "A Elegy to a Brave Buck," purportedly written by a friend of Ridge's who signed his work "A Frend of Bravry wether mong Diggers or white folks." Here again the admiration for the individual Indian seems to be prompted by the belief that noble behavior by a Digger is the rare exception.

Although Ridge considered the Diggers inferior and primitive, he defended them against the whites who persecuted and enslaved them. A January 27, 1858, report in the *National Democrat* describes the hardships the Indians faced during cold weather and their mistreatment when they came into the towns for help. Homeless and ill clothed, they received little help because many whites were afraid aid would be squandered on liquor. Ridge wrote editorials on more serious cases of oppression too, relying on reports from outlying districts to illustrate his views. A good example is a piece published in the New Orleans *Daily True Delta*.[45] Here he recounts several instances of whites' attacking innocent Indians: the massacre of an entire rancheria, or settlement, including men, women, and children; the murder of a captured Indian girl who attempted to escape by jumping into a river; the execution of a six-month-old child; and other atrocities. In his comments on such inhuman acts, Ridge attributes them to "civilized ignorance," a state of mind that seems to "destroy the finest feelings of nature" and at the same time "denies those delicate sensibilities which belong to cultured minds." This "civilized ignorance" characterizes those to whom he refers elsewhere as "a meaner class of whites," who seem to be incited by the California Indians' very vulnerability. He titles an editorial in the *Bee* of July 12, 1857, "Oppression of the Digger Indians" and goes on to relate how "lawless bands" of white men killed Indian parents in order to kidnap their children. The children were subsequently sold, presumably as slaves or indentured servants. These bands of whites were able to escape prosecution by stealing cattle from white ranchers, blaming the Indians, then hunting down and executing the "rustlers." Although their main income from this operation came from stolen cattle, selling Indian children was a lucrative sideline. Ridge's editorial urges the federal government to act out of humanity and stop the practice.

Perhaps it was because of all his diligent work that Ridge needed some time off from his duties for a holiday. An item in the May 5 issue of the *Bee* reports that the editor, his wife, and their daughter were off on a "jaunt" to the mountains "in search of fresh air and amusements," his health being "not as good as we could wish." Acting in his stead was his old partner James Allen. During his ten-day vacation, Ridge served as correspondent to his paper, sending dispatches dated May 6, 9, 10, and 11. The family traveled by stage to the mining district some forty miles from Sacramento. Arriving in Drytown in Amador County, the Ridges stayed at the hotel of D. G. Bell, whom Ridge calls the "Old Chief" and identifies as a Cherokee. Bell, Ridge says, "keeps as excellent a hotel as the mining region affords." This Cherokee and his wife were apparently the soul of affability and hospitality. The trio stayed in the area nearly a week before they returned to Sacramento. Leaving Elizabeth and Alice at home, Ridge then continued his holiday alone and took the train to Folsom. He returned to Sacramento in time to get out the paper on May 15. While traveling, Ridge wrote descriptions of the countryside, often commenting on the effects of the drought that occurred in the mid-1850s. He took a special interest in the relatively new practice of quartz mining in the goldfields and provided an inventory of the water- and steam-driven mills that pulverized the ore. Quartz mining revitalized the goldfields after the more obvious surface deposits had run out. Gold-bearing quartz rock was now mined in tunnels and shafts, requiring large doses of capital and technology. The new gold-mining methods drew Ridge's attention for two reasons. First, as a former miner, he was interested in new technology in the field. Second, as a businessman with a stake in the area, he welcomed quartz mining for the boost it gave the economy. In Folsom, Ridge stayed at Patterson and Waters's Hotel. In his dispatch to the *Bee* from there, he comments on the Sacramento-to-Folsom train, with its full load of freight and passengers. Always a booster of progress, he describes the mining operations in this area in some detail too, as well as major improvements such as a suspension bridge nearing completion and a new reservoir built by the railroad.

After his return to Sacramento, Ridge stayed on at the *Bee* for another two months. In July the newspaper was sold to James McClatchy, whose family has operated it ever since. Apparently the Ridge family's plans were not firm after the sale of the newspaper. The San Francisco *Daily Alta California* reported in its July 29, 1857, issue that the Ridges were moving to Oroville, but their actual destination was Marysville, where Ridge became editor of the *California Express*. The *Express* was published by W. F. Hicks and Company both daily and weekly out of its office in the Express Building on First Street. The publishing company was made up of Lloyd Magruder, S. Addington, J. Laird, and W. F. Hicks, local businessmen. Hicks was a printer by trade. Magruder was involved in politics, and while a candidate for Congress in Idaho Territory in 1863, he was murdered. The *Express* was the "official" paper for Yuba County, which usually meant that its proprietors held the county printing contract. Far from the politically independent organ the *Bee* purported to be, the *Express* was staunchly Democratic; the platform of the California Democratic party was printed on the front page of every issue.

By the time he became editor of the Marysville newspaper, Ridge had acquired a fine literary and journalistic reputation. The *Alta California*, one of the state's most popular journals, quoted the editor of the Sacramento *Age* as Ridge was about to leave the capital to return to Marysville:

> Before his announcement as editor of that paper [*Bee*], he was well known as "Yellow Bird," and is a popular literary writer; since then his writings have been distinguished by dig-

nity, ability and good sense, and, when touching on subjects
that admit the exercise of his peculiar genius, he has shown a
capacity which few writers possess—to touch the citadel of the
soul. His talent charms and has secured the respect of the profession, and his generosity and manliness and heart have made
him friends of all good men who know him.[46]

Alonzo Delano, a popular California writer who published under the
name "Old Block," called Ridge in 1856 "one of California's most popular writers," citing *Joaquín* and his articles in the New Orleans *True Delta*,
and said he was a "writer of many beautiful powers."[47] Ridge was to
demonstrate in the *Express* that his reputation was well deserved. For
example, a New Year's Day essay published in 1858 speaks eloquently
of the influence of each individual intelligence on "the universal mass of
mind." It is a piece that stresses the cultivation of the intellect and the
appreciation of well-written and well-spoken language. Other essays in
a philosophical vein establish the differences between talent and genius
and define greatness. He also published a piece in his newspaper titled
"Literary Statesmen of Britain," in which he disagrees with the proposition that the pursuit of literature disqualifies a person for the active
business of life, either professional or political. He cites as proof Disraeli,
Palmerston, Walpole, and other Englishmen, and he probably had himself in mind as well. In the New Year's Day issue, however, he also shows
his talent for whimsy. He wrote a poem "In the ancient Finnish measure— / In the Scandinavian rhythm— / In the metre of Longfellow"
asking readers to contribute "discs of silver." The verse is a reminder that
January 1 is the time to renew subscriptions.

But for the most part, while at the *Express* Ridge turned his talent
toward political comment. During this time he was to turn increasingly
to the positions held by Stephen A. Douglas, senator from Illinois and
presidential hopeful. In the turbulent years leading up to the Civil War,
he was a vocal supporter of the "Douglas Democracy" and opposed
many of the policies of the Buchanan administration. One of the major
issues during the time Ridge edited the *Express* was whether the new

territory of Kansas, created under the 1854 Douglas-backed Kansas-
Nebraska Act, would be slave or free. Douglas, and Ridge, contended
that the question should be settled by the principle of popular sovereignty—letting the citizens of each new territory or state vote on the
matter. In Kansas the problem was compounded by the influx into that
area of both pro- and antislavery settlers. Both camps produced state
constitutions and submitted them to the United States Senate. The antislavery document, the Topeka constitution, was rejected by that body,
but the Lecompton charter, which would have allowed slavery, was accepted. Kansas would have been accepted into the Union as a slave
state had the Buchanan administration had its way, but Douglas, following his principle of popular sovereignty, insisted that the people of
Kansas vote on the constitution. The Lecompton document was voted
down overwhelmingly. Ridge's editorials on the issue followed pretty
much the Douglas line. He did not support the Free-Staters, since, he
said, they would not participate in the constitutional convention held
at Lecompton but elected to hold a rump session at Topeka. Although
he supported the terms of the Lecompton constitution, he would not
support its adoption unless a majority of the people in Kansas voted for
it. Thus he opposed the Buchanan-backed senators who voted to accept
the document as the state constitution. Ridge argued eloquently for the
Douglas position almost daily in the pages of the *Express* during the first
six months of 1858. In some ways it is surprising that Ridge, in the hundreds of column inches the *Express* devoted to the Kansas question, never
mentioned that Douglas and the other framers of the Kansas-Nebraska
Act totally ignored the American Indians who held claim to that area
under numerous treaties. Apparently Ridge's views on Manifest Destiny
and the assimilation of Indians into white society were so well formed
by that time that he did not regard the treaties as a problem. It is ironic,
however, that the Indian groups displaced by the whites' settlement of
Kansas were eventually given land in the Cherokee Nation. The land was
provided in the treaty that John Rollin Ridge had a part in negotiating
at the end of the Civil War.

Ridge's *Express* editorials argued other current issues as well. One
offers a legal opinion on the status of a slave brought to California by

his master. The slave, known as Arch, claimed to be free once in California, since California was a free state. Ridge says the case does not come under the fugitive slave law, since Arch was brought to the state by his master and did not escape. The Dred Scott case does apply, Ridge argues. If Scott had declared himself free in Illinois instead of waiting until he returned to Missouri, he would have been free, since he was under the laws of Illinois while in that state. Arch had claimed freedom under the laws of California while in California, Ridge reasons, and so he is free.[48] Ridge also continued his attacks on the Mormons. By the time he became editor of the *Express*, the federal/territorial government rift had widened and Buchanan was forced to send in troops. Ridge, in a tortured bit of logic in one editorial, says the federal government should not make a judgment on polygamy, since that is a local issue and its legality should be determined through popular sovereignty. When women are held as wives against their wills, however, the Mormons are depriving them of liberty without due process, a violation of the United States Constitution. Since Ridge is certain that "young girls" were detained by Mormon "high priests and apostles" and made their "sealed wives," the United States government should step in. He also accuses the Mormons of "treason against the government" and of creating a "system of oppression, robbery and murder, under a blending of hierarchal and civil power" that was imposed not only on Mormons and those they called "apostates," but on "American citizens temporarily residing in the Territory or passing through it."[49] Throughout his editorship at the *California Express*, Ridge called for building a transcontinental railroad. He argued that it would have the obvious benefits of expanding commerce and communication but would also help bring civilization to the Indians of the West and allow emigrants to Oregon and California to avoid Utah Territory. Ridge continued, too, to express his profilibuster views during this period. At various times he advocated buying Sonora, placing all of Mexico under a United States "protectorship," and annexing Cuba. Ridge continued as editor of the *California Express* until August 4, 1858. On August 12 of that year the *Daily National Democrat* appeared in Marysville, with John Rollin Ridge as editor.

8

National Democrat

In summer 1858 Ridge became affiliated with the publishers of the Marysville *News*, whose editor had been General James Allen. A new company was formed under the leadership of A. S. Randall, the other principals of the undertaking being Samuel B. Christian, J. F. Whitaker, Walker Boulware, and John O. Heatley. All these men had worked on the *News* and its predecessors, the *Herald* and the *Inquirer*. Whitaker had been a printer for the Marysville *Express* in 1853. The *News* was short-lived, running only from January 9 to August 9, 1858. Randall and his partners were eager to revitalize their investment, so they brought in Ridge hoping he would provide the needed shot in the arm. Ridge bought out Allen's share of newspaper, which at the time had a circulation of 3,500. At thirty-one, the editor was full of the requisite youthful energy, but he also had valuable editing experience. An added asset was his growing literary reputation.

The first issue of the *Daily National Democrat* came out on Thursday morning, August 12, with the words "The Voice of the People Is the Voice of God" proudly emblazoned on its banner. The masthead listed John R. Ridge as editor and carried the following line attributed to Thomas Jefferson: "I have sworn on the altar of my country eternal enmity to every form of tyranny over the mind of man." The paper was issued daily except Mondays from its office on the corner of Maiden Lane and Second Street in Marysville's business district. The *Daily Democrat* carried reprinted poetry, advertising for local merchants and various products, short local news items, reports from surrounding communities concerning mining and other businesses, and news dispatches from the East, San Francisco, Sacramento, and other California cities. Page 2 usually carried a nearly full-column editorial plus another column of news items, both written by Ridge. The total number of words composed each day averaged more than two thousand.

Of course Ridge was well known as a writer in Marysville by this time, being the celebrated author of *Joaquín Murieta* and having composed several poems that had appeared in the local press. So it was natural for him to write a commemorative poem on the laying of the transatlantic cable between the United States and the United Kingdom, to be delivered at a public celebration of that event in Marysville. A version of the poem was published in the September 23 issue of the *Daily Democrat*, four days before the holiday. And holiday it was, with all the city's business "from the heaviest banking house down to the humblest rag-picker" suspended, according to the newspaper's account published on September 28. The townspeople gathered at 1:00 P.M. in front of city hall to begin the festivities, as cannons were shot off and church bells rang. The grand marshal led a parade, headed by a band and marchers bearing the flags of various European nations. At this point there occurred the only trouble to mar an otherwise perfect day. Ridge reports the "slight interruption" this way:

> As the procession moved off, the Chinese delegation, which formed a very attractive feature, finding themselves in the rear —(a very unenviable position to occupy in a retreating army, but a very appropriate one in this case)—and probably remembering the precedent set for them not long since by their pale-faced superiors—*bolted* from the ranks of the main procession;

all explanations and promises of a more prominent position in the ranks could not shake the mulish stubbornness of the outraged "Johns," and they slunk off to their own more congenial hovels, muttering curses loud and deep on "Melican men" generally.[1]

The "precedent" alluded to is not clear, but clashes often occurred between the Chinese and the Americans, many of whom had convinced themselves that Orientals were taking all the gold from the goldfields.

The rest of the parade then formed up and proceeded on its route up and down the streets of Marysville until it reached the pavilion in the city park. This part of the celebration was opened by the Choral Harmonie Association's singing "God Save the Queen," followed by a prayer by a local clergyman. After the invocation the Liederkranz Society broke into "The Marseillaise," setting the stage for Ridge's dramatic reading. After the applause for the singers died down, the poet was introduced by Mayor Peter Decker. Ridge strode confidently to the podium, his long black hair flowing, as Elizabeth and Alice watched proudly. He then read his "Poem on the Atlantic Cable," his voice resonant as he measured out the stately cadences of his heroic couplets. His verse, tracing the history of human communication, underscored his audience's sense that they were celebrating an auspicious event, further proof that the march of progress was leading to human perfection. As Ridge delivered his final line, "A throbbing heart-string of HUMANITY!" the crowd broke into enthusiastic applause. The poet bowed and, turning, returned to his seat as the Liederkranz Society began to sing the national anthem of Germany. Once the group had finished, the mayor introduced the day's next speaker. E. D. Wheeler then delivered his oration, a speech that touched on the wonders of modern science and its role in improving the lot of the human race. Wheeler finished his remarks by expressing the hope that the transcontinental railroad and telegraph would both soon be completed. The coast-to-coast telegraph was finished in 1861, eight years before the railroad and five years before Cyrus Field's Atlantic cable was to operate reliably.

But the Marysville festival was a celebration of the primacy of progress, and after the applause for Wheeler's speech subsided, the program moved on to its next stage, the reading of telegrams sent to various parts of the state, along with replies received. One telegram from "the Press Gang of Marysville to the Press Gang down below" was sent to the Sacramento *Union* by Ridge and the Marysville *Express* editor A. C. Russell. Its message read as follows: "Lightning is our best and fastest reporter and is sure to have a permanent situation. The Press should keep the Atlantic and Pacific Telegraph enterprise before the people." Other telegrams were sent by Mayor Decker to officials in Sacramento, Stockton, Placerville, Weaverville, and San Francisco, which were all holding similar celebrations. The band played throughout the rest of the afternoon as the townspeople picnicked and visited. The Ridge family greeted a number of well-wishers before retiring to their home that evening.

The next two years were relatively quiet ones for Ridge, punctuated by occasional family outings but filled mostly with work at the *Daily Democrat*. He seems not to have taken vacations other than the odd day off. Even after he was injured in a serious accident, he refused to take time off to recover. The June 8, 1860, issue of the newspaper reported that as Rollin and Elizabeth were returning from the funeral of Judge Henry P. Haun, one of the shafts of their buggy came loose and hit the horse. The animal bolted, upsetting the carriage and spilling its passengers onto the pavement of C Street. Elizabeth was cut severely on the face and suffered bruises over a good part of her body; the report on her husband says only that he was "pretty badly hurt." Whatever his condition, he refused to be confined to the house.

The newspaper seems to have been doing well during this period, since before its first year was out, it—or rather its editor—had drawn the ire of the better-established *Express*. The resulting exchanges doubtless provided the major excitement in Ridge's life at the time. The editor of the *Express*, Andrew Campbell Russell, worked on a number of papers during his career and had been involved in several physically violent incidents arising from editorials he had written. Russell had been wounded in a knife attack over an article, had fought a duel with Captain Joseph Folsom in 1851, and had been hurt in another altercation prompted by one of his editorials in 1852. The rivalry between the two papers came to a head over the local July 4 orations in 1859 and was to remain heated during Ridge's tenure on the *Daily Democrat*, even after Russell left his editorship. The *Express* published the speeches delivered at the Independence Day celebration in Marysville, praising them for their eloquence and patriotism. The next day, Ridge used his editorial column to ridicule the speeches for their many grammatical and rhetorical errors. When the *Express* in turn defended the orators, Ridge issued another editorial on the subject. His thesis was simple:

> The idea that empty puerility, nonsensical bombast, high-falutin froth and declamatory fury, and that not even redeemable by the leaven of a little, a very little, knowledge of the proper construction of that language in which the Declaration of Independence was itself promulged, are to be tolerated by an intelligent assemblage of American citizens, simply because it is only on occasion of the celebration of the Fourth of July, is the most ridiculous assumption heard of among a civilized people.[2]

He then goes on to insist that an editor has both the right and the responsibility to comment on and criticize orators and even preachers.

From here the war of words escalated, with Ridge charging that the proprietors of the *Express* were "old line Know Nothings" and that one of their number was an "unnaturalized denizen." A person who refused to become a citizen, Ridge contended, must have an aversion to American institutions and no sympathy with the principles of American government. At this point, whether he knew it or not, Ridge himself was taking a position very close to that of the Know-Nothings. As was quite common in the newspaper wars of the era, the battle became personal. In one of his volleys Ridge says that the *Express* editor lacks the "rudiments of an editorial education." In another he describes the rival editor's tactics of using an anonymous correspondent's comments on

Ridge as an act of cowardice. When the *Express*'s correspondent says he possesses "some sweet morsels," items that will not "prove very palatable to the sensitive organs of the would-be great man at the *National Demo-crat*," Ridge responds with typical bravura. He asks that the morsels be brought forward so he can judge whether they prove unpalatable. If so, he goes on, he will see to it that they are made equally unpalatable to his attacker. "We trust he understands us," he says. If not, "we shall endeavor to give him a realizing sense of what we mean."[3] Clearly, Ridge was quick to engage his rival in a battle of words and wit; this readiness was to remain with him throughout his career.

While the rival editors fought it out on the editorial pages, both knew that the exchange sold their products. In addition, they knew to cooperate when it was mutually beneficial. The city printing contract of 1860 is a case in point. Following a relatively new policy, the Marysville city council awarded the contract to one of the city's newspapers after sealed bids had been received and opened. The contract went to the low bidder. Formerly, the city printer had been elected and simply billed the city for his services. The contract not only involved publishing official notices but included all the municipality's printing business as well. In addition, the paper awarded the contract got to refer to itself as the "official" city newspaper. Until 1860 the *Express* and the *Daily Democrat* strove to underbid each other, the former doing the work for $1,500 in 1858 and the latter for $1,200 the following year. The bidding war resulted in "ruinous sacrifice" for both papers, in Ridge's terms, and had to be stopped. When the council opened the bids in April 1860, it found that both bids were much higher than previous ones. Outraged, its members charged the newspapers with collusion to fix prices. Ridge denied the charge but said the newspapers could not do the work for what they had charged before.[4]

Apparently, Ridge's comments on the 1859 Fourth of July speeches made an impression on the city officials who planned the affair; either that or Ridge was issued a challenge to do better, for when the 1860 celebration was planned, it was announced that John Rollin Ridge would be the main speaker. The events began early, with bells ringing from the church steeples for a few minutes at midnight and again at sunrise. Cannons were fired at sunrise and again at noon and sunset. At 10:30 A.M. a parade, consisting of bands, the Liederkranz Society, and carriages full of dignitaries, proceeded to the pavilion in the city park. The Society and children's choirs sang, and the Rev. Mr. McClary gave the invocation. Vandyke Hubbard read the Declaration of Independence, after which a poem was read by B. P. Avery. After another song, John Rollin Ridge delivered his patriotic address without notes and, the July 6 issue of the Marysville *Daily Appeal* reports, "in a strain of dignified eloquence, discanting upon the growth of the Confederacy [Union] and the duty of its citizens, and earnestly enjoining the cultivation of a broad national patriotism." His address was brief and "interrupted once by the breaking of some benches, but it was listened to with pleasure and heartily applauded." Quite possibly the benches were broken by disgruntled supporters of the previous year's speakers. That evening the Ridges joined the crowd at Cortez Square to watch the fireworks. Rollin's fame as a public speaker spread, and in September 1860 he was invited to present a poem, written by him for the occasion, to the Agricultural, Horticultural, and Mechanics' Society of the Northern District of California. In June 1861 he read a poem, again written for the occasion, at the College of California commencement at Oakland. He also presented a poem at the Fourth of July celebration in San Francisco in 1861. The July 9 issue of the Marysville *Daily Appeal* described the poem as "remarkable for its sustained dignity of style, loftiness of thought and imagery and strong glowing patriotism."

These three poems, along with "The Atlantic Cable," can be termed Ridge's "philosophical" poems, since they comprise some of his major statements on the history of civilization and the impact of history on contemporary societies. Ridge, like many thinkers in the nineteenth century, believed that civilization is an evolutionary process. Societies, races, and nations are caught up in the inevitable march of progress and are constantly evolving toward higher and higher levels. The march is not merely technological; human intelligence and even human spirituality move upward. Implicit in this belief is the idea that the various contemporary societies, races, and nations have reached different plateaus on the evolutionary scale because of environment and other factors. Some of the hunter-gatherer societies, indeed, have barely begun the climb of progress. The Western nations, on the other hand, including the United States, have reached the highest levels and are at the cutting edge of the evolutionary process. And the theory could be supported empirically; one could look around and see the technological advances being made every day in the developed countries and compare this activity with the antique stagnation of less advanced societies. Among the many implications of such a system is the premise that the "advanced" nations are morally obligated to spread their ideas and methods to the "benighted" peoples of the world. A corollary of this idea is that less advanced people should accept these offerings wholeheartedly and learn to live like their more civilized counterparts. The message for American Indians is obvious. By the time Ridge wrote these poems, he believed his family had made the transition in only three generations from a primitive aboriginal existence to a modern civilized one. The four works—two called simply "Poem," plus "The Atlantic Cable" and "California"—are expressions of Ridge's basic philosophical beliefs.

The longest of his works in verse (324 lines), the first "Poem" reveals some interesting insights into Ridge's views. It demonstrates his deep-seated belief in progress and at the same time praises Indian culture; his praise, however, is directed not toward contemporary Indian nations, but rather toward the old Aztec and Inca civilizations. The poet also includes an antiwar statement as well as a prediction for the future.

Delivered before the Agricultural, Horticultural, and Mechanics' Society of the Northern District of California on August 5, 1860, the poem begins with a song of praise for the plow. The plow is the symbol of agriculture, which makes possible civilization and progress. Indeed, all the achievements of the human race, all the arts and sciences, have depended and still depend on farming. Having made this assertion in the opening lines, the poet then traces the history of civilization, as he sees it, from the beginning:

> The Nations justly vaunted now and great—
> Old days beheld them in the hunter state,

When clad in skins and quivers on their backs,
They followed on the wild deer's bounding tracks;
Or sought, through wood and brake and fen,
The fierce and gnashing boar within his den.

(Lines 28–33)

From this hunter-gatherer society evolved, according to Ridge's scheme, an existence that relied on keeping flocks and herds. This change made life somewhat easier for ancient people, since it removed them a step from total dependency on nature and shifted their reliance to their own craft and skill. But it was still a precarious way to make a living:

Next came the pastoral days, when men less roved,
But pitched their camps by pleasant springs, nor moved
Till pasture failed or rival flocks their bounds
Did press, intrusive on their chosen grounds.
Still, 't was a roving life, surrounded too
By Foes and daily dangers not a few.

(Lines 43–48)

The nomadic herding gave way to yet a higher, more stable existence with the advent of agriculture. Agriculture, according to Ridge, made it possible for people to control nature for the first time, or at least to coexist peacefully with it.

But came in turn the third and better state,
With cheering omens of a higher fate.
Then, did the restless Nomad cease to roam—
His hardships o'er, he found at last his home.

(Lines 51–54)

Ridge then describes the historical forces that permitted the advance of civilization. When people recognized that they shared "mutual interests and needs" (line 65), human communities were possible. One of these needs was defense against less civilized beings: "Against the still untamed and savage man / The armed alliance of the few began" (lines 67–68). With peace at home and security against foreign enemies, society was able to advance further. This progress was predicated on the people's "New wants," a sort of latent consumerism rising to public consciousness. These material desires led to invention, on the one hand, and to a body of laws on the other. Invention was necessary to supply the people's wants, and the laws were vital to keep them from being too aggressive in their pursuit of happiness.

With the spread of agriculture, civilized communities sprang up in various places. Invention and the human propensity for a materially higher standard of living soon led to commerce. Trade led to higher expectations and more invention, so the impetus to progress—at least on the materialistic and technological level—was supplied.

> Thus commerce rose, and, stimulating art,
> Gave impulse to Invention and a new start
> To all improvements that a Nation raise
> And make a people's glory, wealth and praise.
>
> (Lines 85–88)

Ridge traces these developments to ancient Tuscany and Rome as well as to Egypt. Although these states reached a high degree of civilization, further progress was retarded by their fondness for war. He sees war as causing the fall of the great ancient societies; he describes the process in the following passage:

> They fell—
> As fell the grand old Rome—because too well
> They loved the bannered pomp of conquering war,
> Neglecting arts of peace more glorious far,
> While fought the soldier at a despot's will,
> The rusting plow within the field stood still,
> And hosts, returning from a vanquished land,
> Spread vice and luxury on every hand.
>
> (Lines 97–104)

The historical forces that drive the engine of progress were not confined to the Old World, according to Ridge. In America, too, great nations were coming into being, presumably through natural means and not through influences from Europe or northern Africa. The next two sections, some seventy-three lines, are devoted to descriptions of the high state of civilization reached by the Aztecs of Mexico and the Incas of Peru. The poet praises the labor and ingenuity of the Indian nations and shows that the results of their work were similar to those in Old World communities still admired for their high achievement. The "cultured plain" was rich with crops, "deep canals" aided commerce, the "cities vast" were served by aqueducts, and the technology of irrigation was in common use on the farms. The arts also were in full flower and manifested themselves in architecture, sculpture, and tapestry that rivaled the works of the Old World.

It is at this point in the poem that Ridge takes the opportunity to make a positive statement on the old Indian civilizations. First he makes it clear that Indian achievements should not be ignored because of race:

> Was art, that built those cities vast, less art,
> Because of Aztec genius 't was part?
> Was patient toil, that led thro' channels deep,
> And aqueducts, and 'long the rocky steep,
> The streams a thousand fertile fields supplied,
> Less toil, because no white man's arm was tried?
> Were peace and plenty but the Spaniard's right?
> The Aztec *barbarous* because not *white*?
>
> (Lines 125–32)

Yet the greatest of all the Indian achievements was not the "temples blazing rich with gold," but rather the Indians' political and economic system. This system was based on the idea that "government is wisest that's designed / For good of greatest number of the kind" (lines 159–60), a concept espoused by many of the Western democracies of the nineteenth century. Under the Incan plan, Ridge says, each person got an equal portion of the land to work, and each was guaranteed an equal share of its products so that none went hungry. The Incas not only provided freedom from want but enjoyed a social security system that surpassed the modern welfare-state schemes:

If sickness fell or any evil fate,
The State provided, not as charity
But right, for him whose former industry,
Still looking to the common weal in this,
Had swelled her coffers and her granaries.

(Lines 170–74)

For Ridge, the Peruvian Indian society had reached the pinnacle of civilization, a point of development where all the community's members were happy and secure.

The upward spiral of progress carries along whole societies, at least those dedicated to "Agriculture and the arts of peace" (line 185), but it has other effects too. The evolutionary process is at work in human nature itself, providing for a growth of "The mind and heart" (line 187). Just as "New forms" (line 193) of life appeared on earth, "The human soul, the Man expanded too, / And found in realms of thought the strange and new" (lines 197–98).

Having traced "the history of the plow" (line 200), Ridge turns to California, a land he believed would soon rival the glories of ancient Greece and Rome and even Peru. Agriculture, with its attendant arts and sciences, would cause the desert to bloom and the people to prosper:

The land shall blossom with its edens fair,
The fruitful hills make fragrant all the air,
And breezy valleys wave their yellow hair,
For mark you, Art, with Science aid, shall make
Spots fertile which the ignorant forsake.

(Lines 304–8)

The poem ends with a confident passage predicting the imminent fulfillment of California's promise.

"The Atlantic Cable" also offers insights into Ridge's social and political views. This work celebrates one of the major technical achievements of the century. Ridge regarded the event as a significant milestone in the march of progress, and his poem boldly explores the implications of such an advance in communications. It begins with an announcement of his major themes: that nature operates according to a plan governed by slow but inexorable progress, that all people are kindred, and that communication supplies the means for people to act like brothers and sisters.

> Let all mankind rejoice! for time nor space
> Shall check the progress of the human race!
> Though Nature heaved the Continents apart,
> She cast in one great mould the human heart.
> (Lines 3–6)

Communication among distant peoples seems to the poet to be a basic urge, felt by ancients and moderns alike. Typically, he gives an account of the history of human communication that helps make his point. In prehistoric times, he says, "skin-clad heralds" were sent "to thread the woods, / Scale mountain peaks, or win the sudden floods, / And bear their messages of peace or war" (lines 17–19). He recounts how couriers on foot were replaced by messengers on horseback and how water travel evolved from oars to sail to steam. This progress, "Improvement's race" (line 25), contributed to relations among people:

> Then, sea-divided nations nearer came,
> Stood face to face, spake each the other's name,
> In friendship grew, and learned the truth sublime,
> That Man is Man in every age and clime!
> (Lines 30–33)

But as great an advance as steam power was, it was surpassed by the harnessing of electricity—for Ridge perhaps the ultimate achievement in the human race's attempts to control nature. Electricity is "A mightier monarch" that gives "to human thought a thought-swift wing" (lines 48–49). That elemental power of the universe, which so terrified the premoderns, now is controlled by people.

Ridge finds it appropriate that it was Americans who brought electricity under human control, mentioning Benjamin Franklin, Samuel S. B. Morse, and Cyrus W. Field as contributors to the achievement, men who gave "the lightning's voice to Liberty" (line 85). For Ridge believed that the advanced form of communication the cable afforded would preach the gospel of democracy and its progressive idealism all over the world. The cable would "wing the heralds of Earth's happiness, / And sing, beneath the ever-sounding sea, / The fair the bright millenial days to be" (lines 86–88).

In the final verse, Ridge expands on what is possible in the future, the sort of world that lies at the end of the path of progress. Here, as in "Poem," Ridge emphasizes that peace is necessary to the progress of the human race.

> Now may, ere long, the sword be sheathed to rust,
> The helmet laid in undistinguished dust;
> The thund'rous chariot pause in mad career,
> Its crimsoned wheels no more through blood to steer.
>
> (Lines 89–92)

"California" and the "Poem" delivered at the Oakland College commencement treat the theme of progress too. Both deal specifically with progress made in California and with the contribution of the American pioneers who settled there after the Mexican War and during the gold rush of 1849. The first thirty lines of "California" describe the state's natural riches, then the poem goes on to praise the accomplishments of its people. The natural resources of California, exploited by the "Arts and Labor" (line 40) of the citizens, have led to new heights of civilization, the symbol of which is San Francisco:

> With mien
> Majestic as of right her look should be,
> She sits like Tyre of old beside the sea;
> And, while the messengers of commerce wait,
> She opens wide and free her Golden Gate.
>
> (Lines 43–47)

Here Ridge reiterates his theme that modern people control the environment and dominate nature. Like other nineteenth-century prophets of progress, he ignores the ecological implications of such an attitude and praises those who chop down forests, change the course of rivers, and level mountains in the name of progress.

Similar ideas are expressed in the poem Ridge read at Oakland College on June 6, 1861. Here he salutes the "Adventurers" who worked the goldfields—men who, stricken with a "fever-rage for gold" (line 46), left behind their families and friends. Most of these, Ridge knew from experience, were not successful in their quest for riches, and many sacrificed their health or even their lives. Yet he maintains that their efforts were necessary and led directly to the American settlement of the state and the establishment of civilization in the region. The rugged pioneers also made possible the learning environment:

> Lo! Peace hath built her quiet nest;
> And "mild-eyed Science" roves,
> As was her wont when Greece was blest,
> In academic groves.
>
> (Lines 93–96)

As we have seen, the "Digger" Indians, indigenous to California, held a special fascination for Ridge. He identifies them in his commentaries on American Indians as a primitive people far down the evolutionary ladder from more "civilized" groups like the Cherokees. In "Poem," however, the California natives are treated more kindly. The Digger did not recognize the worth of the gold that lay at his feet, and "The dream of greatness never rose / Upon his simple brain" (lines 9–10). However, Ridge points out, these people were content with their lives, at least until the coming of the whites.

> But happier perchance by far
> Still digging for his roots,
> Than thousand paler wanderers are
> Whose toil hath had no fruits.
>
> (Lines 21–24)

Ridge's comments on the Diggers reflect his sometimes ambivalent attitude toward the assimilation of American Indians into white society.

While he celebrates progress, he also hold the typical romantic idea of an ancient golden age, an innocent past in which people were spared the vicissitudes of modern life. This golden past is attractive, Ridge acknowledged, but he also recognizes that returning to it is impossible. For contemporary people living under primitive conditions, the truth is harsh but simple: assimilate, adopt modern methods and mores, or perish. This choice is as inexorable as the march of progress itself. And the path of progress is not to be trodden reluctantly. Less advanced people, in his estimation, need to provide an education for their children equal to that received by whites. They also need to adopt modern methods of agriculture, commerce, business, and manufacture. In short, they are to become assimilated in white society much as Ridge himself has done.

Ridge's views were not unusual for someone in nineteenth-century America, especially one who regarded himself as a pioneer in the new world of promise—California. They are not unusual, either, for an American Indian who saw himself as successfully entering white society. In many ways his views reflect the ideas of his father and grandfather, who believed it was futile for the Cherokees to resist the pressure exerted on them by whites. Adapt or die was the message of three generations of Ridges to their fellows.

Ridge's fame grew in other areas too. He acquired a reputation as a crack shot; it was reported that he often bragged about his prowess with firearms, and he doubtless enjoyed the image as part of the romantic persona he cultivated. In one of his newspaper pieces he describes a hunt on the Feather River undertaken by members of the *Democrat* staff. After traveling some eight or ten miles upriver, he reports, the five-man party split up, with Ridge and John Heatley setting out in search of game. When they came upon some rabbits, both hunters fired their shotguns but missed. A little farther on, Ridge again fired and missed. At this point, he writes, he was a bit mortified, since he could see that Heatley was beginning to doubt Ridge's assertions about his marksmanship. By this time, though, Ridge hit his stride, felling two rabbits running in opposite directions with two shots. He then put on a show for Heatley, hitting a third rabbit by aiming the gun over his shoulder and shooting

another while lying on his back on the ground. With his fellow newspaperman finally impressed, Ridge called off the hunt, declaring that
they had bagged enough game.[5] In another incident we get a glimpse
of Ridge's popularity at the time, as well as his marksmanship. The
Daily Appeal gave the following account in its issue of October 9, 1860:
"From the Hydraulic Press we learn that Bro. Ridge was treated with
hospitality while on his recent tour in the mountains. Lager flowed free,
turkey shoots were gotten up in honor of the distinguished visitor, and
the poet and editor showed himself so excellent a marksman, that the
San Juaners were quite astounded. Good for John R." The editor knew
that his shooter's reputation, in addition to contributing to his romantic
image, served as a deterrent in the rough-and-tumble environment of
frontier journalism and politics.

But by this time Ridge was on good terms with the men who ran
the other Marysville papers, the *Express* and the *Appeal*. The September 8, 1860, issue of the *Appeal* notes that "the three Marysville editors are hanging out like brothers." The same issue reported that James
Heath of Marysville was displaying a large group of "sun-pictures," or
photographs worked in india ink. The editor remarks, "A portrait of
Mrs. John R. Ridge in this collection, is the most expressive and classical head we have seen in a long time." Similar gracious and friendly
utterances were exchanged among the three newsmen during the next
months.

In the May 19, 1860, issue of his paper, Ridge had the unpleasant
task of reporting that his old mentor, Cephas Washburn, and his son
Edward P. Washburn had died of pneumonia within a short time of
each other. In an obituary titled "Distinguished Arkansians Dead," he
traces some of the main events of his teacher's long life and notes the
accomplishments of his son, who had achieved some fame as an artist.
Rollin and Elizabeth felt the loss all the more acutely because another
of Washburn's sons, J. W. Washbourne (who had changed the spelling
of his family name), was married to Ridge's sister and had been a friend
and ally in Rollin's Arkansas days.

The love of literature Ridge had acquired in Arkansas studying the classics and English masters under Washburn stayed with him during his time in Marysville. His newspaper pieces were peppered with literary allusions; it is evident from his own writing that he had the habit of reading one work by an author, then moving on to other works by that same poet or novelist. For example, during the first months of 1859 Ridge was reading Alexander Pope and quoting liberally from his works. In fall 1860, he was reading and quoting from Edmund Spenser; he insisted, however, that during the presidential election he would leave off secular literature and read nothing but the Bible. As a writer he was of course attuned to the state of letters in his own locale. Although he admitted that the first American settlers in California were little interested in art and literature, that situation seemed to have changed. At first "the great mass of the people were rushing too madly forward in the great race for wealth, to pause by the wayside and refresh their fevered minds at the founts of art and learning," he wrote in 1859. But by the end of the first decade of statehood, the quest for riches seemed to have subsided, and the public were turning to literature, especially what appeared in the periodical press. Ridge went on to list some of the popular journals of the day, including *Hesperian, Home Journal, Hutchings's California Magazine*, and *Golden Era*.[6]

Some of Ridge's newspaper articles written during this period demonstrate critical skill along with a solid sense of literary history. In one essay he defends contemporary literature against charges by clergymen and others that modern writers produce immoral works that corrupt the nation's youth. Ridge retorts that while some examples of contemporary writing might appeal to the prurient, the problem is not so acute as in former times. He cites Lord Byron and the English Restoration writers as examples, throwing in Shakespeare's "Venus and Adonis" and certain of Chaucer's works for good measure. But, he says, no writers in the modern languages could match the classical authors for pure licentiousness. Sappho, he says, wrote things that could not be read in the mid-nineteenth century in "the most abandoned circles." And Horace, he goes on, described scenes that, if translated today, would get the translator a jail term under present obscenity laws.[7] In another literary

piece, "Sneering at American Genius,"[8] he answers an attack on Henry
Wadsworth Longfellow that appeared in the English journal *Athenaeum*.
He traces the history of British criticism of American writers and says
that most reputable English journals have now recognized the genius of
Oliver Wendell Holmes, Washington Irving, and Longfellow. He says
that the *Athenaeum* alone seems to persist in outmoded prejudice against
Americans. He likens Longfellow's work to that of Walter Scott in that,
like Scott, the American poet has taken what is noteworthy and valuable in the early history of his native land and rendered it into romance.
Probably because of his own situation and ambitions, Ridge had an
interest in the relation between literature and politics, a much-debated
issue in Victorian Britain and America. He had addressed the subject
before in Sacramento, commenting on politician-novelists in England.
In an 1859 essay he turned to politics and poetry, two seemingly in-
compatible "sciences," as he called them. The subject came up, he says,
because in many of the newspapers and magazines recently received in
the *Democrat* office, he noticed a great many articles disparaging politicians in general and political editors in particular. Though many people
see political editing as being obnoxious to anyone with a "refined and
exulted nature," Ridge says just the opposite is true. "Wherever there is
a great exaltation of feeling, from any cause whatever, a strong infusion
of sentiment, a lively effort of the imagination, a more than ordinary eloquence of expression, the poetical spirit is present." Thus even political
writing and oratory can be poetical under his definition. He goes on to
cite poets who were politicians—William Cullen Bryant, James Russell
Lowell, and Albert Pike of Arkansas—and asserts that the "purest and
loftiest intellects of our country are engaged in political journalism."[9]
Doubtless Ridge meant to include himself.

Just as he took literature seriously, he was concerned about the profession of journalism. In a piece called "Political Editing,"[10] he declares
that in a democracy, political newspapers are a necessity. In America, he
writes, each person is a politician in a sense and is much more attuned
to political happenings than, say, someone living under a monarchy or
an oligarchy. As a result, the American public needs the news and intel-

ligent commentary that such newspapers provide. Although political newspapers abound in the United States, Ridge says that unfortunately some of them are run by what he calls "campaign editors," people who care only for the election of favorite candidates or parties. These inferior journalists, he writes, rely on falsehoods and distortion to help them reach their ends. He then sets out the criteria he believes are necessary for the "respectable" editor, the antithesis of the "campaign editor." These include the ability to argue logically, a thorough knowledge of history and current events, a talent for satire, and a propensity for telling the truth. If the newspapers of the lower sorts of editors are allowed to exist, it is the fault of the people. Readers are intelligent enough to know when they are being deceived, he says, and when they see that they are, they should refrain from subscribing to that newspaper.

If Ridge was married to the profession of writing, then politics was his mistress. He had been weaned on public affairs and public debate in the Cherokee Nation, after all, and politics were quite naturally in his blood. But while many political people are practical, pragmatic, and willing to compromise for the sake of getting things done, Ridge was not. He was opinionated and stubborn and found it difficult if not impossible to back down from a position. On the other hand, he was extremely loyal to both men and ideas, had an extraordinary sense of history, and could argue logically and forcefully. Behind it all was a passionate intensity, fired by a determination to fight for whatever he believed was right. This cast of mind could lead to some interesting contradictions. The "mudsill" issue is a good example.

Shortly after Ridge began his editorship in Marysville, he reacted in an editorial to a statement by Senator James Hammond of South Carolina, a supporter of the Lecompton constitution for Kansas, to the effect that workingmen in the North were no better off than black slaves in the South. The implication of Hammond's remarks was that the white northern workers—whom he called "mudsills"—were on the same social level as the southern slaves. Ridge and others saw this as an insult to white workers in both sections of the nation, North and South. He responded with outrage, charging that Hammond and other members of the Lecomptonite party were elitists, determined to remove what Ridge called "popular liberty," or the right of all white males past the age of majority to participate in the affairs of government. In venting his hostility to the Lecomptonite position as he defined it, Ridge praised those who earn their bread by the sweat of their brows and thundered his determination to defend the working classes against their enemies. Though Ridge's most immediate aim was to line up workers' support for the anti-Lecompton forces, the philosophical position he adopted in defending the rights of the laborers was consistent with other political stands he took, such as the "settlerism" issue he had campaigned for earlier in Sacramento. At various other times, Ridge's editorials supported the working men and women of California. His basic theme was that working people should be proud of their status, since it is essential to society. He was intensely hostile to those he suspected of wanting to introduce any form of class privilege and vowed to resist any attempt to establish an "aristocracy" in the country. Yet his "mudsill" position is inherently racist in that it insists blacks are inferior to whites. In a subsequent editorial on the same subject,[11] Ridge quotes some southern editors who, he says, are supporters of Hammond. These remarks support the senator's contention that workers in the North are no better than slaves and are not fit for polite society. One goes so far as to say that slavery is a natural condition and soon will be introduced into the North. Although Ridge deprecates these statements, at no time does he come out against slavery. He defends the rights of white people on the lowest rung of the economic and social ladder, yet he cannot condone freedom for the slaves.

Ridge's old animosity toward the Mormons continued in the prewar years. In a May 12, 1859, account of the deaths of two "apostate" Mormons, Ridge speculates that an inquest held by the Mormon authorities was really a cover-up. He says the deaths occurred at the "instigation of the Mormon Church—that monster which grows and fattens under the sanction of our government." He inveighs against President Buchanan and his appointee, territorial governor Cummings, who are being deceived by Brigham Young, and calls for the dismissal of the Utah Indian agent, whom he accuses of fraud. By the next year Ridge was so inflamed at the Mormons that he proposed the United States government wage war against them. The basis for this extraordinary proposal from a proponent of popular sovereignty was Ridge's claim that the Mormons were inciting the Indians of Utah against the non-Mormon whites and supplying them with arms and ammunition. He also claimed that Mormons harbored a "deep-seated animosity" toward the American government and people.[12] Although he favored an invasion of Utah, he rejected, ironically, a suggestion by William H. Seward that Congress legislate against polygamy, citing the principle of popular sovereignty. His position was that anything not specifically outlawed by the United States Constitution should be decided by a vote of the citizens of each state or territory. Ridge's hostility toward the Mormons continued for the rest of his life.

9

Douglas Democrat

During this period in Marysville, in the years immediately preceding the Civil War, Ridge's support for Stephen A. Douglas grew. As early as December 1858 the paper carried these words on its masthead: "For President in 1860, STEPHEN A. DOUGLAS, OF ILLINOIS, Subject to the decision of the Democratic National Convention at Charleston." Ridge saw Douglas as someone who avoided the two extremes in national politics—abolitionism on the one hand, and advocating the expansion of slavery on the other. Though it may be difficult to regard John Rollin Ridge as a moderate, especially in view of his later Copperhead activities, that is exactly how he saw himself. Before the Civil War he made repeated statements on the necessity of preserving the Union at all costs. He condemned the radicals of the Republican party who in their zeal to free the slaves threatened to split the country. To free the slaves would also violate the due process clause of the United States Constitution, according to Ridge. On the other hand, he opposed southerners' attempts to expand slavery into the territories after the Dred Scott decision invalidated the Missouri Compromise. If slavery was to be expanded at all, it should be into portions of Mexico, Central

America, or Cuba annexed to the United States through the efforts of the filibusters. Extending slavery to northern territories was impractical, he said, and the South should be content to continue as it had done under the protection of the Constitution.

Ridge adhered strictly to the Douglas Democrats' position of popular sovereignty, insisting that the people of the territories were entitled to decide the issue of slavery, not Congress or the national government. People who lived in an area that was organized into a territory, he reasoned, were not represented in Congress. Thus, to allow Congress to fashion laws for them would be equivalent to allowing the British Parliament to enact laws governing the American colonists. In Ridge's mind, Douglas's position was the middle way of American politics and deserved the support of all who would preserve the Union and the Constitution.

But his support for Douglas turned out to involve him in one more losing cause. Popular sovereignty had contributed greatly to the deterioration of the situation in "bleeding Kansas" as both southerners and northerners flooded into the area, each side determined to dominate the other. As the proslavery forces fought it out with the Free-Soilers, the Indians and their treaties were being ignored. American Indian tribes that had been removed from the Old Northwest as well as groups indigenous to the area held claim in perpetuity to most of what became Kansas and Nebraska through treaties with the federal government. But the Indians were forced onto small reservations or removed to Indian Territory south of Kansas. The popular sovereignty issue that Ridge so passionately defended led to chaos among the whites who sought to settle in the new territories; similarly, the Kansas-Nebraska Act, championed by his hero Stephen A. Douglas, led to more injustice heaped on Indian heads as treaties were ignored or abrogated, and once more Indian people were forced off their land.

Still, Ridge stuck with his man and the local Douglas Democrats. He campaigned hard for candidates in Yuba City and Marysville before the 1858 elections and was exuberant when Douglas men swept the voting in Yuba City and fared very well in Marysville. He had a personal interest in their success; contemporary newspaper accounts report that Ridge presided over the meetings of the Union Democrats from 1858 to 1861. He was becoming a force in the party.

In 1858, too, he followed the Lincoln-Douglas debates taking place in Illinois, where the Republican lawyer Abraham Lincoln was trying to unseat Senator Douglas. Much of the debate centered on the slavery question, with Lincoln seeing it as a national problem and Douglas proclaiming it a sectional issue to be settled by popular vote in each state or territory. In the opening speech of the 1858 campaign, Lincoln made his famous statement that the government could not "endure permanently, half *slave* and half *free*." His warning of an impending, inevitable crisis was addressed in October 1858 by William H. Seward's statement that "it is an irrepressible conflict between opposing and enduring forces, and it means that the United States must and will, sooner or later, become either entirely a slaveholding nation, or entirely a free-labor nation."

Ridge regarded the remarks of both Lincoln and Seward as inflammatory. He argued that conflict between the North and South was not inevitable as long as people from one section of the country were not allowed to impose their wills on people from another. Ridge was just as vehemently opposed to southerners who wished to extend slavery over the western territories. He argued with those who, like Senator David R. Atchison of Missouri, supported the Lecompton constitution in Kansas and saw it as a first step toward expanding slavery to the Pacific Ocean.

Ridge saw the whole question as involving basic democratic principles; he believed that the people ruled the country and made their will known through the ballot. But in spite of this deep-seated sense of democracy, Ridge could not see how the institution of slavery violated the very essence of the democratic spirit. The reason for this contradiction almost certainly lies in Ridge's view of human history and the various cultures it produced. This view, tied closely to his belief in the primacy of progress, held that the distinct human groups had progressed to different levels of civilization. Some were "civilized" enough for self-government, for democracy, while others were not. Some groups of Indians, like the Creeks and Cherokees, were capable of joining white civilization and becoming assimilated into it. Other groups, like the native California tribes, were not. Black Africans, he believed, were simply not ready for any kind of self-determination and were destined, at least for the immediate future, to live under the domination of the more "advanced" whites. How a culture was to progress under conditions of slavery, Ridge never explained.

The *Daily Democrat* continued to support Douglas during the 1858 campaign, defending the positions he took in his speeches and refuting those taken by Lincoln. On November 11 Ridge accused President Buchanan of secretly supporting Lincoln, motivated by the desire to remove Douglas as a rival. After Douglas's victory in Illinois, Ridge continued to tout him for president in 1860 and predicted he would easily carry the South.

During spring 1859 the newspaper continued to attack Buchanan and his wing of the Democratic party. Editorials claimed the president was losing supporters every day owing to wrongheaded administration policies such as support for the Lecompton constitution. Ridge accused Buchanan of appointing corrupt officials in Illinois and elsewhere. He attacked the rival wing of the party, accusing it of attempting to reinstitute "federalism," which he defined as a system that removes power from the people and concentrates it in the hands of a few who claim the right to dictate to the masses. This system, Ridge claimed, was the aim of the Lecomptonites. Citing Senator James Hammond, one of Buchanan's supporters, Ridge says in a May 21 editorial that a basic premise of the rival Democrats is that the equality of the various classes in the North is unnatural and will lead to discord. The Lecomptonites, Ridge writes, believe that the "only condition of society is where the relation exists of master and slave, in an absolute and unqualified form"; the implication here is that the intention of the other wing is "the complete subjection" of the northern workers. He goes on to list the achievements of former "poor boys" Daniel Webster, Henry Clay, and Benjamin Franklin.

With equal vigor, the editor opposed the Republicans and abolitionists. In a January 5, 1859, piece titled "The Bloody Programme," Ridge sets forth what he sees as the plan of the abolitionists and predicts what will happen if they are allowed to put it into force. The first step is for Congress to refuse to admit any more slave states to the Union. To achieve this, the Free Soilers would have to compose a majority in the national legislature. Step two is to "remodel" the Supreme Court over a period of time, then to reverse the decision that recognizes slaves as property under the Constitution. The final step is to amend the Constitution to abolish slavery in the United States. "Truly, this is a fearful vision to contemplate," Ridge writes. The three-part plan to abolish slavery would lead quickly and inevitably to civil war and to insurrection by blacks, resulting in "murder and conflagration" in the South and "woe over the whole Union."

He also editorialized against the actions of those he labeled "incendiaries" and called for hanging John Brown and for suppressing books like *The Impending Crisis*, addressed to the "inhabitants of the benighted South," which challenged southerners to repent of their sin and root out slavery. In a February 3, 1860, editorial, Ridge called the book "a mission of evil." As proof of how the South would react to freeing the slaves, Ridge printed a speech by Jefferson Davis to the Mississippi legislature calling for secession if an abolitionist president was elected. Davis exacerbated the problem, Ridge charged, by insisting that slavery be extended into all the western territories because of the Supreme Court's declaration that slaves are regarded as property under the Constitution. Again he reiterated his position that the only hope for the country was to adopt the 1856 Democratic platform advocating popular sovereignty and to elect its main proponent, Stephen A. Douglas.

It was not only his editorial pen that Ridge used to promote the Douglas ticket, but also his literary one. On February 12, 1859, a political poem appeared in the pages of the *Daily National Democrat*. Ridge was reading Alexander Pope during the early months of that year, and the satirical little verse "The Douglas Star" shows the eighteenth-century poet's heavy influence. The first stanza reads:

> To your souls ye laid the flattering thought,
> Ye knavish burrs to POWER stuck,
> That gold would break what Douglas wrought,

And virtue bend the knee to BUCK;
But swiftly flashing through the night,
The lightning's news your visions mar,
And, though your souls abhor the sight,
Still brightly shines the DOUGLAS star.

Clearly not one of Ridge's best poetic efforts, the verse gloats about Douglas's victory in Illinois over both Lincoln and the supporters of Buchanan, whom he accuses of trying to buy Democratic votes for Lincoln in order to remove Douglas from his seat in the United States Senate. The poet seems even more elated by the win over the Buckaneers—Ridge's derisive term for Buchanan supporters—than by Douglas's victory over the Republicans.

But cheer over the victory in Illinois was short-lived. Despite Ridge's prediction that the South would stand solidly behind the senator, Douglas was repudiated by the delegations from several southern states at the national Democratic convention of 1860. The proslavery forces had lost Kansas to the Free Soilers, and many blamed Douglas and his stand on popular sovereignty. Southern leaders like Jefferson Davis and William L. Yancey of Alabama called for Democratic platform planks that supported the extension of slavery into every territory. Yancey even demanded the convention declare "that slavery was right."[1] When the northern delegations refused to include the extreme proslavery planks Davis proposed, the convention split. Delegations from eight southern states withdrew on April 30, and the convention at Charleston adjourned. In June the conclave was reconvened at Baltimore, this time without the southerners, and nominated Douglas for president. The southern delegations, meeting in a rump convention at Vicksburg, nominated Buchanan's vice president, John C. Breckinridge of Kentucky. Meanwhile the Republicans had convened in May and nominated Abraham Lincoln. To complicate matters, a new party, the National Constitutional Union, was formed and nominated John Bell of Tennessee as its standard-bearer.

In the months leading up to the 1860 election, Ridge struck out at both the Republicans and the southern Democrats. For the Republicans to insist on debating the abstract question of slavery is immoral, Ridge charges in an August 22 editorial, since the "presentation and argumentation" of the question arouses people like John Brown and thus is dangerous to the country. This is an untenable position, of course, especially for a political editor whose many statements on the sanctity of the press insisted on the necessity for the free discussion of ideas in a democracy. He continued to insist that it was immoral for the northern abolitionists to impose their will on the rest of the country.

In a June 1860 editorial called "The Rail-Splitting and Union-Splitting Candidate," Ridge argues against Lincoln's half-slave and half-free position and opposes Seward's "irrepressible conflict" idea. Yet the southerners who demand the right to extend slavery are making war on the "best interests of the country," he declares on September 13. Southerners who call for dissolving the Union and establishing a southern confederacy are attempting a personal power grab. The South must realize that a breakup of the Union would harm them, he argues, because slaves could escape north with no fugitive slave law to bring them back. Slaves would thus have no value along the border. Ridge called for Breckinridge to withdraw during October and November, declaring that such a move would ensure Douglas's election. Shortly before the election, he promised to support whoever was elected, insisting that secession was treason and that the Union must be preserved. This was a promise Ridge was not to keep.

Once the votes were counted, it was clear that Lincoln had carried every free state; only Missouri went for Douglas. Lincoln received 180 electoral votes to 12 for Douglas, even though the Illinois senator was a close second in the popular vote. Breckinridge carried 9 southern states, along with Maryland and Delaware, and Bell took Virginia, Kentucky, and Tennessee. Ridge's immediate reaction was to blame Buchanan, since his actions had split the Democratic party. He was right to the extent that Lincoln's opponents had garnered a million more of the popular votes than the president-elect had. His editorials also urged calm in the South, arguing that Lincoln could not institute radical policies, since the Republicans did not control Congress. The only action that

could effectively disturb the status quo was secession, he declared, and
that act would inevitably lead to civil war. In that prediction, of course,
Ridge was dead right. He urged against secession, declaring that it was
not the way to redress grievances. "Whenever there is an intolerable act
of oppression upon the South by the Republican Administration, and
no prospect of a remedy at the ballot-box, then we concede the right of
revolution, but nothing more." At that point, he says, "we concede that
the Confederacy [Union] is a failure, and that the fond anticipations of
mankind in regard to free Government must go out in darkness."[2] This
is an important political statement for Ridge in that it provides the rationale for his involvement with the Knights of the Golden Circle and with
Copperhead activities in general. On December 18, he notes that there
has been some talk about setting up the state of California as a separate
Republic of the Pacific. He rejects this notion, since it is as much secessionist as efforts to establish a southern confederacy. Later, however, he
was to reverse this position and endorse the idea of a California republic.

By February 1861, however, the Confederacy had been established.
Ridge's position at first was to join others in urging Buchanan, then in
the last days of his presidency, to send troops to put down the insurgents.
Buchanan's response to all who counseled action was that the federal
government could not declare war on a state. Ridge, believing the Union
must be preserved, then threw his editorial support to the Crittenden
compromise, a proposal that would have institutionalized slavery in the
South, compensated owners for unrecovered fugitive slaves, and extended the Missouri Compromise line of 36°30' between free and slave
states to the Pacific. When Ridge was ridiculed by rival papers for this
apparent repudiation of the principle of popular sovereignty, he replied
that preserving the Union was more important than other consider-
ations in the current desperate circumstances. The Crittenden compromise was in any event rejected. Lincoln could not agree on the extension
of slavery that was inherent in the proposal, and the secessionists proved
intransigent.

In the mid-1850s the Yuba Indians, native to the area around Marysville, were being subjected to the same treatment the Cherokees had

gone through in Georgia during the 1830s. The Yubas were being forced off their traditional lands and relocated on one of the reservations being established in California at the time. Colonel Henley, in charge of the army's removal force, appealed to the main Yuba leader, Waukeetaw, saying that on the reservation the people would be provided with better care and food. He also said that if the Indians remained where they were, they would all die. Waukeetaw's reported reply was, "Die here, good; go away and die, no good." At that point Henley, seeing that persuasion would not work, told the old chief that the "great chief" in Washington had given him orders to remove the Yubas by force if necessary. Waukeetaw, convinced of the United States Army's military superiority, prepared his people for removal. As in many other removal situations, the Indians split, some giving in to what they considered inevitable and some vowing to fight to the death. Many of the latter were arrested by the Marysville police and put aboard the *Cleopatra*, the boat that was to carry the Yubas to the reservation. The others burned the rancheria where they lived and voluntarily boarded the *Cleopatra*. The Yubas were not happy on the reservation, however, and began to drift back to the Feather River area. By 1860 most had returned to Yuba and Sutter counties. Ridge, who wrote many articles on the Indians in his newspapers, published a report in January 1861 that Waukeetaw was dead, killed by Indians on the Empire Ranch as he was returning from the reservation. He praised the old chief and expressed regret at his death.

A few days later Ridge received a letter bearing Waukeetaw's name, denying that he was dead. Just after Ridge got the letter, he was visited by a group of Yubas from Sutter County who told him they had heard of Waukeetaw's death and were determined to seek revenge. They had armed themselves and prepared to travel to the Empire Ranch to seek out the killers, but before they left they had decided to question the source of their information to find out if the report was true. Ridge communicated with them as best he could, telling them how he had gotten the story and also about the letter from the Empire Ranch purportedly dictated by Waukeetaw. The Yubas decided to send runners to the ranch to find out the truth. Ridge wrote them a letter addressed to the whites there, which explained the runners' mission and asked that they be well treated.[3]

Ridge also used his newspapers in Marysville to editorialize on the plight of the California Indians. He was especially outraged at the treatment of Indian women. A January 15, 1858, editorial in the *National Democrat* reports that "hundreds and hundreds" of white men were living with Indian women and fathering "half-blooded Digger children." He asserts that some white men are so eager to "intermarry" with native women that "they commit almost any outrage" on "some terrified, half-starved squaw," including kidnapping and rape. Although he says that the California Indians are only a "few degrees above the Pigmies of Africa," he denounces the practice and calls for an end to it. On December 4 of the same year he takes up the subject again, this time exposing the problem of abandonment. White men would take Indians as temporary wives, produce one or more children, then move on, leaving both women and offspring. Ridge cites one dramatic case in which a woman and child were left behind when a miner returned to the East. When the miner did not return as promised, the woman "grieved herself to death," according to the account. Ridge closes by saying that even the poorest of God's creatures deserve better treatment.

Ridge reported outrages on the Indians of California during this period, and he also made specific recommendations on Indian policy. His discussions were wide ranging but usually focused on a few inter-related topics: the Indian wars in Oregon and Washington being waged by the federal government, the treatment of California Indians, the need to assimilate all Indian groups into the larger society, and the organization of Indian lands in present-day Oklahoma into a state that would be the prototype for other Indian states.

Ridge was vehement in opposing the policy of sending United States troops against Indian groups in Washington and Oregon territories. His opposition was based on three premises: that profiteering whites had duped the government into attacking the Indians, that the vast majority of Indians were not hostile, and that the government had failed to carry out its promises to native groups. Earlier, in a February 20, 1857, editorial in the *Bee*, he had charged that the "difficulties" leading up to the war "were gotten up expressly for the purpose of a general system of speculation." Whites in the area expected to profit from the commitment of federal troops, through government contracts for transporting supplies, by provisioning the soldiers and their animals, and "in a thousand different ways." In addition, the army could be expected to remove the Indians from land the whites wanted. Ridge wrote that even though the settlers "insulted and abused" them, most Indians were "anxious to be friendly." Nonetheless, he charged territorial governor Stevens, at the head of his "volunteer" forces, prosecuted "deliberately, systematically, and avowedly, a *war of extermination* against them," causing the Indians to react in self-defense. This reaction, in turn, precipitated the call for federal troops.

Further, Ridge asserted, the Indians had every right to repel settlers from their lands if they chose to do so. The government had acquired 62 million acres of land from them, promising to pay $2 million and to send teachers, physicians, and farmers to hasten the process of civilization. Three years after the land cession, the government still had not made good its promise. In an editorial in the October 13, 1858, issue of the *National Democrat*, Ridge agreed that hostile actions by Indians could not be tolerated but said that most times they were caused by the actions or misrepresentations of whites. He castigated the Buchanan administration for not acting in good faith toward Indian groups as previous presidents had done. The best policy, he warned, was "to respect the Indian title, where they really have a title, recognize them in their national capacity, and keep faith with them."

Ridge, however, does not appear to have considered the native population of California one nation or to have regarded their "title" to land in the same way as that of the more "civilized" tribes like the Choctaws and Cherokees. Further, his writings present varying solutions to the "problem" of "what to do with them." When it was proposed to give the state of California control over the Indians in spite of its dubious record of dealing with them, Ridge did not object. The plan, reported in the February 24, 1860, edition of the *National Democrat*, provided for a threefold policy: the first part was to remove Indians, especially those who had been hostile to whites, to remote reservations. (A later Ridge editorial suggests land near Walla Walla, Washington.) An apprenticeship program would be made available for other, presumably more friendly, Indians. The third part of the policy called for the remaining Indians to be assigned to reservations in California run by private citizens who would contract with the state to train their charges in the "basic arts of civilization." In his comments on this plan, Ridge warned against allowing the apprenticeship plan to deteriorate into a system of involuntary servitude. In 1860 his position seemed to be that slavery was acceptable for blacks but intolerable for Indians, even the lowly "Diggers."

Later that spring another plan was announced, one that Ridge embraced. This program would have removed all the Indians from California and put them on one large reservation where, Ridge reasoned, they could be better controlled and educated. He dismissed attacks on the federal reservation system by saying it had been mismanaged but offered the best hope for "civilizing" the Indians. What was needed, he said in a *National Democrat* editorial on April 14, was firm government commitment and better supervision of reservation personnel. On July 1 in the same newspaper Ridge came out in favor of a system of leasing reservations to "responsible persons," saying it would be better than leaving them in the hands of government agents. The "responsible persons" would be under the control of a supervisor who would answer directly to the secretary of the interior. The editor endorsed the plan, which he believed would cut down on the swindling going on under the current system.

Implicit in Ridge's support for a reservation system was a belief that assimilation into the dominant culture was the best, and ultimately the only, solution to the "Indian question." He agreed with what he saw as the basic United States Indian policy, which he described in an *Express* editorial of January 6, 1858: "To civilize the Indian tribes as soon as possible, and to circumscribe them, by a gradual extinction of their title, to limits simply sufficient for their support by the industry of their own hands, and to prepare the more intellectual of the tribes for citizenship of the U.S." Specifically, he supported giving individuals allotments so each would have a homestead that could not be taken away legally. Before land was allotted in severalty, however, the Indians must be taught how to cultivate it using modern methods, to raise livestock, and to emulate other white practices. These skills could be taught on reservations by dedicated whites. At present, though, too many of the reservations were in the hands of people looking for a quick profit at the expense of the Indians, the government, or both. But the system had worked in the past, Ridge said, and under proper supervision it continued to work. He cited a report of the secretary of the interior as proof in the July 15, 1860, issue of the *National Democrat*. The report outlined the success of an allotment program set up on several small reservations in Minnesota. There the Sioux had discarded their "barbarous costumes" and adopted "the industrial habits by which civilization is made and maintained." Ridge lauded the program and declared that "the true policy for civilizing the wild Indian tribes [had] been discovered." The rest, he said, was easy: "Giving them their lands in severalty, instead of in common, and feeling the dignity that every owner of land in his own absolute right naturally does feel, they will be stimulated to industry and sobriety."

To those who maintained that assimilation was impossible because the Indians could not be civilized, Ridge countered that the Cherokees had progressed in sixty years from a state of barbarity to one of civility and refinement and that other tribes had made similar advances. His essay, printed in the November 16, 1860, issue of the *National Democrat*, goes on to cite the British historian Thomas Macaulay on the long march to civilization undertaken by the inhabitants of Britain. Those who believe the Indian cannot be civilized, Ridge writes, suppose "that the savageism of the Indian is peculiar to himself, instead of common, as it is, to all barbarous nations alike." Each nation, he says, has had to hike up the long road of progress; the Indians are fortunate that they have white Americans to assist them on the journey. Ridge believed not only that Indian societies and cultures would give way in the face of inexorable Euro-American expansionism, but that what he saw as the distinct race of American Indians would be dissolved through a process he identified as "amalgamation." As he had expressed it earlier, in a *Bee* editorial of March 17, 1857, the process was inevitable: "Wherever the white race goes, amalgamation takes place. It has progressed with the march of civilization on the continent and it *will* with the certainty of an inevitable law, solve the destiny of the races."

Related to the idea of assimilation or "amalgamation" of the American Indians was the issue of giving them United States citizenship. Ridge embraced the idea of making Indians equal citizens, defending it on both practical and legal grounds. From a practical standpoint, he wrote, many of the tribes were already civilized and were ready for full citizenship. In fact, he said, many civilized Indians had not only become citizens, but held public office as well. An April 24, 1859, article called "Indian Citizens," published in the *National Democrat*, says there is a "strong desire" in southern and western states to grant statehood to the Indian territories "lying along the waters of the Missouri and Arkansas, into the American Confederacy [Union] and to make, by a sweeping act of legislation, all its Indian inhabitants citizens of the United States." Ridge insists that such an act would bring happiness and prosperity to the Indians affected and that the new state would be a model for similar Indian states as other tribes were civilized. No legal barriers exist, he writes, and he argues that the principle has already been established in the Indian policy of the Jefferson administration and by the pronouncements of the Supreme Court in the Dred Scott decision. The legal implications of Indian citizenship and statehood are addressed in a Ridge article in the October 23, 1859, issue of the *National Democrat*. The piece "Political Status of the North American Indians, West of the Missouri and Arkansas" claims that if Jefferson's policy of civilizing Indians and granting them citizenship had been systematically followed, "several Indian States would already have been admitted into the Union." He then goes into a lengthy examination of the portion of the Dred Scott opinion that deals with the political status of the Indians. Ridge cites Chief Justice Roger B. Taney's assertion that Indian tribes were sovereign nations and had so been regarded since white contact. Further, Taney declared that citizens of Indian nations were considered foreigners and thus, "like the citizens of any other foreign government, may be naturalized, by the authority of Congress, and become citizens of the United States." Since no constitutional barrier exists, Ridge argues, it would take a simple act of admission for Congress to create an Indian state, a move he would fully support. His ideas on Indian statehood and citizenship were completely consistent with his views on assimilation.

Although he was physically hundreds of miles from the Cherokee Nation, Ridge kept abreast of major developments there, especially those relating to the rivalry between the Ross and Ridge factions. He received copies of his cousin Elias Cornelius Boudinot's newspaper the *Arkansian*, and he corresponded with family members such as Josiah Woodward Washbourne. The *Arkansian*, published at Fayetteville in 1859 and 1860, espoused the same assimilationist ideas as Ridge did, and Boudinot was an early advocate of statehood for the Indian territories west of the Arkansas line. The *Arkansian* was also a voice for the anti-Ross faction of the Cherokees. Rollin Ridge, of course, had denounced Ross and his followers in pieces published in area newspapers when he lived in Arkansas and at Honey Creek; he continued the practice while he was in California, determined not to let his physical separation from the Nation deter him from speaking out against his rivals. Nor would he allow distance to temper his bitterness.

Two articles written in June 1860 for the *National Democrat* reflect Ridge's concern with events in the Cherokee Nation. The first, printed on June 16, deals with John Ross's attempt to sell the Neutral Lands bordering Kansas. The majority of Cherokees oppose such a sale, Ridge asserts, but Ross is determined to go through with it. Ross's major motive, the California editor says, is "to put money in his purse," since the "great aim of his schemes" is "the aggrandizement of himself and family." A secondary motive, Ridge declares, is to hand the strip over to the abolitionists, since it would "be at once overrun with the Free-State hordes of Kansas, the moment it was opened to white settlers." Although Ross's proposed sale did not materialize, Ridge predicts future attempts because the Cherokee principal chief had come under the influence of Evan Jones, an abolitionist missionary. Rollin warns that Jones is "a learned and eloquent, but intriguing and dangerous man." He notes that Jones, his son John, and other followers are dedicated to eradicating slavery in the Cherokee Nation by whatever means necessary, and part of their plan is to turn over the Neutral Lands to the Free-Soilers. Jones must and will be resisted by the majority of Cherokees who, Ridge says, favor the institution of slavery. Although Cherokees have generally been friendly to missionaries, he goes on, they will eventually turn against the "Jones band" because of their political activities: "They are no longer preaching the gospel, but Abolitionism. They are no longer attending to the legitimate business on which they came, but are interfering with an institution which has existed for many long years among the Cherokees, and which is as firmly rooted in their midst as it is at this moment in South Carolina or Alabama or Mississippi." Ridge then suggests what should be done with the Joneses: "If Abolitionists are mobbed in those States, tarred and feathered, and hung upon trees, sometimes, what might be expected from a people who, like the Cherokees, have but just tamed the savage in their veins?"

The second article, printed on June 30, continues the attack on Ross and Jones and outlines their connection with the Keetoowah or Nighthawk Society, the predominantly full-blood organization also called "pin Indians." Ridge charges, probably quite accurately, that Ross and Jones are leaders of the organization, though both deny it. A great advantage that Jones has in influencing the full-bloods, Ridge recognizes, is his fluency in the Cherokee language and his ability to print his propaganda in the Cherokee syllabary. The true purpose of the society, the editor goes on, is to promote abolitionism, although this aim is not revealed to the members. The rank and file are told that the mixed-bloods, many of whom are educated in the English language, desire to have "white laws" extended over the Nation. Many of the full-bloods, fearing the loss of their country, are thus persuaded to join the Keetoowahs in their opposition to the mixed-blood slave owners, according to Ridge.

The rift in the Cherokee Nation, however, was along more familiar lines. John Ross, after all, was a mixed-blood slave owner. The rivalry, as always, was between the Ridge-Boudinot-Watie, or Treaty, party and Ross and his supporters. Both Evan and John Jones were solidly in the Ross camp and thus fair game for Ridge's attacks. His article blames them for conspiring to split the Cherokee Nation into armed camps and charges that the Keetoowahs have recruited known outlaws into their ranks to assassinate prominent mixed-bloods. Ridge decries the secret nature of the society and says its meetings are held "at night in the woods and thickets." The full-bloods are being used by Ross and the Joneses for their own nefarious ends, and the uneducated, "poorer classes of Cherokees" cannot see through the ruse. Ridge ends his article with the words of an unnamed correspondent from the Cherokee Nation. This writer, probably Washbourne or Boudinot, concludes that the Nation is on the brink of a civil war that will resemble "bleeding Kansas" and will bring an influx of northern carpetbaggers and the imposition of a territorial government by federal officials. In the end, Ridge's informant says, Evan Jones will be governor. "He will then stand with his foot upon the neck of the poor Cherokee," and the Ross faction will have succeeded in bringing the entire Nation under its yoke. Thus Ridge followed the Treaty party line in his comments on Cherokee Nation affairs. It is interesting yet understandable that no part of his discussion was devoted to Stand Watie's promoting a secret group to rival the Keetoowahs—the Knights of the Golden Circle.

Over a period of two years while he was at Marysville, Ridge published essays on Indian history, customs, and lore in the *National Democrat*. He was planning a long work on the North American Indians, and these essays were most likely the result of his thinking and reading on the subject. Many of them concerned "civilizing" the various Indian groups. The first appeared on October 21, 1858, and commented on the candidacy of a Chickasaw for the United States Congress. Ridge reprinted an announcement from the *Chickasaw and Choctaw Herald* that Emalah Tubbee was running for the post. After describing Tubbee as a fitting candidate, Ridge uses the occasion to comment on the Chickasaws and Choctaws. He outlines their modern form of government and their "highly civilized" life-style. His essay concludes with some remarks contrasting the Chickasaws and Choctaws with the "Diggers" of California who, he relates, subsist on a diet of "grasshoppers and angle-worms."

An essay called "More about the Civilized Indian States" was published on February 24, 1859. The piece sets out to refute the view that North American Indians cannot be civilized. He begins by pointing out that the civilization of "other races . . . was slow and gradual, the tedious work of centuries." But the civilized tribes of North America—the Cherokees, Choctaws, Chickasaws, and Creeks—are

> a people who have leaped, as it were in a moment, from the utter night of barbarism into the broad and perfect day of civilized life. With all their drawbacks—with all their uprootings from their native soil—with all their removals, forcible and violent, from the homes they had hoped were permanent—with all their temptations to relapse into savagery, from the uncertainty of their fate in the hands of the white men—with all these and a thousand other disadvantages, they have marched steadily on the path of improvement.

A description follows of the advances these tribes have made in the areas of government, education, and agriculture. An essay along similar lines was published in the January 20, 1859, *National Democrat* and centered on the long trek the Britons took on the road to civilization, having at one time been in a position relative to Rome similar to the present position of the American Indians relative to Washington.

The May 23, 1860, issue of the *National Democrat* carried a piece titled "Flatheads and Black Feet" that continued the discussion of civilizing the Indians. Ridge, relying on contemporary reports as well as the words of members of the Lewis and Clark expedition, describes some of the characteristics of these peoples. Noting that the Blackfeet had "phrenological advantages," he nonetheless concludes that though their neighbors can be civilized, "the Black Feet will never be." On December 19 of the same year, Ridge published an editorial in the *Democrat* that ridiculed a circular issued by the government of Haiti inviting blacks and Indians to the island nation, offering the emigrants land and "all sorts of privileges." The editor states that though the move might be a good one for blacks, it would not be advantageous for civilized Indians such as the Cherokees, Choctaws, Creeks, and Pottawatomis, who have such a good life on the mainland. Further, to move the Plains Indians to Haiti would be of no advantage to the Haitians, he concludes, since "a few hundred of them would have the scalp of every wooly head in the country, in less than a month."

Throughout the pages of the *National Democrat* while Ridge was editor there appeared shorter references to the American Indians. Some were simply reports of raids, some by white attackers, some by Indians. Others were comments on hostile actions by Indians against wagon trains and camps, which Ridge always deplored. He editorialized against unfair treatment of Indians by whites and gave special attention to incidents in which the Indians were cheated or their treaty rights were denied. As in his longer works, he supported the policy of "civilizing" Indians and predicted that they must assimilate or be exterminated.

John Rollin Ridge's association with the Knights of the Golden Circle began as early as August 30, 1860, when he reprinted an address by the group's leader, George Washington Lamb Binkley. Ridge clearly was not personally acquainted with Binkley at this point, since he spells his name "Brickly." Binkley was a promoter from Cincinnati who had worked as a physician, lawyer, lecturer, and writer and had earlier attempted to organize a group called the Continental Union. This organization was to have been the successor to the Know-Nothing party, but it never attracted many members. During the mid-1850s, Binkley abandoned his Union and began another group, the Knights of the Golden Circle, originally a filibuster organization. His plan was to impose the "superior Anglo-American civilization" on Latin America and to make himself rich by selling memberships at ten dollars apiece. The self-styled "general" called for volunteers to assemble at Fort Ewen, Texas, on the south bank of the Rio Nueces in September 1860 to begin an invasion of Mexico. It was this call that Ridge published, having picked it up from a Richmond newspaper. But the organization was to become more than just another filibuster unit as the Civil War began in earnest. Many northern Democrats, operating under the slogan "The Constitution as it is, the Union as it was," opposed the policies of the abolitionist Republicans, regarding them as too radical. Politically active conservative Democrats came to be called Copperheads; many of them turned to the Knights of the Golden Circle as a means of acting on their opposition to the Republican administration.[4]

Since the organization was a secret one, rumors circulated rapidly about its size, aims, and actions. Many newspaper editors, seeking sensational stories, published articles on the Knights, blaming them for sabotage, alleged assassination plans for Lincoln and his cabinet, and other treasonous acts. The publicity helped the group find new recruits, and chapters were formed in many parts of the country, particularly the Midwest.

California had its Golden Circle adherents, as did the Cherokee Nation. Many Cherokees had owned slaves in Georgia and took them along to the West when they were forced to remove. In many ways they reacted to the abolitionist movement as the southern planters did. The excitement that gripped the rest of the country just before the Civil War was felt in the Cherokee Nation as much as anywhere. Debates were held on the slavery question, and tempers grew hot on both sides. On the one hand, influential government agents assigned to the Cherokees spread secessionist ideas among the people. On the other hand, many of the missionaries in the Cherokee Nation, among them Evan Jones, opposed slavery and preached the gospel of abolitionism. The old Ridge-Ross split, always present in the Nation, did not help matters, though both families held slaves. In any event, Stand Watie, the leader of the Treaty party, organized a chapter of Knights. The organization was formed for two reasons: to oppose the abolitionists who threatened an economic system favored by the slaveholders, and to combat the influence of an older secret society among the Cherokees—the Keetoowahs, organized by John Ross and Evan Jones. The Keetoowahs, or Nighthawks, were a group of full-bloods recruited to limit the power of the Ridge faction. They were also called "pin" Indians because their symbol was a pin worn on the coat, shirt, or vest. The Keetoowahs had control of the Cherokee Light Horse, or police force, led by a Ross man, Cah-Skeh-New Mankiller. Members of the Ridge faction complained that the laws were not being enforced against members of the Ross party who committed crimes against their rivals. The Knights of the Golden Circle was formed partly to counteract the acts of the Light Horse and to protect the Treaty party.[5]

Ridge knew what was going on in the Cherokee Nation, and the founding of the Knights there no doubt influenced his decision to find out more about the group. This was not hard to do; the political circles Ridge traveled in included many former Know-Nothings and anti-Republican Douglas Democrats. Though at no time did he admit membership in the secret society, it is all but certain that Ridge was a leader in the movement. The difficulty in finding specific information on Ridge's ties to the group is, of course, that it was a *secret* society. Accordingly, members avoided holding large meetings. The officers would meet to initiate new members and to formulate plans, but these clandestine activities were never publicized, nor were records kept. At various times, though, Ridge defended the organization in print, maintaining that since Republican groups were arming for self-protection, it was only right that their rivals should be allowed to do the same. His columns also downplayed rumors concerning the Knights' activities or intentions. But he was certainly accused of being one of the leaders of the organization in California at various times, the earliest being the first months of 1861. The accusations were enough to induce him to move from Marysville.

Although Ridge was apparently investigated by local authorities for his involvement in the Knights' activities in early 1861, nothing was found to show that he had committed any illegal act.[6] Hurt by the charges and the investigation, he decided to leave Marysville and seek friendlier surroundings. Apparently Ridge's place in the community had not been damaged to any great extent by the investigation. The rival *Appeal* issued a statement as he prepared to leave Marysville. The editor praises Ridge, who had published the *Daily National Democrat* since its establishment in 1858 "with great ability and rare devotion to principle." He goes on to say that Ridge is leaving the city and makes this comment on his departure: "We are sorry to lose Brother Ridge from the local press, and we believe, our regret is shared by every citizen."[7] But Ridge was determined to leave. Needing money to relocate his family, he secured a mortgage on his share of the A. S. Randall Company, consisting of one-eighth part of "all the Printing Presses, Type, Furniture, fixtures, apparatus, and material for printing" owned by the newspaper. The $700 loan, taken out on March 7, 1861, was made by Henry C. Everts, who was in the shipping business in Marysville.[8] Ridge was replaced as editor by George C. Gorham on April 23, 1861. Ironically, after Ridge left the *Daily National Democrat*, it was merged with the *Appeal*, a rival Republican newspaper. Their affairs all settled, the family loaded up their belongings, left their home at 131 D Street, and headed for San Francisco. As it turned out, the choice of cities was not propitious.

10

Antiabolitionist

In May 1861 Ridge became editor of the San Francisco *Evening Journal*, an anti-Lincoln and antiabolitionist newspaper in—unfortunately for the *Journal* and its editor—a bastion of loyal Republicanism. He was associated with Calvin B. McDonald, former editor of the Weaverville *Trinity Journal* and other newspapers, including *Sign and Grip*, a paper put out in Sacramento by the Order of Odd Fellows. In his statement of editorial policy, Ridge declared that the *Evening Journal* would be strictly independent of any political party, though he pledged to support the Union, declaring it the best hope for humanity. Lincoln and the abolitionists, Ridge believed, were bent on destroying the Union. In spite of their opposition to his political views, many of the contemporary journalists on rival newspapers seemed to like and admire Ridge personally. The editor of the *Daily Alta California*, a paper extremely loyal to Lincoln and his policies, had this to say upon his arrival in the Bay City:

> Our contemporary, the Evening Journal, is fortunate in having secured the editorial cooperation of John R. Ridge. This gentle-

man has, as editor of the National Democrat, at Marysville, shown himself to be a vigorous writer, and an uncompromising Union man. His editorial articles are always terse, perspicuous, free from prejudice and clothed in elegant English. Mr. Ridge is more fortunate than some of the fraternity, inasmuch as he is a poet of no mean pretensions. His verses on "Mount Shasta" have a widespread popularity, and may be justly classed amongst the brilliant gems of the more celebrated of American poets.[1]

His association with the *Evening Journal* was short-lived, and in July he moved to the San Francisco *National Herald*, a newspaper known for its vehement anti-Lincoln stance. He was invited to write for the *Herald* by George Whitney Guthrie, proprietor of the paper. Guthrie was involved in Democratic politics and served as deputy surveyor of the port of San Francisco. In his first editorial in that newspaper, Ridge makes his antiadministration views known: "We war against the Republican party, not because it is for sustaining the laws and the Government, but because in its hands there is no wand of peace saving as it may there be put by the Union-loving Democracy of the nation."[2]

While at the *Herald*, Ridge's main assignment was to write on political affairs. This he did in a column called "Topics of the Day," where he regularly attacked the Republicans, asserting that they were dragging the country into war. He also commented on foreign affairs and warned against intervention in American problems, especially by England. After the battle of Bull Run, Ridge's column was still calling for compromise, declaring it was not too late to come to terms with the South. Many moderate Democrats in the South would welcome a settlement of the hostilities, he believed. By September, though, he recognized that full-scale war was inevitable. At one point he turned his attention to Indian territory and reviewed Albert Pike's mission to bring the Indians in on the Confederate side, expressing the hope that the Cherokees, at least, would remain neutral.

While editor of the *Herald*, Ridge was active in local and state politics too. "Topics of the Day" defended the Union Democratic candidates against attacks by the Republican papers, and Ridge turned his editorial guns on rival politicians. He became personally involved when he and Guthrie attended the state Democratic convention in July. At that meeting he was nominated for state printer, a lucrative and influential post for any newspaperman, but he was defeated in the Republican victory that resulted in the election of Governor Leland Stanford and his slate of candidates for state office.

During this period Ridge was writing poetry, but he turned his hand to patriotic verse, including "Ode to the National Flag" and "Poem," delivered at San Francisco in 1861 as part of that city's July 4 celebration. The "Ode to the National Flag" first appeared on September 29, 1861, in the Marysville *Daily Appeal*. It was published with an introduction under the title "A Fine Poem": "The following stirring apostrophe to our national banner from the pen of Jno. R. Ridge, was delivered by its accomplished author, a few weeks ago, before a large and brilliant assemblage in the Hall of the Dashaway Society, in San Francisco, and is the out burst of a loyal heart." The poem consists of thirteen stanzas identifying the flag as the national symbol, an emblem inseparable from the concept of liberty. The poem expresses the hope that both the flag and what it represents will continue. It is an emotional work—not unexpected a few months after the attack on Fort Sumpter.

Ridge delivered another patriotic poem that volatile summer, and it differs markedly in tone and emphasis from the "Ode." "Poem" approaches the vituperative rhetoric of some of Ridge's most acerbic political editorials. Though the work begins with a paean to America, symbolized by the dome of the national capitol, the reader's attention is soon drawn to forces that threaten the country:

> But in our dome the eagle builds its nest,
> And with our banner flies with armored breast;
> Yet, crawling round those pillars white, we've seen
> Beneath his perch, those meaner things unclean.
>
> (Lines 46–49)

These "meaner things" are described as reptiles that have "slimed Mount Vernon's consecrated sod" (line 51). These reptilian characters are not merely minor politicians: "Where sat a Washington, but late we found / The meanest reptile of them all inwound" (lines 54–55). Here Ridge is attacking Presidents James Buchanan and Abraham Lincoln, whose policies he abhors. But the chief monster, the "many-headed sire" of the Republicans (line 58), even now raises his head in the country: "Yea, Treason rears / Aloft his snaky front" (lines 58–59). Though the situation is perilous, in the end the rebels will be put down. The national flag "Shall never sink before you rebel crew— / Shall never bow, vile traitors, unto you!" (lines 70–71). This section of the poem expresses Ridge's thesis that though secession is treason, the southerners were forced into such drastic action by intractable Republican policies, policies that themselves constitute treason. He goes on to say that the "evil days" (line 73) that have come upon the nation would not have dawned had Andrew Jackson, Daniel Webster, Henry Clay, or "the gallant, glorious Douglas" (line 90) been alive. Ridge then breaks into a hymn of praise for the late Stephen A. Douglas. The poem closes with a prediction that in the end the nation will survive and treason—presumably both the Republican and the secessionist varieties—will be stamped out.

Ridge remained with the *Herald* until after the September 1861 elections, under the terms he and Guthrie set when he took the job of political editor. When he left the San Francisco daily, Ridge's reputation as an outspoken editor who was well liked and respected by his colleagues, even his rivals, seemed intact. His old rival at the *Appeal* published the following notice:

> During his connection with the Herald, the Appeal was compelled by its sense of duty to criticise frequently and sharply the views of that journal, which we deemed illiberal and jaundiced concerning the policy and course of the National Administration, and inconsistent with Union Democracy. We never impugned nor suspected the loyalty of its editor, though others did who mistook his excessive and unwise partizanship for

something worse, and have the animosities to bury, but renew
to our old friend and neighbor previously expressed wishes for
his constant welfare.[3]

Unfortunately, this high personal regard for the Cherokee editor was
not to survive in later years.

The September 23, 1861, issue of the *National Herald* was the last to
bear Ridge's name as editor, but he was determined to continue his fight
for the Democratic party and its principles and to oppose the Lincoln administration and what he considered its treasonous policies. By this time
Ridge's enthusiasm and his confidence in eventual success had began
to wane, and he was beginning to take an increasingly bitter outlook.
The frustrated desire for revenge on his father's killers festered too. One
evening before he left San Francisco, Rollin was drinking with some of
his fellow editors in the gallery of Hays Pavilion. He recounted the story
of the murder, then claimed that the face of each of the killers was etched
on his memory. He went on to say that he had subsequently learned each
of their names and had kept track of them all. According to his story,
only four were still alive in 1861. He also told his colleagues that his
own sense of revenge was so strong he had traveled to Weaverville to
investigate a rumor that one of Ross's men was there.[4]

The family remained in San Francisco from September 1861 until the
end of May 1862. During this time Ridge worked on a series of articles
on the North American Indians for *Hesperian* magazine, which came out
in the March, April, and May issues. He had a long association with
Hesperian, having published poetry in the magazine in the late 1850s.

It is clear that Ridge intended to write a long, comprehensive trea-
tise on the American Indian and that these three installments were the
beginning of that work. The full title of the series gives an idea of
its scope: "The North American Indians. What They Have Been and
What They Are. Their Relations with the United States in the Existing
National Crisis. The Modifications of Their Character by the Infusion
of White Blood and the Contact with Civilization. Their Probable Des-

tiny." Exactly why the series was discontinued is not known, but the project probably was laid aside in May 1862 when Ridge and his family moved from San Francisco to Red Bluff, where he became temporary editor of the *Beacon*. His subsequent political and editorial work most likely left him little time for scholarship. The constraints of time, along with the lack of the reading materials he needed for his research, probably made him abandon the project. The three articles that were published, however, give a fair indication of how he intended to proceed.

The first article in the series begins by speculating on the origins of the American Indians, reaching no conclusion except that they are clearly a race distinct from all others. Ridge notes that the Indians hold religious beliefs similar to those of Orientals but points out that some of their tenets also resemble those of the ancient Greeks, Persians, Jews, and Chaldeans, so little can be concluded from such comparisons. After the discussion of origins, Ridge goes on to declare that the Indians who live west of the Rockies are inferior to the tribes of the East, an argument he previously made in his discussions of the "Diggers." He expresses doubt that "they belong at all to the same stock" and determines to discuss the western Indians separately in a subsequent article. The groups he includes in his first piece are "the Athabascan, the Algonquin, the Iroquois, the Achalaquas, the Decotah, the Apalachian, the Chicorean, and the Natchez." It is clear that Ridge, in his discussion of each group, is following contemporary anthropological beliefs gleaned from his reading rather than any special knowledge or insight. For example, he cites a long-disproved theory speculating that all the groups he names except the Athabascans are descended from the Mexican Toltec tribes, who were believed to be the builders of the Mississippi valley mounds.

Relying on his reading of nineteenth-century ethnologists, Ridge describes the physical characteristics of these Indian groups, including their skin colors and skull shapes. He also discusses the practice of skull compression or flattening among various tribes. Then follow Ridge's comments on the intellectual traits of the Native Americans. Citing several accounts by early French explorers, he relates their impressions of the Indian mind and writes that these accounts "agree that the intellectual reach and scope of the Indian was by no means inferior to that of the uneducated classes of civilized nations, and that, in the faculty of expressing himself on public occasions, in a dignified and elegant manner, he was far superior to them." Ridge's argument is that if the Indians' intellectual capacity has developed to such an extent, only education is lacking to bring them—at least the "superior" eastern tribes, presumably—to a level of civilization equal to that of their neighbors. The last pages of the article carry a discussion of the Indians' great courage and stoicism, both of which Ridge obviously admired.

The series' second article appeared in the April 1862 issue and centered on the "religious belief and peculiarly mythological notions of the Indians, belonging to the groups designated in the previous number." Ridge begins by noting that most of the tribes had worshiped the sun and moon and traces this practice to their early connections with the Toltecs and, through them, back to the Incas of Peru. Most of the tribes now, however, regard the sun as a symbol of the Great Spirit, and not as the deity itself. The Great Spirit is opposed by an evil spirit whose symbol is darkness. Lesser gods on both sides inhabit the universe, according to Ridge, and engage in a Manichaean battle for control of human lives. Ridge illustrates his discussion with undocumented examples or anecdotes through all three articles, but in the second he takes the unusual step of quoting passages from Henry Wadsworth Longfellow's *Hiawatha*. He uses some two hundred lines from the poem to illustrate the Indians' belief in metempsychosis, or transmigration of souls. A short passage on various Indian festivals concludes the article. Ridge mentions the "Planting Festival" and the "Green Corn festival and dance," but he does not elaborate beyond saying they were important. He goes into more detail in discussing the ceremony in which a white dog is sacrificed. He discounts here the conjecture that this rite proves the Indians are one of the lost tribes of Israel, since many races had the custom of burnt offerings. The lost tribes theory was widely held by missionaries and others until the middle of the nineteenth century.

Ridge continues on the subject of religion and mythology in the article published in the May 1862 issue of *Hesperian*. His focus here is on Indian priests, prophets, and medicine men and their practices. The two major "institutions" of Indian religion Ridge identifies as the Medawin and the Jeesukawin; both are of ancient origin and exist in all the tribes from the Atlantic to the Rockies. The Medawin are the magicians and are closely connected with and sometimes identical to the medicine men. The Jeesukawin, on the other hand, are the prophets. After a general description of both groups, Ridge gives an account of a ceremony performed by the Wabeno, a group of Medawin. His source is "copies of papers furnished to the Indian Department at Washington"; Ridge seems not to be personally familiar with the rites, since at several junctures he professes ignorance about exactly what is going on. After his description, he comments on the extreme secrecy of the Medawin, but the next sentence seems to contradict that idea: "The secret grips and signs [of the Medawin] have been recognized as identical with some of the grips and signs of Free Masonry." He then relates a fantastic anecdote purportedly told by a friend who was a Mason. The friend was traveling on the plains east of the Rocky Mountains when he was surrounded by a band of Dakotas. Finding himself at a disadvantage, the friend "rode in front of the chief and gave the Masonic sign of supplication. To his surprise and delight, the chief returned the true response." The white man then shook hands with the Indian leader, using the Masonic grip, which was returned in proper fashion.

Ridge next gives his account of the secret rites of the Medicine Feast and concludes that the Medawin possess "the secret of Mesmerism." This is followed by a discussion of "the aboriginal idea of a future state," which he says differs from the Christian concepts of heaven and hell. Ridge asserts that any concepts of reward or punishment in the future life were introduced by early Christian missionaries and are not indigenous. Most Indians believe in a "land of souls," he says, a counterpart of this world, where people and animals go after death. Happiness in this other world is the general rule.

Ridge concludes his three-part series with comments on the Indians' reaction to the preaching of the missionaries. "The reply of Red Jacket, Chief of the Six Nations," he says, "to the speech of 'Black Robe,' (the Christian missionary), who in the presence of the assembled Council of the Iroquois had proclaimed the 'true Gospel,' is a fair sample of the general reasoning of the Indian mind upon the subject of the white man's religion." Ridge then reprints the famous passage in which Red Jacket questions the idea that only the whites possess the revealed will of God and asserts that so far the whites have not adhered to their own tenets—have not, in effect, practiced what they preach.

The Ridges left San Francisco in May and traveled to Red Bluff, where Ridge was to edit the *Beacon*, a Democratic paper established in 1857. This was another temporary position, beginning in June 1862. The editor, C. E. Fisher, had traveled to the East on business, and Ridge edited the newspaper until his return in October 1862. The *Beacon* billed itself as "A Weekly Journal, devoted to Politics, Literature, Education, Agriculture, General Intelligence, Etc., Etc." Clearly this newspaper with its eclectic interests was right up Ridge's alley. Some of the old enthusiasm returned, and he jumped into attacking the Republicans. His name appeared on the masthead of the June 19, 1862, issue along with the Union Democratic slogan, "The Constitution as it is, the Union as it was." His first editorial set the tone for his editorship. He blames the war on the "fanatical" "hostility of the Republicans to the Constitution" and refuses to support the administration. "We shall not hug to our bosom the viper of the North, while we strike vindictive blows at the dragon of the South." The Republicans threaten to convert a war for the Union into a war for the subjugation of states and the emancipation of the blacks, he writes. Later he asserts that Republican policies— the abolition of slavery in the District of Columbia, for example, and the prohibition against slavery in the territories—are grounds for revolution. Labeling Lincoln the "great public enemy of the Constitution," he calls on Democrats to resist attempts to merge their party with the Republicans. It is possible, he declares, to be anti-administration and yet to be a loyal citizen. He also defends the right of the press to differ with the government and denies that the Copperhead newspapers give aid and comfort to the enemy. When Lincoln issued his Emancipation

Proclamation, Ridge thundered that that action "completely overturns our system of government." His point was that the president had no right to govern by proclamation.

During his tenure at the *Beacon*, Ridge commented on Cherokee affairs too. He published a reprint of a brief history of the Cherokees from the Leavenworth *Conservative* in which the signers of the New Echota treaty are not treated kindly. He defends their action by saying that they "gave their individual consent without pretending to speak for the rest of the Nation." In another article, "What of John Ross?" he comments on two reports about the Cherokee chief, one saying that Ross is backing the Union and another claiming he has gone over to the Confederates. This is not contradictory, Ridge writes, if you know Ross. He went with the Confederates when it was popular in the Nation to do so, but he quickly changed sides when the Union army arrived and raided the Cherokee treasury. "The most loathsome reptile" cares nothing for the Union, the Confederacy, or the Cherokees, Ridge asserts. Ross cares only for gold, "His bloody hands . . . eagerly stretched forth for some of our money in the U.S. Treasury."

Whether Ridge participated in the Knights of the Golden Circle during his sojourn in Tehama County is not certain, but certain pronouncements of his make it probable that he did. His bitter attacks on Lincoln, his repeated charges that Republican policies were destroying the Constitution, and his statements that revolution was not only possible but desirable suggest he was thinking along the same lines as the Knights. In an editorial called "A Question of Right," he reports that a letter had been written to the San Francisco *Call* telling of a plot by southern sympathizers to organize a military force to annex Nevada, Utah, and New Mexico to the South. The *Call*'s editor admonishes the letter writer that it is his patriotic duty to come forward and identify his informant. Ridge advises the writer to keep quiet, since it is wrong to reveal a private confidence. If he was not working directly with the Knights, he was certainly sympathetic to their cause.

Ridge left the *Beacon* on October 9, 1862. His next project was to come to the aid of his party and establish a Democratic paper at Weaverville in Trinity County, a Democratic stronghold in the years leading up to the Civil War. Once hostilities started, however, there had been a distinct shift in political affiliation, with most of the county's Union Democrats going over to the Republican ranks. Most were motivated by the wish to demonstrate their loyalty to the Union. The democratic leadership in California and elsewhere was justifiably alarmed and sought to stem the flow of Democrats to their rivals. John Rollin Ridge, loyal Democratic editor, was persuaded to establish a newspaper in Weaverville and to attempt, by means of his skills in rhetoric and logic, to lure the prodigal Democrats back to the fold. He established the Weaverville *Trinity National* in 1863 but soon found out that the political change there had been profound and permanent. His accusations of treason against Abraham Lincoln were not well received by people who had voted for the Illinoisan, and the newspaper failed after only a few issues.

He found few supporters and fewer subscribers in the Trinity County goldfields. One report tells how the "majestic Cherokee" traveled to the mining camps along the Trinity River between Junction City and Taylor's Flat. He spent the night at the North Fork Hotel and repaired to the bar after dinner, where he invited some men to join him in a drink. As they sipped, Ridge showed them a buckskin gold-dust sack nearly a foot long that he carried folded in his pocket. He boasted that when he returned from the gold camps, the sack would have been filled by subscribers. One of the drinkers then made the remark that if Ridge indeed did fill the sack, it would be with Republican money, since there were few Democrats about. Ridge was obviously chagrined and replied, "Must be a ——— poor lot of Democrats." When he returned from the trip, he had taken only nine subscriptions.[5]

11

The Civil War
and After

After the demise of the *Trinity National*, Ridge found himself back working as a traveling agent, this time for Beriah Brown's *Press*, a Democratic
paper. Brown's newspaper followed the same editorial line Ridge had
advocated at Weaverville, declaring that the Republicans were usurpers
of power and deserved to be overthrown. While he traveled solicit-
ing subscriptions, Ridge was accused of organizing for the Knights of
the Golden Circle. The Marysville *Daily Appeal* published a rumor that
Ridge had established lodges at Marysville, North San Juan, and Grass
Valley in May 1864. The *Appeal*'s editor called for his arrest if the rumor
turned out to be true.[1] By the middle of the next month Ridge was
again editing a newspaper; on June 17 he bought a one-fourth interest
in the Grass Valley *National*. At first Ridge was coeditor of the triweekly,
sharing the duties with William S. Byrne. The other members of the
publishing partnership known as Byrne and Company were John P. Skelton, the business manager, and Charles S. Wells, a local businessman. On
August 1, 1864, the *National* went daily, and John Rollin Ridge became
its sole editor.

The Grass Valley *National* had been founded in September 1853 as

the *Telegraph*, the name it carried until 1858. The *National* was published
almost continuously from its founding and chronicled the boom-and-
bust activities of Grass Valley and Nevada County. A weekly at first,
the *National* became a triweekly in August 1861. On April 24, 1862,
the paper's publisher William Watt sold his share to Byrne and Skelton.
Watt's partner, Warren B. Ewer, retained his share of the company. The
three partners modernized the printing plant and published the newspaper until June 11, 1862, when their office burned down. Since they
had not taken out insurance, it appeared that the *National* was doomed,
but the people of Grass Valley raised $900 and lent it to the newspaper,
an indication of the community's high esteem for the publication. Publishing was resumed on July 19, 1862, with new equipment and in new
quarters. Ewer sold his interest to C. S. Wells in August 1863. When
Ridge joined Byrne and Company in 1864, the *National* was a major
source of news and commentary for both Grass Valley and Nevada City,
California.

The two towns are close to one another in the hills of Nevada
County. They were rivals in the early years, Nevada City being the
county seat. Grass Valley was in an area of ample arable land, oak and
pine timber, and good water. The first settlers to arrive there came over
the plains via the Truckee Route and Emigrant Gap, the route Ridge and
his party later followed. Miners flooded into the area in 1849 soon after
the discovery of gold. The town grew quickly and by 1850 boasted a general store and two lumber mills. Grass Valley survived an Indian attack
in 1850 and a devastating fire in 1855. The community's economy was
based on the quartz mines; the town installed the first mills in California
that could crush quartz ore and extract the gold. Nevada City was settled
in 1849 and by fall 1850 had a population of six thousand. The town was
destroyed by fire in 1851 but soon was rebuilt. In 1856 it survived a second fire that destroyed both wood and "fireproof" brick buildings. Most
of the mining operations around Nevada City were placer mines, which
relied heavily on a steady supply of water. The relative prosperity of the
towns was shaken by the unusual events of 1860–62. In 1860 the Com-
stock Lode was discovered in western Utah, causing an outflow of both

capital and labor across the Sierra Nevada. Speculating mine operators took their money and their most productive miners and headed for the rich new goldfields to the east. The populations of both cities dropped, and many businesses failed. Then in 1861 California was hit by a massive drought. Many of the placer mines of Nevada City were forced to shut down, and Grass Valley residents feared their water supply would disappear. After the drought came the floods of 1862, which greatly disrupted mining operations. In the next year drought struck again, and it seemed the area was locked into a dangerous cycle. By the time Ridge arrived in the summer of 1864, however, the cycle seemed to have been broken. A new prosperity, based on improved methods of quartz mining and milling, was welcomed by the citizens of Grass Valley. Even the miners of Nevada City, eager to share in the new wealth, turned from placer mining and began to build hammer mills to process quartz ore. The mills allowed the miners to exploit new sources of gold, and the local economy revived.[2]

New developments were evident on the political scene in Nevada County as well. By 1863 the political fortunes of California Democrats had fallen to a new low. Republicans were demanding that Democrats unite with the administration party to prove their loyalty to the government during the extreme conditions generated by civil war. The administration put pressure on Democrats in a number of ways, and newspapermen were particularly vulnerable. In California, for example, a number of Democratic newspapers were excluded from the mails in 1862, creating a circulation problem. These included the Stockton *Argus*, Stockton *Democrat*, San Jose *Tribune*, Tulare *Post*, and Visalia *Equal Rights Expositor*. The *Expositor* continued to publish its anti-Lincoln editorials until its presses were destroyed by a mob.[3] Whereas Ridge and others continued to maintain that opposing the policies of the federal government was not tantamount to treason as some Republicans insisted, many Democrats were persuaded and went over to the other side. The Democratic faction that supported Lincoln became known as the Union Democrats. The other faction, the Peace Democrats, openly supported the South by 1863 and called for an end to the war. When Ridge settled in Grass Valley to edit the *National*, he was a leading spokesman for the Peace Democrats.

By the time he arrived in Nevada County, animosity was high between the opposition forces. From the 1862 elections on, Nevada City was firmly in the hands of a Republican–Union Democrat coalition, while the Peace Democrats had control of Grass Valley's city government. Allison Ranch, a settlement of Irish miners in Grass Valley township, was vehemently opposed to the Republicans and allied with the Grass Valley Democrats. During the presidential campaign of 1864, the situation heated up. Various incidents were provoked by both sides. For example, at one point a group of Unionists from Nevada City crowded into a Grass Valley saloon and began to sing Republican songs. In the resulting melee, the town marshal, a Democrat, ordered them to quit singing. When the report of the marshal's action reached Nevada City, the Republicans were outraged. Some hotheaded members of the town militia tried to round up volunteers for a march on the adjoining town, but cooler heads recognized the folly of such an undertaking. The march never materialized, but violence between the rival towns always seemed imminent. It became a mark of manhood to loudly proclaim allegiance to one side or the other in saloons and other public places. The proclaimer, however, always made sure he was heavily armed. Union clubs were formed, and their members allegedly trained with firearms for what seemed almost a certainty—attacks by Copperheads and other southern sympathizers. On the other side, the Knights of the Golden Circle and the related Knights of the Columbian Star armed themselves for the inevitable conflict between the two forces.

Fanning the flames with newsprint from both sides were the editors of Nevada County. These writers dipped their pens in vitriol to produce political columns filled with personal attacks, rumors, and accusations ranging from immorality to treason and murder. As soon as Ridge arrived at the *National*, the rival *Nevada Daily Transcript* fired a salvo at him. Ridge, the editor says, was "once a gentleman" but now is editor of the *National*, implying that one could not be both. "Imperial Caesar at last may be useful to stop a hole, and so may John R. Ridge, after his political demise, answer a purpose more ignoble." The *Transcript* goes on to castigate Ridge for his adherence to the Peace Democrats' principles, saying that when the South seceded, he had urged Buchanan to use force against the rebels. Now Ridge has changed his tune: "The quill of an eagle's wing, of an American eagle, was exchanged by Ridge for the tail feather of a chicken, and we hear from the warrior editor, the defender of the rights of Man in Kansas, the poet, emulous of fame, nothing but the querulous notes of peace, craven peace."[4]

Ridge, hardly one to back away from a war of words, jumped into the fray with both feet. His editorials were as anti-Lincoln as ever, but by this time a marked sympathy for the Confederacy came through. He had taken on one more lost cause. He attacked the personal liberty bills of northern states, which in effect nullified the fugitive slave law, as being unconstitutional. Further, he maintained that the bills gave the South an impetus to secede. He continued to insist that the abolitionists were to blame for secession and thus for the war itself. He called, too, for an end to the hostilities. In an editorial of August 12, 1864, he asks, "When will this madness cease?" Then he goes on to write the following:

> Nothing that this Administration had done has tended to anything but disaster and ruin. Nearly four years of war, and no prospect of its termination; a financial system which has reduced us to bankruptcy; a blood tax which is impoverishing the people; a national graveyard bounded only by the limits of the Union; a land of widows and orphans—these are the mighty results for universal freedom, predicted by those sages of the hour who are to take the places of Washington and Jefferson.

Four days later he says, "The infamous conduct of this Administration, in the prosecution of this war, has so changed the relations of the parties contestant, that the South is not now contending against the Government, but against a usurpation." This usurpation is treason, he insists.

In September, George B. McClellan and George H. Pendleton were nominated for president and vice president on the Democratic ticket.

They were to run on a peace platform, and Ridge's newspaper embraced the candidates and the platform. During the presidential campaign, Ridge defended the practice of slavery and condemned Lincoln and the Republicans for attempting to abolish it. He attacked the abolitionist press for its moralistic stance, especially for its boast that if the North is oppressing the South, "Ours is the oppression that makes men free."[5] Ridge calls this "Puritanical cant," a "Puritanical self-sufficient smirk" and "an oppression which makes the negro free and enslaves the white man—raises the standard of African freedom, while it strikes down Constitutional Liberty."[6] To the abolitionist contention that slavery caused the war, Ridge replies that slavery did not, but "meddling" with slavery did. "Slavery was minding its own business—Abolitionism came along and committed outrage upon it," he contends on November 5, 1864. In an accompanying piece, he estimates the cost of the war and compares that figure with the number of slaves emancipated; he suggests that the abolitionists could have bought all the slaves in the South for half what the war cost and saved the nation untold grief. In the hectic months preceding the election, Ridge's editorials got more and more fevered. He rarely wrote about the Democratic national candidates; instead he repeated dire warnings about the consequences of a second Lincoln victory. The logic of his arguments often became strained, as the preceding examples demonstrate. Some of the heat of Ridge's writing may be accounted for by his personal involvement in the campaign.

This involvement included helping to form a Grass Valley Democratic club and taking control of the Nevada County Peace Democratic organization. The first meeting of the club was held on August 18 at Mazeppa Hall above Corbett's saloon, where a constitution was adopted and officers were elected. Rollin was elected corresponding secretary. Having adopted as its motto the old Democratic slogan "The Constitution as it is, the Union as it was," the group held its second meeting at Temperance Hall on September 24, 1864, the room above the saloon having proved too small to accommodate the crowd. The group listened to speeches by Ridge, Byrne, and others and made plans to get out the vote for McClellan.[7] In the middle of October another rally was held at the hall, and Ridge spoke to the crowd. Ridge's speech was not reprinted in the *National*, but the rival *Nevada Daily Gazette* made it the subject of an editorial in its October 17 issue. The *Gazette* charged that Ridge's speech included treasonable statements, including the assertion that Lincoln's reelection would bring revolution to northern California. The newspaper also reported that Ridge had said a split nation was better than four more years of Lincoln and had advocated the establishment of a Pacific Republic.

On the following Saturday Ridge traveled to Nevada City with some supporters, mounted a stand on Broad Street, and made a speech haranguing the *Gazette*'s editor, W. J. Beggs, for his remarks. The regular *Gazette* editor, Oliver Perry Stidger, was disabled at the time, the victim of a gunshot wound inflicted by an unknown assailant as Stidger was traveling between Nevada City and North San Juan. In his Broad Street comments, Ridge called the substitute editor a coward and a liar and demanded satisfaction in a duel. This was the first of a series of challenges Ridge issued in the next few months, further illustrating how his views changed in a short time. As editor in Marysville, Ridge had deplored what he described as the medieval custom of dueling, maintaining that it had no place in a modern, progressive society. He was particularly outspoken on the issue in 1859, after Senator David C. Broderick was killed in a duel. When Stidger recovered and returned to his post at the *Gazette*, he defended his substitute editor and brought Ridge's wrath down on his own head. The Grass Valley editor went so far as to challenge his Nevada City counterpart, in spite of Stidger's advanced age.

As the campaign advanced, the fighting between the rival newspapers became fiercer. The *Gazette* published a satirical verse, "A Noad to Ridge," on October 24, 1864. It was signed "Jaybird, first cousin to Yellowbird, poet laureate of the Cherokee Nation." The first of five verses reads as follows:

O John R. Ridge, 'tis understood
    Before you grow much older,
You'll strap your knapsack on your back,

Your gun upon your shoulder;
Against the Government you'll fight—
    Your "dander it has riz"—*
For a rebellion you are "in,"
    You'd better tend to "biz."
O Johnny Ridge, you hadn't ought to go,
You shouldn't go rebelling, no, Johnny Ridge, oh no.
*Original Cherokee

The Nevada City Republican newspapers referred to Ridge as a "half-breed Indian," and one of them even questioned his citizenship. The October 17 and 18 issues of the *Nevada Daily Gazette* carried articles with identical headlines: "Is John R. Ridge a Legal Voter?" The first piece cites section 1, article 2, of the California constitution, which limits suffrage to white males. The *Gazette* editor writes that Ridge claims to be a Cherokee and thus "has no more right to vote than a Digger Indian." The implicit equation of native California Indians and the Cherokees was meant as an insult. The second article asserts that the Cherokees are a separate nation and that Ridge should vote there instead of in California. Apparently Ridge took what appears to be harassment as a serious threat to his right to vote. He defended himself in the October 22 issue of the *National*:

> The skulking coward of the Nevada *Gazette*, "sub," crub, or whatever he is, alludes to our Native American ancestry as something to disqualify us from voting. He shows his ignorance. John Randolph, and thousands of others of Indian descent, have not only voted but held high official position under Federal and State governments. The Supreme Court of the United States has declared a doctrine which fully sustains that right.

On October 28 Ridge acknowledged the presence of a new newspaper in Grass Valley, the *Union*, a Republican daily established just ten days before the election. The proprietors, M. Blumenthal, James W. E.

Townsend, and H. C. Bennett, all strangers in the area, were sent into Grass Valley by the Republicans in a last-ditch effort to get votes away from the Democrats. Ridge wished the Union "as much success as it deserves" and dismissed the rival paper as inconsequential. He had considerably more interest in the *Union* than he let on, however. A bizarre sequence of events took place on the eve of the election. Not surprisingly, there are two versions of the story. First, Blumenthal's.

The *Union* came out on the Sunday morning before the election carrying a story that the *National* challenged the next day. The *Union*'s version states that editor Blumenthal had been approached by his partner Townsend with a proposal that they could both make some money by selling out to Ridge. Blumenthal refused, but Townsend came to him again, saying that Ridge had told him the pair could "name their own price" for substituting the McClellan ticket for the Lincoln slate and transferring ownership to the *National*. Blumenthal's alleged reply was, "There was not enough money in the world to induce me to take such an action." On Saturday night Townsend was scheduled to speak to the Lincoln-Johnson club, but he failed to show up. One of the men from the *Union* went to the office to investigate. There he caught Townsend in the act of transferring the forms for the next day's edition to the *National* office, where Lincoln's name would be replaced by McClellan's. Townsend escaped, but the edition was saved and the *Union*'s integrity remained intact. Now for Ridge's version.

The *National*'s reaction was published on November 7 and included a statement purportedly written by Townsend and one written by Ridge. Townsend provides some background by noting that the *Union* had been founded as both a political and a business venture. He goes on to say that financial support promised by the Republicans had not been forthcoming. Townsend also makes the dubious claim of having been converted to the McClellan cause as the election approached. Thus, when Ridge made an offer to buy the *Union* he was inclined to accept for both political and financial reasons. When he presented the offer to Blumenthal, however, "this pink of political purity reared up at the proposition, *though at the same time he was negotiating with certain parties to sell out the whole concern and deliver it on Saturday evening* to the Democrats." Townsend's self-serving story is suspect for two reasons. First, the "certain parties" were never identified. Second, if Democrats were negotiating to buy a newspaper in Grass Valley, Ridge, as a newspaperman and a party leader, would have known about it. Townsend's story corroborated Ridge's statement, which surprised no one.

Ridge begins his account by accusing Blumenthal of lying. He writes that he was first approached by Blumenthal, "through Townsend," who offered to sell the *Union* to Ridge. Ridge then went to Blumenthal, who explained that he wanted to sell because the promised Republican financial support had not come through. When asked what price he would accept, the editor named too high a price, Ridge writes. Ridge then made a counteroffer of a "bonus" for "the use of his columns" to promote McClellan. Blumenthal did not consent to this arrangement, but on Saturday night he offered to sell out for $900. When this was refused he lowered the price to $800, according to Ridge. Ridge did not accept, since he wanted to think over the situation. In the meantime the *National* editor was again approached by Townsend, who told him of his new convictions concerning McClellan and of his plans to change the paper's affiliation on his own without consulting his partners. "It was understood between him and Ridge to that effect, and that was all Ridge had to do with the affair," Ridge goes on to say.

Both sides substantially agree on what happened next, though they disagree on the motive. On the morning of November 7, Ridge and two other men marched out of the *National* office on the northwest corner of Main and North Church streets and headed down Main. They climbed the stairs of the Bennett Building at Main and Mill and burst into the *Union* office. An argument followed, during which Ridge challenged Blumenthal to a duel. Blumenthal refused, whereupon Ridge began beating him with his walking stick, all the time urging his victim to fight back. Although the basic facts of the incident are not disputed, the reasons for Ridge's actions are. Blumenthal and others subsequently maintained that Ridge had paid Townsend a sum of money for the *Union* and was upset when Blumenthal refused to turn over the paper or at least

defect to the Democratic side. Ridge denied this and claimed he was
motivated by a sense of honor. His November 7 statement concluded
with the following: "For his 'cheeky' use of Ridge's name in connection
with this affair, and his series of lies with reference to this matter, Ridge
went into his office this morning and whaled him. Blumenthal, begging
for mercy which he received, with the admonition that if he would not
fight, he would do better to get some man in his place who would."

On the following Tuesday the election was held, with predictable
results: Lincoln carried Nevada County, sweeping Nevada City. The city
and township of Grass Valley went for McClellan by a slim margin,
with Allison Ranch's unanimous Democratic vote making the differ-
ence. Although the election was settled, the battle between Ridge and
the Republicans continued and, if anything, intensified. The rhetoric was
blistering: Ridge was "villanous, debauched, vagabondish, and seedy,"
according to the *Gazette* on January 11, 1865; the editor of the *Union*
was a fool, a coward, and a knave in the eyes of the *National*'s editor.

The rivalry between the *National* and the *Union* soon deteriorated
into a running feud. The fault seems not to be all Ridge's, though his
actions could by no means be construed as restrained. Blumenthal, em-
barrassed and outraged at the beating he had received from Ridge, hired
a new editor, H. C. Bennett, probably to provoke a confrontation with
Ridge. Bennett was brought in with considerable fanfare orchestrated by
Blumenthal, whom Ridge by now was calling "Bombastes Blumenthal,
our local Falstaff." After joining the *Union* staff in December 1864, Bennett let it be known that in addition to his considerable intellectual and
journalistic skills, already attested by Blumenthal's advance publicity, he
was an accomplished "shootist." Just the match for John Rollin Ridge.
Bennett immediately took editorial aim at the "Copperhead traitors" in
Nevada County and announced that any of them who interfered with
him would be disposed of as he would shoot troublesome dogs. Bennett sprinkled his columns with similar statements, prompting warlike
replies from the easily excited editor of the *National*. The issue came to
a head on Thursday, January 12, 1865, when Ridge walked down to the
Union office to confront Bennett about one of the allegations made in

his column. At this time Ridge was under heavy attack from the *Union* and the *Nevada Daily Gazette*, both of which accused him of organizing armed groups to fight against the Republicans. When he reached the second-floor office, he found that Bennett was in Nevada City on business, so he returned to his own office. Blumenthal, seeing an opportunity for a showdown, immediately telegraphed the neighboring town and told Bennett to return at once. Bennett did, and the pair walked the short distance up Main Street to the *National* office, where they found Ridge standing on the porch. At that point Ridge challenged Bennett to a gunfight, daring him to draw his weapon. Bennett refused, noting the dangers to passersby and citing a city law against dueling. Ridge then drew his own pistol but held it down at his side, all the time urging his rival to draw. Bennett replied that he would fight Ridge "anywhere but on the street." The incident ended with no shots fired, but the feud expanded.[8]

Ridge called Bennett a liar, coward, scoundrel, poltroon, and various other deprecatory names in his columns, while Bennett wrote that Ridge had promised to fight him at the edge of town on the morning after the incident but had not appeared. Ridge denied any such appointment. An attempt was then made to effect some conciliation between the two editors. A friend of Ridge's, George D. Roberts, met with a friend of Bennett's, S. D. Bosworth, and suggested that Bosworth act as intermediary. Ridge and Bennett continued to jockey for position, both in their newspapers and in conversations with Bosworth, however, and no compromise could be reached. On January 16, 1865, Ridge received a message from Bennett saying the *Union* editor accepted a challenge supposedly issued by Ridge. Bennett was probably reacting to bellicose statements in the *National*. His letter proposed that the duel be held on the road between Grass Valley and Nevada City—neutral territory that would be convenient for spectators from both towns—at 7:00 the next morning. Bennett's choice of weapons no doubt came as a surprise to Ridge; Bennett elected to use United States regulation military swords, which he would supply. Bennett's letter and Ridge's reply were published in the *National* on January 17. The reply expressed surprise at Bennett's acceptance of a challenge, since according to Ridge, none had been issued. If Bennett wishes to challenge him, the letter goes on, Ridge will accept but will reserve the right to choose the time, place, and weapons. Ridge notes that after sending the letter he has gotten no reply from Bennett. He then calls his rival a fool, a coward, and a knave, saying that "no one but a fool would imagine that, as the challenging party, he had a right to select weapons, time and place." "No one but a coward would assert that he had been challenged when he had not, and no one but a knave would *lie* by making such an assertion." There is no record of Ridge's skill as a swordsman—or his lack of it.

Apparently feeling that he had effectively cowed Bennett, Ridge turned his attention to his other major rival, W. J. Beggs of the *Nevada Daily Gazette*. Recalling that he had denounced Beggs from a stand on Broad Street in Nevada City, Ridge revealed in a January 19 column that the day before he had sent the *Gazette* editor a challenge to a duel. He published both the challenge and its reply. Beggs's answer was to refuse the challenge on the grounds that Ridge still had his matter pending with Bennett and it would not be proper to fight a second duel before the first was out of the way. Ridge pronounced the letter a "cowardly subterfuge" and denounced Beggs as a "poltroon and a scoundrel," two of his favorite epithets during this period. On the following day Beggs published a statement that had Ridge offered him a second challenge, he would have accepted. To no one's surprise, Ridge fired off another challenge. Delivery of this note, he reports on January 21, was refused by Beggs, who told the messenger he would accept no more notes from Ridge but would defend himself if attacked on the street. In the January 20 issue of the *Gazette* Beggs says he did refuse Ridge's note, adding that "we now assert that the white-livered craven, John R. Ridge, is beneath the contempt of anything wearing the outward semblance of a man," and that he will have nothing more to do with him. In spite of the rhetoric, Ridge felt vindicated, since both his rivals had refused a public challenge.

These public challenges may have been a way of diverting attention from the serious charges being made against him by the Republican papers. After the 1864 election he was accused of raising secret armed groups of southern sympathizers, known variously as the Knights of the Golden Circle, the Knights of the Columbian Star, the Sons of Liberty, and the Defenders of the Constitution. Republican newspapers like the *Union*, *Gazette*, and Marysville *Appeal* called for Ridge's arrest and his imprisonment in Alcatraz. The Republican papers issued dire warnings about Copperhead secret societies and their plans to annihilate Union loyalists. Every crime committed in northern California at the time was attributed to members of these groups. When two men were arrested for murder at Allison's Ranch in January 1865, for example, the *Gazette* claimed they belonged to the Knights of the Columbian Star, "of which Colonel Ridge is an officer."[9] It also reported that it was "pretty definitely ascertained" that the gang that had robbed stages and murdered an officer in El Dorado County, the murderers of Union men in Fresno County, and outlaw Mike Hayes's gang were outgrowths of the Knights. Ridge was allegedly a major recruiter for the rebel groups. The *Gazette* reported on January 21, 1865, that "just before the presidential election in November, the half-breed Indian rebel was going through the state organizing bands of secessionist cut-throats under the Knights of the Columbian Star and the Defenders of the Constitution." Armed rebellion was a real threat, according to the Republican editors, and there was a "hellish plot" by "truculent rebels" of Grass Valley, Allison's Ranch, and other "notorious haunts of treason" to "sack and burn" Nevada City. "We have satisfactory evidence of the disposition of 'Colonel' Ridge and his 'Knights' to make the attempt, whenever it is feasible."[10] Despite the "satisfactory evidence," the *Gazette* reports that the police are "apathetic" and refuse to arrest Ridge and "other leaders of the Confederate cut-throat gang."

Although Ridge never admitted any of the actions the Republican editors accused him of, he did comment on citizens' arming themselves, the reaction of the government, and the "threat" to Nevada City. A piece in the August 9, 1864, *National*, called "Arming for Democrats," comments on the order by the federal military commander in the region concerning armed groups that are not part of the army or regular militia.

General McDowell, Ridge says, has outlawed such groups, yet the "inner circles of the Union Leagues" have been supplied with government-issue weapons, so the order is aimed solely at Democrats. He quotes Beggs from the *Gazette*: "Every Union man in the State should purchase for himself a first-rate rifle, or a double-barrelled shot-gun, and a Colt's revolver. The probabilities are that before the end of sixty days these arms will be required." The *Gazette*'s rationale for urging such purchases is that the Democrats are secretly arming themselves to resist a draft. This is not true, Ridge asserts, yet the Democrats must also arm themselves because the Unionists have. The situation was rapidly becoming a North-South arms race, albeit a local one. Ridge went on to say that the Democrats, "if they arm at all," must do it secretly to avoid the "'eagle eye' of the military authority." He also cites a decree by the "Abolitionist Governor" that members of the militia were to bring their arms home and have them ready for an emergency. His last paragraph mentions the constitutional right to bear arms. McDowell's order violates the Constitution, Ridge reasons, since it allows Republicans to arm but not Democrats. His logic is that if the order is unconstitutional, it can be ignored. The implication of Ridge's article is that Democrats must be able to resist if the Unionists take action against them by arresting their leaders, closing their newspapers, or preventing them from voting.

The *National*'s editor was immediately attacked for his August 9 article and was accused of trying to incite resistance to the draft and generally stir up trouble. He denied the allegations in a lead article in the August 19 issue. On the draft, however, he has this to say:

> But we would ask reasonable men, men descended from a race with whom liberty is as natural as the air they breathe—men descended from those proud European and English stocks, which have illumined history with historic deeds in the cause of constitutional freedom, if they believe that American freemen, so descended and so crowned with the traditional glory of their ancestors, are a class to be driven, dragged or manacled at the hands of military tyrants.

Certainly many Americans, especially those who had emigrated from Europe to escape conscription there, could agree with the sentiment of this statement.

On September 27, 1864, Ridge reacted coyly to a frantic report in the *Gazette* that the Knights were organized at Moore's Flat in Nevada County and that the group met for "secret drill" one or two evenings a week. His response begins by ridiculing the *Gazette*'s alarm: "To arms! to arms! ye dauntless Leaguers! Your firesides, your families, your government pap is in danger." But then he goes on to relay a rumor he has heard about Democrats' arming in the county, under the aegis of either the Knights of the Golden Circle or the Knights of the Brazen Cross. The rumor was that 900 men were armed at Moore's Flat, 450 at Woolsey, 2,000 at San Juan, 33 at Jones' Bar, 1,500 at Birchville, and 57 at Lake City. He finishes his article by writing, "We fear that it must be said of the *Gazette*'s rumor, in the language of Artemus Ward, 'too troo.'"

Ridge published a tongue-in-cheek description of an initiation into the "Knights of the Golden Opportunity," allegedly supplied by an informant, in the September 29 *National*. In his account the initiate is led into a cave, usually a saltpeter cave, and "after expressing a hearty desire to feed on Abolitionists, either in the form of a stew, a boil, a roast, a broil, or a fricassee, he is administered a copious draught of Shoddy blood." He then is obliged "to do the simple trapeze act, turn a flip-flop, balance a small-size crockery establishment on his chin, and walk a tightrope with two of Quantrell's men suspended from his legs." After this "light exercise," he is given a steam bath, dried in a "fiery furnace," and questioned as to his ability to annex California and Canada to the Confederacy. Then he must promise to capture federal vessels patrolling Deer Creek and South Wolf Creek and to perform other terrorist acts. Ridge finishes by writing, "Other horrible designs have been hinted at but we forebear giving more particulars at present, being opposed to creating further panic in our midst." After the election, Ridge flatly denied the existence of any such organizations and ridiculed the Republican paper for alarming the local citizens.[11] When the predicted invasion of Nevada

City did not materialize, Beggs and Bennett became the laughingstock of the county.

By April 1865 the war was over, and shortly afterward Lincoln was assassinated. Because the news reached Grass Valley shortly before press time, the tragedy was reported briefly in a black box in the *National's* April 15 issue. On April 17, though, the entire newspaper carried black-bordered columns. In an editorial, Ridge expressed "profound regret" for the death of the man he had so often reviled. The regret was probably genuine; in the procession at Grass Valley mourning Lincoln's demise, John Rollin Ridge and M. Blumenthal marched arm in arm.[12] Soon after the death Ridge began a series on the history of assassinations, beginning with that of Caesar. He wrote a running narrative through several issues on the emperor's death and the events that followed.

On April 10 William S. Byrne retired from the *National* and sold his interest to Charles S. Wells. It is clear from his "Valedictory" published that day that he and Ridge severed their partnership on good terms. In fact, Byrne and Ridge were to be business partners again. On Christmas Eve 1865, the two bought a quartz mine along with sixteen other persons. The claim, known as the William Heard Ledge, was two miles east of Grass Valley in the township. The ledge was reportedly 1,900 feet long.[13]

By September 1865 Ridge was once again involved in Cherokee affairs. He had been in touch with Stand Watie and Elias Cornelius Boudinot, both of whom had played important roles in the Confederacy. Watie had raised a regiment of cavalry, had fought for the South until the end, and had been made a general. Boudinot, the son of Elias Boudinot, was a lawyer who had served in the Confederate army under Watie, rising to the rank of major, and was elected Cherokee delegate to the Confederate Congress in Richmond. At the end of the war the United States government wished to treat with the Cherokees and other Indian groups who had allied with the South during the war. Watie, Boudinot, and eventually Ridge were to take part in the negotiations.

A general council of Indians living in the territory west of Arkan-

sas was called by Dennis N. Cooley, the commissioner of Indian affairs at Fort Smith, Arkansas, for September 8, 1865. Delegations from
the Creeks, Osages, Senecas, Cherokees, Seminoles, Shawnees, Wyan-
dottes, Quapaws, Chickasaws, and Choctaws attended, as did five commissioners appointed by President Andrew Johnson. Cooley himself
presided and presented the Indians with an agenda that included the
following: each tribal group must treat with the government because of
secessionist activities by some of their number; the tribes must help the
government in making peace with the "wild" Indians; slavery must be
abolished; freedmen must be incorporated into the various tribes and
be given equality with tribal members; lands in Kansas and elsewhere
must be relinquished for allocation to Indian groups being removed
from other parts of the country; the separate nations in present-day eastern Oklahoma would be incorporated into a newly organized Indian
Territory. These and other issues were discussed by the delegates until
September 21, when the council was adjourned sine die. Before adjournment, however, plans were made for each of the nations to treat with
the federal government.[14]

The Cherokee delegation to the Fort Smith council was unique in
at least one respect: it was made up of two rival factions, the "Northern"
delegates and the "Southern." Of course, at the heart of the split was the
old animosity between the Ridge, or Treaty, party and the Ross faction.
The Ridge, or Southern, delegates favored a division of the Cherokee
Nation along party lines. The Northern faction opposed this idea. The
titles "Northern" and "Southern" came about because of the particular
actions of both groups during the war. Both Watie and Ross had led
their followers to side with the South at the beginning of the war, each
believing the Confederacy would succeed. Both men, of course, had
built up considerable fortunes, much of it through the labor of black
slaves. When federal troops entered the Cherokee Nation, however, Ross
and his followers embraced the Union cause, outraging Rollin in far-off
California. The Ross party's claim was that they had only pretended to
join the southerners as a "diplomatic ruse" to enable them to hold out
until federal troops arrived.[15] After federal occupation of the Cherokee

Nation, the Ross faction began a campaign to confiscate the lands and property of the Treaty party men who still fought for the South. Members of the Ridge faction remained faithful to the Confederacy—Stand Watie was the last southern general to surrender. When it was time to negotiate with the government, both Ross and Watie claimed the title of principal chief, though Watie later modified his claim to "Chief of the Southern Cherokees." The government recognized both delegations and, as it has done countless times before and since, commenced to use factionalism within an Indian group to gain concessions.

Ridge was being kept informed of developments in the Cherokee Nation by correspondence with his family and with Boudinot and the Waties. Some of this intelligence apparently became garbled, because just days after the adjournment of the Fort Smith council, he sent a letter to President Johnson, applying for the position of "Provisional Governor of the Cherokee Territory." Apparently he had heard from Boudinot or Saladin Watie that the government intended to establish an Indian territory and misinterpreted the message. His letter to Johnson was sent from Grass Valley and dated September 25, 1865.[16] At the time, both Ridge and his friends and relatives in the Nation were contemplating his return. The time seemed propitious. He had participated in several losing political battles in California, yet he had succeeded in building up a considerable literary and journalistic reputation, which was probably even better in the Cherokee Nation than in California. To be called back to take a leadership role among his people just when they were entering another troubled period was an attractive prospect to him, especially since his friends were predicting a rosy economic future after the new treaty was signed.

It was Josiah Woodward Washbourne, son of Cephas Washburn and husband of Rollin's sister Susan, who first advanced the idea of Ridge's joining the Southern delegation. Washbourne, a lawyer, dreamer, and heavy drinker, was appointed clerk of the negotiating party and, right after Christmas 1865, had traveled to Washington to take up his post. In a letter to his wife dated January 16, 1866, he speaks of the opportunities that seemed to lie just ahead for Ridge. "He [Ridge] might do a great

deal of good were he here now, in framing our treaty," he writes. He
then adds,

> I wrote to Rollin to come immediately here and to make up his
> mind to live in Arkansas. He can be anything he wants. He is
> the only one of our family not accused of attaint [*sic*] of trea-
> son and he can be at the head of orators, have at the head of
> the press, can be U.S. Senator if he will come out and try. He
> will have all of Boudinot's influence and all of [J. M.] Tibbett's
> and it will be very great and he can, with his great California
> reputation be anything he desires. I beg of him to come here
> and press these great advantages and raise again the fallen for-
> tunes of our family—He can do it with his reputation, latent
> genius.[17]

He goes on to urge his wife to write to Rollin, saying, "A word from his
favorite sister will weigh upon him stronger than all else." Both Washbourne and Elias Cornelius Boudinot wrote to Ridge from Washington
inviting him to come there to start a triumphant new career as a leader
of his people. The pair also applied to Stand Watie to appoint Ridge a
member of the Southern delegation.

By February 21 Rollin had consented to travel to Washington to
join the Southern Cherokee negotiators. Stand Watie appointed him to
the delegation on that day. Previously he had appointed his son Saladin, E. C. Boudinot, J. A. Scales, William P. Adair, and Richard Fields.
Washbourne continued to make plans for the future of the family. He
wrote to his wife envisioning the time when "our family will soon grow
rich again" saying, "Boudinot [and I] are about to buy the old Free
Democrat office and go to editing and publishing a paper right away.
We look for Rollin to join us. I expect to buy the necessary paper, ink,
etc., on my way home. I expect to move to Little Rock with you all."[18]

Late in April, Stand Watie and J. A. Scales returned to the Cherokee
Nation. Shortly after, about May 10, Ridge arrived in Washington and
was immediately elected chief of the delegation in Watie's absence.[19] By
this time spirits were high among the Southern delegates, who fully ex-

pected the government to sign a treaty giving the Ridge party a pro rata share of Cherokee funds and allowing them to set up an independent Southern Cherokee territory in the Canadian district.[20] The government had reported that it had given up trying to deal with the Northern delegates by late April and had made good its threat to turn to the Southern group to complete the treaty. The Ridge delegation was elated at this series of events and predicted victory.

On May 17 Ridge was empowered to negotiate for the Cherokee Indians who lived east of the Mississippi. An affidavit filed by Johnson K. Rogers, who had power of attorney for the eastern band, authorized him to act on behalf of those Cherokees who might wish to "rejoin their brethren in the West, and who have not forfeited any rights in that Nation but who have refrained from taking their legal position in the Cherokee Territory, as guaranteed to them by treaties."[21] On the day before, the Southern delegates had met with President Johnson, who apparently assured them that the government was ready to negotiate.

Ridge wrote to Cooley the day after the meeting with the president. His letter gives some idea of what was discussed at the White House. After requesting a copy of Cooley's annual report, which he compliments, Ridge says that he needs the information contained in the document for a history of the Cherokees he is writing. This is no doubt the contemplated "true story of our people" Ridge wrote to Watie about back in 1854. Then he gets to the heart of the matter and requests that Cooley talk to Johnson and explain a point Ridge had tried to make in the meeting. Rollin says he fears the president misunderstood him when he "spoke of the bloodshed which would ensue in the Cherokee Country, if the Government delivered us over into the hands of the Ross dynasty." Ridge was clearly making an argument for the partition of the Cherokee Nation, asserting that the majority Ross faction would be in control were the Nation not divided and, if true to form, would continue its persecution of the Ridge party. He goes on to say, "I did not mean— and *did not say*—that *we,* the Ridges, Boudinots and Waties, would raise the flag of war and begin difficulties, but that the Ross faction would certainly renew upon *us* the oppression of old and dig graves for us as they did for our immediate ancestors, or try to dig them, and that in that case, we were men enough to resist, and that we *would* resist, if it drenched the land in blood."[22] Ridge tells Cooley that he thinks this observation "was just, manly, and true," but that Johnson might have misunderstood it. He closes by asking the commissioner to be sure his point is made to the president.

All the time, of course, the Northern faction was arguing against separation of the Nation and was lobbying in the Senate to prevent it. On May 26, 1866, the Southern delegation issued a document, *Comments on the Objections of Certain Cherokee Delegates to the Proposition of the Government to Separate the Hostile Parties of the Cherokee Nation*, which argued for partition. It appeared in the form of a sixteen-page printed booklet and outlined the history of the strife between the two factions. A graphic description of John Ridge's assassination was included, along with accounts of other atrocities committed by the "pin Indians" and members of the Light Horse. The booklet, signed by Ridge, Fields, Adair, Watie, and Boudinot, was written principally by Boudinot, with Ridge making a sizable contribution.[23]

In June a treaty was signed by the Southern delegation and administration officials. Its key provisions in Ridge's eyes were these: the stipulation that the Southern party, while not separated from the nation, would be allowed the Canadian district for "their exclusive use and occupancy," and the award of a pro rata share of the financial settlement to the 7,000 members of the Southern faction.[24] This treaty, however, was never brought to the Senate for ratification. The Northern faction, alarmed at the possibility that the government might treat with the enemy, reopened negotiations, though on less firm footing than before. By July 19 the government concluded a treaty with the Ross party, giving the Ridge faction the Canadian district. The followers of the Waties, Ridges, and Boudinots who chose to live in the district would be allowed to elect their own judges, make their own police regulations, and send delegates to the national council. The major concession the Southerners sought, however, was not forthcoming. They wanted a share of the Cherokee treasury and of any money the Nation would receive as part of the settlement. John Ross, though he was close to death at the time, would not concede on that point, and thus the treasury remained in the hands of the majority party. The loss on this issue made the treaty seem a failure to the Ridge delegation in spite of the other gains they had made.

Although it was rare for him to admit it, money was always a prime motivation for John Rollin Ridge. In his affinity for gold he was joined by most other members of his family, including his cousin E. C. Boudinot. Perhaps this is natural for people living in a frontier economy where speculating and exploiting resources were the order of the day. As it turned out, however, money was the cause of a falling-out between Ridge and Boudinot during their last days together in Washington. And that argument was the reason the dreams of Josiah Woodward Washbourne for success and riches for them all were never realized.

After the treaty was ratified, the only money the delegation received was an appropriation for expenses amounting to $28,825. Apparently no formal method of disbursement or distribution was set up by either the delegation or Commissioner Cooley's office, and this lack of organization led to the argument. On October 31, after approving the delegation's expense account, Cooley gave Ridge, Adair, Fields, and Saladin Watie $10,000 as an initial payment, the remaining $18,825 to be paid when Congress appropriated it from the sale of tribal land in Kansas. Scales and Stand Watie were to receive equal shares, but they were back in the Nation. Boudinot, too, who also was to get a share, was absent from Washington at the time the disbursement was made. When he returned from Arkansas, Boudinot demanded his share, asserting that he had not received any of the $10,000 or any other money from the government. Ridge, however, objected to his statement in a "certificate" he wrote and sent to the other members of the delegation and to the Office of Indian Affairs. In that document Ridge charged that Boudinot had "sold himself" and "made $1500 off the other delegates and no telling how much more."[25] Ridge went on to say that Cooley told him Boudinot had gotten $1,500 of the $6,000 paid to the Southern delegation's attorney, Perry Fuller.

Boudinot reacted angrily, rejecting Ridge's charges. In a November 15 letter sent from Little Rock to the secretary of the interior, O. H. Browning, Boudinot asserted that he had been "grossly swindled by my brother delegates under a misrepresentation of Mr. Ridge." Boudinot charged that the money had been given to Fields, acting as attorney for Ridge, Adair, and Saladin Watie, and that the four had split the payment equally. He made a claim for one-fifth of any money paid out to the delegation, apparently ignoring the claims of Scales and Stand Watie. He also requested that Browning hold up payment of the remaining $18,825 until Boudinot got his share of the $10,000. The delegation eventually split over the controversy, with Ridge and Fields on one side and Adair and Saladin Watie backing Boudinot's claims.[26] Boudinot also wrote to Cooley and Fuller asking them to sign enclosed statements denying Ridge's charges.[27] Boudinot was furious with Ridge and sent the following letter to him in Grass Valley:

> Sir:
>
> I have been fully informed through Watie and Fields of the malicious and dishonest part you played in my absence to injure my reputation and steal my money.
>
> I have written to your wife, brother and sisters, that all friendly relations between you and me have ceased forever, and that you have proved yourself a faithless and ungrateful friend, a slanderer and a liar, a thief and a coward.[28]

Boudinot, of course, had been an editor, too—of the *Arkansian* in Fayetteville and of the *Arkansas True Democrat* at Little Rock. He had obviously picked up all the name-calling skills needed by the competent nineteenth-century journalist. He goes on, defending his reputation:

> I have lived twelve years in North West Ark. and am known well to the people of the state and the Cherokee Nation; I have had many enemies, but not even the bitterest have ever accused me of dishonesty or of unfaithfullness to my friends; but *you,* after an acquaintance of a few weeks, discovered that I was a traitor to the cause. I had so much at heart and for which I had labored

so long and unselfishly, and that I was dealing dishonestly with those I considered my best friends.

He tells how Ridge succeeded in alienating for a time his good friends and allies, Fields, Adair, and Saladin Watie, but says that now they have seen through Ridge's subterfuge. He then questions Ridge's intentions:

What motive under Heaven could have moved you to this insane and futile attempt to malign and injure me? I would have laid my energies and my means at your feet to have advanced your personal and political fortunes. *You had no excuse;* the pitiful sum of $500, justly belonging to me, which you put in your pocket was, it seems a sufficient temptation for perjury and theft. It has been said that "all men have their price"; this *may* be true; but my price, must be more than $500.

The $500 is a one-fourth share of the $2,000 that Boudinot claimed from the initial $10,000 payment. Boudinot then writes that he has proved Ridge's allegations wrong and ridicules his pretensions:

It is high time you were done with your favorite theme of "blood and high birth"; were it possible I would let out of my veins every drop of Ridge blood that courses through them; the penitentiaries of your state are full of men of more gentle blood than *you* have exhibited in your transaction with me.

Boudinot has one last piece of business to transact before he signs off:

In conclusion let me remind you that you owe me $30, which you borrowed a few days before I left Washington; if it is convenient, please forward it by mail to me here. Care of Commr. Ind. Affr.

The great plans of Washbourne, Ridge, and Boudinot were never to be. Boudinot spent the winter of 1866–67 appealing for his share of the expense money, claiming a total of $4,569.56. On April 10 he received one-fifth of the $18,825 owed the delegation. The remainder was disbursed to Richard Fields for distribution to the other delegates.[29] Apparently Stand Watie never received his share, partly because of John Ross's objection. Before his death on August 1, 1866, the old chief was able to deliver one last blow against his old enemy.[30]

After Ridge's return to Grass Valley, little was heard from him. He continued to edit the *Daily Democrat*, speaking out against the Reconstruction policies of the Republicans. By this time Ridge was suffering from a condition known at the time as "softening of the brain." Expense records show that he received medical treatment during his stay in Washington, but his ailment is not identified. The condition occurs in people suffering from stroke, gout, alcoholism, or syphilis; its symptoms are dullness of intellect, drowsiness, absent-mindedness, emotional episodes, and finally dementia and death, all caused by damaged blood vessels in the brain. The disease advanced throughout the spring and summer of 1867, and in the last two weeks of September Ridge was disabled and bedridden. Tended by his wife and daughter, he remained in a feverish state, often lapsing into incoherence. On October 5, 1867, John Rollin Ridge died. The immediate cause of death was diagnosed as "brain fever," or encephalitis lethargia, involving inflammation and hemorrhaging of the brain.[31] He was buried in the Greenwood Cemetery at Grass Valley at 3:00 P.M. on October 7.

His obituaries were lengthy and for the most part laudatory, even from rival newspapers. For example, the San Francisco *Alta California*, opposed to Ridge during the war, had this to say about him: "Mr. Ridge was a man of generous and warm nature, and was gifted with high intellectual endowments. As a poet, he deserves a prominent position, and as a general writer he was forcible, elegant and polished, his chief forte being that of politics."[32] The Marysville *Daily Appeal* called him a "dignified, courteous and forcible political writer" and said that "his poetical effusions were marked by a strength of imagination and vigor of expression." "Yellow Bird" had a "cultured taste in letters, was a noted shot, and made many warm friendships," the *Appeal* concluded.[33] This reputation is one that Ridge would certainly have wished for himself, and his wife worked to perpetuate it.

Elizabeth Wilson Ridge lived until 1905. In 1868 she published a volume of her husband's poems. It is introduced with a sketch of Ridge's life and remains the only collection of his poetical works. Alice Ridge married Francis Gibson Beatty and lived in Grass Valley until her death in 1912. Andrew Jackson Ridge, Rollin's brother, moved to California and practiced law in Grass Valley for a number of years after his brother's death. The bodies of Elizabeth, Alice, Francis Beatty, and Andrew Jackson Ridge and his wife and family are all interred in the family plot where Rollin is buried. On May 16, 1933, the Native Sons of the Golden West erected a marker on his grave bearing the following inscription: "John Rollin Ridge—California Poet, Author of "Mount Shasta" and Other Poems. Born March 19, 1827, in Cherokee Nation, near what is now Rome, Georgia. Died in Grass Valley, October 5, 1867. In Grateful Memory."

Epilogue

John Rollin Ridge's life was full of contradictions. He was proud of his Cherokee heritage, yet he totally espoused the Euro-American doctrine of progress, with all its racial baggage. He saw himself as a cavalier and a gentleman but was quick to defend the common people, the "mudsills" and "squatters." He fought prejudice against Indians and Spanish Americans, yet he was active in the Know-Nothing party and the Knights of the Golden Circle. His art was important to him—he was proud to be known as a poet—but financial success was equally important. His opinions were sometimes contradictory, too. For example, he supported the reservation system but also came out for the establishment of an Indian state and, presumably, self-government for its citizens. All this is puzzling but perhaps is understandable within the context of Ridge's life.

Ridge's life was shaped in many ways by historical events. First of all, he was born in the Cherokee Nation during a tumultuous time. Whites were pressing into Indian lands in ever-increasing numbers, and the state of Georgia was attempting to impose its sovereignty on the Nation. The Cherokees appealed to the federal government for protection and waged a public relations war in the East, hoping to stop the incursions, but the pressure to remove proved too much. Failing to win the support of the Jackson administration, the Cherokees knew that the situation was desperate. The only choice seemed to be to move out of range of white encroachment or to physically resist and prepare to die for their homeland. Rollin's family was in the thick of all this, and he grew up hearing the hot political debates on the subject that took place in his father's house. Eventually those debates had disastrous consequences for him and the rest of the family.

Major and John Ridge's roles in formulating and approving the Treaty of New Echota affected all the Cherokees, but especially the Ridges themselves. The assassinations that resulted brought emotional and financial hardship to all of them. Forced to flee to Arkansas and leave behind many of their possessions, the family was never able to regain its status. Another effect of the political situation in the Nation was the shooting of David Kell, the direct cause of Rollin's exile from his family, land, and people.

Reaction to earlier historical events led to decisions by family members even before Rollin's birth that were to affect his makeup. His grandparents left the traditional Cherokee ways and adopted the practices of their white neighbors, since they reasoned that this path would lead to a better life. The Ridges farmed and raised stock, always working to improve and increase their property. They became slave owners and engaged in trade and commerce, embracing the contemporary "civilization" of white society in the southeastern United States. It is not surprising, then, that Ridge grew up to espouse assimilation as a remedy for the Indians' troubles. Also, Major and Susanna Ridge were early adherents in the Cherokee Nation of "English" education, centered on the English language and European arts and science. Rollin received a good education, especially for one growing up on the frontier, and demonstrated a reverence for learning all through his life. The decision to embrace white education and lifeways had important implications for all the Ridge offspring. The traditional Cherokee customs and mores had to be abandoned and replaced by Euro-American values. These new values were, of course, transmitted to the younger Ridges and especially to Rollin, who was expected to be the family standard-bearer. Taught by his parents and teachers, he learned his lessons well. Belief in the prevalent nineteenth-century doctrine of progress permeates his poetry and prose.

After killing David Kell, Rollin was once again swept up in the currents of history. It would have made sense for him to turn east, as Stand Watie had suggested, to escape prosecution by the Ross faction and take refuge with his mother's family in Massachusetts or with friends in Connecticut. But it was 1849, and a land of golden opportunity glittered in the West. The lure of riches and the chance to restore the family to its rightful place overcame the desire for a safer, albeit more mundane, solution to his problems, so he joined the wagon trains for California. Once there, he participated in the politics of that new land, at first only through his pen but later in person. He was caught up in the Know-Nothing movement, then joined the Douglas Democrats as the American party petered out. Regarding the abolitionism of Lincoln's party as too radical, he took the Peace Democrats' side during the Civil War, as had Stand Watie, E. C. Boudinot, and most of his friends and relatives back in the Cherokee Nation. As his own politics became more and more radical, he became a Copperhead organizer and finally became involved in the fringe group known as the Knights of the Golden Circle, among other names. In a final political move that proved his penchant for picking the losing side was still intact, Ridge joined the Southern Cherokee delegation that was trying to reach a settlement with the federal government after the war. This last attempt to become a political figure in the Cherokee Nation and to restore his family's lost fortunes ended in yet another defeat.

John Rollin Ridge's life was full of frustrations, too. He often saw himself as beset by outside forces. For example, he was the eldest child of a lost leader of the Cherokee Nation and the first grandson of a legendary figure in their history. From his early years he expected to advance the family's fortunes, both financially and in its leadership role in the Cherokee Nation. He was never able to achieve these lofty goals. Like other literary figures before and since, Rollin Ridge cultivated his image as a lonely, misunderstood romantic genius, especially in California. The right ingredients were there: by the time he reached the West, he was already a published poet. His background was mysterious, and according to his own story, his character had been forged in the crucible of the Cherokee internecine war of the 1840s. He was a crack shot, and his gun carried a notch marking the death of a man who had dared to cross him. He was a handsome outcast who yearned to return to his people and avenge his father's and grandfather's deaths. He had a fiery temper, an accomplished eloquence, a fierce loyalty, and an air of reckless bravery, all contributing to the image he successfully cultivated.

But there was substance to the man as well. He successfully edited and published several newspapers. His essays discussed passionately yet cogently the major local, state, and national issues of the day. Although he became more and more politically radical as time went on, his arguments were almost always logical, and his rhetoric was compelling. His writing on the American Indians was largely sympathetic to them—with the notable exception of his discussions of the natives of California—and based on human history as he understood it as well as on the ethnology of the period. He was also a successful poet and romance writer.

Ridge's *Joaquín Murieta* was the first of a series of versions of the now-famous legend. Although the work is based to some extent on contemporaneous accounts, Ridge's imagination furnished much of its content. Indeed, the romance's protagonist resembles the writer in many ways: both men were dark and handsome, both saw themselves as leaders of minority groups, both harbored a thirst for revenge for undeserved wrongs, and both were outcasts. If Ridge can be said to have created Joaquín, he did so in his own image. The influence of the book goes beyond fiction and romance and even colors California history. *Joaquín* is a tribute to Ridge's substantial narrative talent and his ability to synthesize information from several sources.

As a poet, Ridge probably fits somewhere in the middle ranks of nineteenth-century American writers. His work conformed to many of the romantic conventions of the period, but some of it carried Ridge's special stamp. Many of the poems set in California—"Mount Shasta," for example—demonstrate a well-developed sense of place. He often waxes lyrical or plaintive in his autobiographical poems, in the best tradition of romantic expressionism. His range even extends to the satirical, as evidenced by "The Arkansaw Root Doctor," his only attempt at humorous folk verse. As a poet, he seems to have had the almost universal, if sometimes grudging, admiration of his contemporaries.

In the end, Ridge was one of the first modern American Indian writers. Like most of them, he found himself caught between two worlds, discovering sympathy and hostility in both. Ridge felt a need to involve himself in politics, especially those that related to white-Indian affairs, just as American Indian writers do today.

John Rollin Ridge knew an inner conflict as well, which found his sense of Indian identity at odds with the need to survive in a white-dominated society. He never fully resolved that conflict.

Notes

CHAPTER ONE

1   Wilkins, *Cherokee Tragedy*, 3–4.
2   Ibid., 29.
3   Ibid., 100–101.
4   Tracy, *History of the American Board*, 68–69.
5   Wilkins, *Cherokee Tragedy*, 107.
6   Tracy, *History of the American Board*, 63–64.
7   *First Ten Reports of the American Board of Commissioners for Foreign Missions* (Boston: Crocker and Brewster, 1834), 136.
8   Wilkins, *Cherokee Tragedy*, 122.
9   Records of the American Board of Commissioners for Foreign Missions, Houghton Library, Harvard University (cited hereafter as ABCFM), 18.3.1, vol. 3, pt. 2, Moody Hall to Jeremiah Evarts, September 25, 1818.
10 Wilkins, *Cherokee Tragedy*, 125.
11 ABCFM, 18.3.1, vol. 1, pt. 1, diary of William Chamberlain.
12 Records of the Cornwall ABCFM School, Cornwall Historical Society, Cornwall, Connecticut (cited hereafter as Cornwall School Records).
13 ABCFM, 18.3.1, vol. 4, John Ridge to Elizur Butler, July 7, 1826.

CHAPTER TWO

1   Wilkins, *Cherokee Tragedy*, 144–45, 184.
2   Ridge, *Poems*, 6.
3   Foreman, "Sophia Sawyer," 395, 399.
4   Ibid.
5   Marion L. Starkey, *The Cherokee Nation* (New York: Alfred A. Knopf, 1946), 172.
6   ABCFM, 18.3.1, vol. 7, Sophia Sawyer to David Greene, December 29, 1833.
7   Ibid.
8   Ibid., Harriet Gold Boudinot to Benjamin B. Wisner, July 4, 1834.
9   Ibid., Sophia Sawyer to David Greene, July 4, 1834.
10 Ibid., Letter from Mary Fields included in Sophia Sawyer to David Greene, June 15, 1835.
11 Tracy, *History of the American Board*, 131.
12 ABCFM, 18.3.1, vol. 7, Sophia Sawyer to Jeremiah Evarts, July 28, 1827.
13 Starkey, *Cherokee Nation*, 173.
14 Ibid., 253.
15 Wilkins, *Cherokee Tragedy*, 229.
16 Ibid., 257–58, 278.
17 Cornwall School Records, John Ridge to Eliza Northrup, November 1, 1836.
18 ABCFM, 18.3.1, vol. 7, John Ridge to David Greene, May 17, 1837.
19 Ibid., Sophia Sawyer to David Greene, November 7, 1835, and July 2, 1836.
20 Wilkins, *Cherokee Tragedy*, 196.
21 Ibid., 296–97.
22 Starkey, *Cherokee Nation*, 303.
23 Foreman, "Sophia Sawyer," 395.
24 ABCFM, 18.3.1, vol. 7, Sophia Sawyer to David Greene, June 7, 1837.
25 Ridge Family File, Arkansas History Commission, Little Rock.
26 Ibid.
27 Wilkins, *Cherokee Tragedy*, 315.
28 Ibid.
29 Starkey, *Cherokee Nation*, 305.
30 Ridge, *Poems*, 7.
31 Wilkins, *Cherokee Tragedy*, 322.
32 Ridge, *Poems*, 8.

CHAPTER THREE

1   Ridge Family File, Arkansas History Commission, June 7, 1842.

2   Ibid.

3   Report of the ABCFM, 1840, 170.

4   ABCFM, 18.3.1, vol. 10, December 7, 1839.

5   Peel, "Romance from the Records."

6   *Flashback* 3 (July 1957): 38, a publication of the Washington County (Arkansas) Historical Society.

7   Foreman, "Sophia Sawyer," 399–400.

8   ABCFM, 18.3.1, vol. 10, Sophia Sawyer to David Greene, January 20, 1841; ibid., January 4, 1842.

9   Debo, "John Rollin Ridge," 59–71.

10 George Edwin MacLean, *History of Great Barrington* (Great Barrington, Mass.: Town of Great Barrington, 1928), 312.

11 V. Nieberding File, Western History Collections, University of Oklahoma Library, November 7, 1844.

12 Josiah Hazen Shinn, *History of Education in Arkansas* (Washington, D.C.: Government Printing Office, 1900), 25.

13 Dorsey D. Jones, "Cephas Washburn and His Work in Arkansas," *Arkansas Historical Quarterly* 3 (Summer 1944): 126–31.

14 Walter John Lemke, *Early Colleges and Academies of Washington County, Arkansas* (Fayetteville, Ark.: Washington County Historical Society, 1954), 14.

15 Deane G. Carter, "Some Historical Notes on Far West Seminary," *Arkansas Historical Quarterly* 29 (Winter 1970): 345.

16 Ibid.

17 Little Rock *Arkansas Gazette*, February 28, 1844, p. 1, col. 4.

18 Ibid.

19 Ibid.

20 Ibid.

21 *Arkansas Gazette*, March 17, 1845, p. 2, col. 2, and March 24, 1845, p. 2, col. 1.

22 Lemke, *Early Colleges and Academies*, 13.

23 Dale and Litton, *Cherokee Cavaliers*, 35–36.

24 Rinaldini was the hero of a romance, *Rinaldo Rinaldini, the Border Captain*, written by Christian August Vulpius in 1797. Ridge also makes reference to this work in connection with his own romance, *The Life and Adventures of Joaquín Murieta, the Celebrated California Bandit.*

25 Dale and Litton, *Cherokee Cavaliers*, 38–39.

26 Twenty-sixth Congress, 1st sess., House Document 129, serial 365, 54–55.
27 *Arkansas Gazette*, August 21, 1839, p. 2, cols. 4–5.
28 Wilkins, *Cherokee Tragedy*, 327.
29 Franks, *Stand Watie*, 69, 72.
30 Wilkins, *Cherokee Tragedy*, 327.
31 George W. Paschal, "The Trial of Stand Watie," ed. Grant Foreman, *Chronicles of Oklahoma* 12(1934): 313–17.
32 Stand Watie Miscellaneous File, Western History Collections, University of Oklahoma Library, Sarah C. Watie to James M. Bell, April 16, 1846.
33 Farmer and Strickland, *Trumpet of Our Own*, 19, and Walker, "Yellow Bird," 19.
34 Ridge, *Poems*, 9.
35 Dale and Litton, *Cherokee Cavaliers*, 36.
36 Mabel Washbourne Anderson, *Life of General Stand Watie* (Pryor, Okla.: Mayes County Republican, 1915), 35.
37 Ridge Family File, Arkansas History Commission.
38 Ibid.
39 Ibid.
40 *Flashback* 3(July 1957): 4.
41 "Fatal Recontre in the Cherokee Nation," Fort Smith, Arkansas, *Herald*, June 6, 1849, p. 2, col. 5; reprinted from the *Arkansas Intelligencer*.
42 Dale and Litton, *Cherokee Cavaliers*, 63–64.
43 Ibid., 65–66.
44 Ibid., 71.
45 Ibid., 66–67.
46 Stand Watie Miscellaneous File, Western History Collections, University of Oklahoma Library, March 27, 1850.

CHAPTER FOUR

1 Foreman, "Bushyhead and Ridge," 296–97.
2 Fayetteville *Northwest Arkansas Times*, March 10, 1973, p. 1, col. 1. Reprinted from the Fort Smith *Herald*, January 24 and 31, 1851.
3 Ibid.
4 Ibid., March 12, 1973, p. 6, col. 1.
5 Ibid.
6 Ibid.
7 Ibid., March 13, 1973, p. 9, col. 1.
8 Ibid., March 14, 1973, p. 14, col. 1.

9   Ibid.

10 Ibid.

11 New Orleans *True Delta*, March 25, 1851.

12 Ibid.

13 "A California Writer," *California Chronicle*, April 30, 1856, p. 1, col. 5.

14 Ibid.

15 Ibid.

16 Ibid.

17 Ibid.

18 Sacramento *Daily Union*, March 19, 1851, p. 3, col. 4.

19 Ibid., March 20, 1851, p. 2, col. 1.

20 Foreman, "Bushyhead and Ridge," 303.

21 *History of Sutter County, California, with Illustrations Descriptive of Its Scenery, Residences, Public Buildings, Fine Blocks and Manufactories* (N.p.: Thompson and West, 1879). The poem is called "Yuba City" in *Poems*.

CHAPTER FIVE

1   Foreman, "Bushyhead and Ridge," 303.

2   Walker, *Literary Frontier*.

3   All poetry quotations are from Ridge's *Poems* (1868) unless otherwise noted.

4   *Hutchings's California Magazine*, April 1859.

5   May Wentworth, ed., *Poetry of the Pacific* (San Francisco: Hubert H. Bancroft, 1866). Cited in Walker, *San Francisco's Literary Frontier*, 218.

6   Stand Watie Miscellaneous File, Western History Collections, University of Oklahoma Library, September 23, 1853.

7   C. P. Hale and Fred Emory, *Hale and Emory's Marysville City Directory* (Marysville, Calif.: Marysville Herald Office, 1853), 38.

8   Stand Watie Miscellaneous File, Western History Collections, University of Oklahoma Library, September 23, 1853.

9   Cornwall School Records, S. B. N. Ridge to Eliza Northrup, January 18, 1854.

10 Ibid.

CHAPTER SIX

1   Ridge, *Joaquín Murieta*, ed. Jackson, 7.

2   Clough, *Joaquín Murieta*, xiii–xiv.

3   Ibid., xiv.

4   George Henry Tinkham, *California Men and Events* (Stockton, Calif.: Record, 1915), 127.

5   Ibid., 129.

6   Ridge, *Joaquín Murieta*, ed. Jackson, xvi–xvii.

7   Angus MacLean, *Legends of the California Bandidos* (Fresno, Calif.: Pioneer Press, 1977), 68.

8   Ridge, *Joaquín Murieta*, ed. Jackson, 7.

9   Two good sources for these reports are Tinkham's book and William B. Secrest's *Joaquín* (Fresno, Calif.: Saga-West, 1967). Both contend that Joaquín was a Mexican. Others disagree, claiming he came from South America. See Jay Monaghan, *Chile, Peru, and the California Gold Rush of 1849* (Berkeley: University of California Press, 1973), 214.

10 Tinkham, *Men and Events*, 132–33n.

11 Frank F. Latta, *Joaquín Murieta and His Horse Gangs* (Santa Cruz, Calif.: Bear State Books, 1980), 328.

12 Secrest, *Joaquín*, 32.

13 Ibid.

14 San Francisco *Alta California*, August 23, 1853, quoted in Ridge, *Joaquín Murieta*, ed. Jackson, xxv.

15 *History of Nevada County, California* (N.p.: Thompson and West, 1879), 115.

16 Hugh Sanford Cheney Baker, "The Book Trade in California, 1849–1859," *California Historical Society Quarterly* 30(December 1951): 353.

17 Ibid., 30(September 1951): 251.

18 *Daily Placer Times and Transcript*, August 25–30, p. 4, col. 3.

19 Walker, "Ridge's Editions Compared," 257.

20 *Daily California Chronicle*, August 7, 1954, 2–3.

21 Yellow Bird, "Joaquín Murieta," *Daily Placer Times and Transcript*, August 25, 1854, 4.

22 Dale and Litton, *Cherokee Cavaliers*, 83.

23 Ridge, *Joaquín Murieta*, ed. Jackson, xxxii.

24 Nadeau, *Real Joaquín*, 123.

25 Ridge, *Joaquín Murieta*, ed. Jackson, xxxii.

26 Nadeau, *Real Joaquín*, 124.

27 Ridge, *Joaquín Murieta*, ed. Jackson, xxxii.

28 Nadeau, *Real Joaquín*, 121.

29 Ibid., 124.

30 Cincinnatus Hiner Miller, *Songs of the Sierras* (Boston: Roberts Brother, 1871), 67–105.

31 Joaquin Miller, *The Complete Poetical Works* (San Francisco: Whitaker and Ray, 1897), 40.

32 Hubert Howe Bancroft, *History of California*, vol. 7 (San Francisco: History Company, 1890), 203; and Theodore H. Hittell, *History of California*, vol. 3 (San Francisco: N. J. Stone, 1897), 712–26.

33 Ridge, *Joaquín Murieta*, ed. Jackson, xxvii.

34 MacLean, *Legends*, 69.

35 Ridge, *Joaquín Murieta*, ed. Jackson, 8–9.

36 Robert M. Cowan, "The Twenty Rarest and Most Important Works Dealing with the History of California," *California Historical Society Quarterly* 10(March 1931): 79–83.

CHAPTER SEVEN

1 Stand Watie Miscellaneous File, Western History Collections, University of Oklahoma Library, October 9, 1854.

2 Marysville City Council Minutes, September 25, 1854. Marysville, California, Public Library.

3 Samuel Colville, *Colville's Marysville Directory for the Year Commencing November 1, 1855* (San Francisco: Monson and Valentine, 1855), 61.

4 *History of Yuba County* (N.p.: Thompson and West, 1879), 59.

5 Stand Watie Miscellaneous File, Western History Collections, University of Oklahoma Library, October 5, 1855.

6 Ibid.

7 Ibid.

8 Stand Watie Miscellaneous File, Western History Collections, University of Oklahoma Library, August 19, 1856.

9 Ibid., Charles E. Watie to Stand Watie, August 19, 1856.

10 Edward C. Kemble, *A History of California Newspapers, 1846–1858* (Los Gatos, Calif.: Talisman Press, 1962), 160. Reprinted from the supplement to the Sacramento *Union* of December 25, 1858.

11 Peyton Hurt, "The Rise and Fall of the 'Know Nothings' in California," *California Historical Society Quarterly* 9(March 1930): 24.

12 Ibid., 41.

13 Ibid., 49.

14 For a discussion of this topic, see Andrew F. Rolle, *California: A History* (New York: Thomas Y. Crowell, 1963), 240–50.

15 Herbert G. Florcken, "Law and Order View of Vigilance Committee, 1856," *California Historical Society Quarterly* 15(March 1936): 76.

16 *Sacramento Daily Bee*, February 3, 1857, p. 1, col. 1.

17 Ibid., June 3, 1857, p. 1, col. 1.

18 Ibid., April 5, 1857, p. 1, col. 1.

19 Ibid., May 2, 1857, p. 1, col. 1.

20 Ibid., February 5, 1857, p. 1, col. 2.

21 Ibid., July 20, 1857, p. 1, col. 2.

22 Stand Watie Miscellaneous File, Western History Collections, University of Oklahoma Library, William Quesenbury to Stand Watie, January 27, 1857.

23 *Daily Bee*, July 27, 1857, p. 1, col. 1.

24 Ibid., April 18, 1857, p. 1, col. 2.

25 Ibid., May 26, 1857, p. 1, col. 2.

26 Ibid., June 12, 1857, p. 1, col. 1.

27 Rolle, *California*, 250–51.

28 *Daily Bee*, June 16, 1857, p. 1, col. 1.

29 Rolle, *California*, 256.

30 *Daily Bee*, April 20, 1857, p. 1, col. 2.

31 Ibid., February 8, 1857, p. 1, col. 1.

32 Ibid., May 16, 1857, p. 1, col. 2.

33 Ibid., May 19, 1857, p. 1, col. 2.

34 Morison, *American People*, 548.

35 *Daily Bee*, May 20, 1857, p. 1, col. 2; June 19, 1857, p. 1, col. 2; July 17, 1857, p. 1, col. 3.

36 Ibid., May 23, 1857, p. 1, col. 1.

37 For a discussion of the issue, see Rolle, *California*, 298–307.

38 *Daily Bee*, July 16, 1857, p. 1, col. 2; July 20, 1857, p. 1, col. 1; July 23, 1857, p. 1, col. 2.

39 Kemble, *California Newspapers*, 360.

40 Edward Standiford, *The Pattern of California History* (San Francisco: Carfield Press, 1975), 221.

41 Rolle, *California*, 390.

42 Standiford, *Pattern*, 222.

43 Rolle, *California*, 390.

44 Marysville *Daily National Democrat*, April 15, 1860, p. 2, col. 3.

45 Farmer and Strickland, *Yellow Bird*, 60–63.

46 John McDonald, quoted in the San Francisco *Daily Alta California*, July 29, 1857, p. 2, col. 6.

47 San Francisco *Daily California Chronicle*, April 30, 1856, p. 1, col. 2.

48 *Marysville California Express*, January 14, 1858, p. 2, col. 2.

49 Ibid. January 28, 1858, p. 2, col. 2.

CHAPTER EIGHT

1   Marysville *Daily National Democrat*, September 29, 1858, p. 2, col. 1.
2   Ibid., July 9, 1859, p. 2, col. 2.
3   Ibid., July 21, 1859, p. 2, col. 2.
4   Ibid., April 12, 1860, p. 2, col. 2.
5   Ibid., November 1, 1859, p. 2, col. 2.
6   Ibid., September 22, 1859, p. 2, col. 2.
7   December 1, 1859, p. 2, col. 2.
8   Ibid., November 20, 1858, p. 2, col. 2.
9   Ibid., April 7, 1859, p. 2, col. 3.
10 Ibid., November 13, 1858, p. 2, col. 2.
11 Ibid., August 15, 1858, p. 2, col. 2; August 26, 1858, p. 2, col. 2.
12 Ibid., May 17, 1860, p. 2, col. 2.

CHAPTER NINE

1   Morison, *American People*, 603.
2   Marysville *Daily National Democrat*, November 21, 1860, p. 2, col. 2.
3   Earl Ramey, "Wau-Kee-Taw, Chief of the Yubas," Sutter County Historical Society *News Bulletin* 3 (January 16, 1962): 5–6.
4   For a discussion of the Knights, see Frank L. Klement, *The Copperheads in the Middle West* (Gloucester, Mass.: Peter Smith, 1972), 135–69.
5   Stand Watie Miscellaneous File, Western History Collections, University of Oklahoma Library, William P. Adair to Stand Watie, July 17, 1860.
6   Stephen G. Hust, "Biography, Yuba City, John Rollin Ridge," September 25, 1951. Vertical File, Yuba City, California, Public Library.
7   Marysville *Daily Appeal*, April 23, 1861, p. 2, col. 1.
8   Chattel Mortgages, Yuba County, California, Clerk's Recording Office, book 1, 401–2.

CHAPTER TEN

1   San Francisco *Daily Alta California*, May 27, 1861, p. 2, col. 1.
2   San Francisco *National Herald*, July 13, 1861, p. 2, col. 4.
3   Ibid., September 26, 1861, p. 2, col. 1.
4   Walker, *Literary Frontier*, 48.
5   Ranck, "Ridge in California," 64.

CHAPTER ELEVEN

1   Marysville *Daily Appeal*, June 3, 1864, p. 2, col. 3.

2   Hugh B. Thompson, "Historical Review of the Town of Grass Valley," in *Directory of the Cities of Nevada and Grass Valley, 1861* (Nevada City, Calif.: Charles F. Robbins, 1861).

3   Walker, *Literary Frontier*, 111.

4   (Nevada City) *Nevada Daily Transcript*, August 7, 1864, p. 2, col. 2.

5   Grass Valley *Daily National*, August 7, 1864, p. 2, col. 3.

6   *Daily National*, August 10, 1864, p. 2, col. 2.

7   Edmund G. Kinyon, *The Northern Mines* (Grass Valley and Nevada City, Calif.: Union, 1949), 138.

8   For a running account of the feud from both sides, see the *Daily National* for January 13, 1865, p. 3, col. 1; January 14, p. 2, col. 2, and p. 3, col. 1; January 17, p. 2, col. 2; January 19, p. 22, col. 3; and January 21, p. 2, col. 2. Also, the Nevada City *Nevada Daily Gazette* for January 13, 1865, p. 2, col. 1; January 14, p. 2, col. 1; January 19, p. 2, col. 1; January 20, p. 2, col. 2; and January 21, p. 2, col. 1.

9   *Nevada Daily Gazette*, January 14, 1865, p. 2, col. 1.

10 Ibid., January 17, 1865, p. 2, col. 1.

11 *Daily National*, November 10, 1864, p. 2, col. 1.

12 Kinyon, *Northern Mines*, 139.

13 Mining Records of Nevada County, Nevada County, California, Clerk's Records Office, book 3, 305.

14 Grant Foreman, *A History of Oklahoma* (Norman: University of Oklahoma Press, 1942), 133–34.

15 *Report of the Secretary of the Interior, 1866* (Washington, D.C.: Government Printing Office, 1866), 11.

16 Bureau of Indian Affairs (BIA), Washington, D.C., Letters Received, Cherokee, 1865–66, M234, roll 100.

17 Washburn Family File, Arkansas History Commission, Little Rock.

18 Ibid., undated, 1866.

19 Ibid., J. W. Washbourne to J. A. Scales, June 1, 1866.

20 Ibid.

21 BIA, Letters Received, Cherokee, 1865–66, M234, roll 100.

22 Ibid.

23 Washington, D.C.: Intelligencer Printing House, 1866.

24 *Report of the Secretary of the Interior, 1866*, 12.

25 Lois Elizabeth Forde, "Elias Cornelius Boudinot" (Ph.D. diss., Columbia University, 1951), 131.

26 BIA, Letters Received, Cherokee, 1865–66, M234, roll 100.

27 E. C. Boudinot File, Western History Collections, University of Oklahoma Library.

28 Stand Watie Miscellaneous File, Western History Collections, University of Oklahoma Library.

29 BIA, Letters Received, Cherokee, 1865–66, M234, roll 100.

30 E. C. Boudinot File, Western History Collections, University of Oklahoma Library, E. C. Boudinot to N. G. Taylor, Commissioner of Indian Affairs, April 13, 1867.

31 Medical definitions are from William A. R. Thomson, *Black's Medical Dictionary* (New York: Barnes and Noble, 1974), 130.

32 San Francisco *Alta California*, October 8, 1867, p. 2, col. 2.

33 *Daily Appeal*, October 9, 1867, p. 3, col. 1.

Bibliography

WORKS BY JOHN ROLLIN RIDGE

"The Cherokees: Their History—Present Condition and Future Prospects." *Northern Standard* (Clarksville, Tex.), January 20, 1849.

"Harp of Broken Strings." *Herald* (Marysville, Calif.), December 24, 1850.

"Still, Small, Voice." *Herald* (Marysville, Calif.), March 28, 1851.

To A*****." *Herald* (Marysville, Calif.), April 15, 1851.

"The Woods." *Union* (Sacramento), May 27, 1853.

"Eyes." *Daily Evening Herald* (Marysville, Calif.), August 12, 1853.

"Mount Shasta." *Daily Evening Herald* (Marysville, Calif.), November 8, 1853.

The Life and Adventures of Joaquín Murieta, the Celebrated California Bandit. 1st ed. San Francisco: W. B. Cooke, 1854.

"North American Indians." *Hesperian* 8(March 1862): 1–18.

"North American Indians." *Hesperian* 8(April 1862): 51–60.

"North American Indians." *Hesperian* 8(May 1862): 99–109.

Poems. San Francisco: Henry Payot, 1868.

The Life and Adventures of Joaquín Murieta, the Celebrated California Bandit. Ed. Joseph Henry Jackson. Norman: University of Oklahoma Press, 1986.

SECONDARY SOURCES

Browne, Juanita K. "John Rollin Ridge." *California Highway Patrolman* 42(October 1978): 13, 57–63.

Clough, Charles W. *Joaquín Murieta, the Brigand Chief of California*. Fresno: Valley Publishing, 1969.

Dale, Edward Everett, and Gaston Litton. *Cherokee Cavaliers: Forty Years of Cherokee History as Told in the Correspondence of the Ridge-Watie-Boudinot Family*. Norman: University of Oklahoma Press, 1939.

Debo, Angie. "John Rollin Ridge." *Southwest Review* 17(1931): 59–71.

Farmer, David, and Rennard Strickland. *A Trumpet of Our Own: Yellow Bird's Essays on the North American Indian*. San Francisco: Book Club of California, 1981.

Foreman, Carolyn Thomas. "Edward W. Bushyhead and John Rollin Ridge." *Chronicles of Oklahoma* 14(September 1936): 295–311.

———. "Miss Sophia Sawyer and Her School." *Chronicles of Oklahoma* 32(Winter 1954–55): 395–413.

Franks, Kenny A. *Stand Watie and the Agony of the Cherokee Nation*. Memphis: Memphis State University Press, 1979.

McLoughlin, William. *Cherokee Renascence, 1794–1833*. Princeton: Princeton University Press, 1987.

———. *Cherokees and Missionaries*. New Haven: Yale University Press, 1984.

McSwaim, Elizabeth. "Member of a Minority." *Arkansas Gazette* (Little Rock), July 20, 1941, p. 8, col. 1.

Morison, Samuel Eliot. *The Oxford History of the American People*. New York: Oxford University Press, 1965.

Nadeau, Remi. *The Real Joaquín Murieta: Robin Hood Hero or Gold Rush Gangster?* Trans-Anglo Books, 1974.

Peel, Zillah Cross. "Romance from the Records." *Arkansas Gazette* (Little Rock), December 16, 1934, p. 3, col. 1.

Ranck, M. A. "John Rollin Ridge in California." *Chronicles of Oklahoma* 10(December 1932): 560–69.

Tracy, Joseph. *History of the American Board of Commissioners of Foreign Missions*. New York: M. W. Dodd, 1842.

Walker, Franklin. "Ridge's Life of Joaquín Murieta, the First and Revised Editions Compared." *California Historical Society Quarterly* 16(September 1937): 257–80.

———. *San Francisco's Literary Frontier*. Seattle: University of Washington Press, 1939.

———. "Yellow Bird." *Westways* 30(November 1938): 18–19.

Wilkins, Thurman. *Cherokee Tragedy: The Story of the Ridge Family and the Decimation of a People*. New York: Macmillan, 1970.

Index

assassination of, 229–31; estate of, 35, 53–54

Ridge, John Rollin: association with Knights of the Golden Circle, 180–82, 195, 208–11; birth of, 13; on California Indians, 132–33; death of, 220; description of, 72–74, 184–85; and dueling, 201, 205–8; as editor of Grass Valley *National*, 196ff.; as editor of Marysville *National Democrat*, 140ff.; as editor of Red Bluff *Beacon*, 192–93; as editor of Sacramento *Bee*, 120ff.; as editor of Sacramento *California American*, 116–20; as editor of San Francisco *Evening Journal*, 184–85; as editor of San Francisco *National Herald*, 185–88; as editor of Weaverville *Trinity National*, 194; education of, 1–2, 14–18, 24, 27, 34–35, 36–44; and 1840s conflicts, 50–51; emigration of, to California, 60–69; family origins of, 3–5; flight of, to Missouri, 55–60; at Great Barrington, 36–39; handwriting sample of, 23–24; on Indian policy, 171–76; inheritance of, 54; on journalism, 121; as Know-Nothing editor, 116–19; letters of, 34–35, 37–38, 45–46, 52, 56–58, 59, 63–68, 92–94; love verse of, 81–84; as marksman, 155–56; marriage of, 53–54; as member of Southern delegation of Cherokees, 211–20; as miner, 69–71; monument to, 221; nature poems of, 84–91; obituaries of, 220; and plans for Indian newspaper, 113–16; on poetry, 122–23; as political candidate, 186; political

ideas of, 124; on progress, 146ff.; rank as poet, 225–26; revenge desired by, 30–31, 37, 45–46, 51, 56–57, 188; romantic influence on, 84–91; satire in writings of, 186–87, 210, 226; shooting by, 55; speeches by, 146, 154, 201; study of law by, 44, 114–15

—works of: "Arkansaw Root Doctor," 226; "The Atlantic Cable," 142–43, 147ff.; autobiographical poems of, 77–81; "The Bloody Programme," 165–66; "California," 147ff.; "A Cherokee Love Song," 81; "Do I Love Thee?" 82; "The Douglas Star," 166; "Eyes," 91–92; "False But Beautiful," 83; "Flatheads and Black Feet Indians," 179; "The Forgiven Dead," 83; "The Harp of Broken Strings," 75, 78–79; "The Humboldt Desert," 90–91; "Humboldt River," 90; "Indian Citizens," 175; "A June Morning," 91, 122; *The Life and Adventures of Joaquín Murieta, the Celebrated California Bandit*, 2, 95–112; "Lines on Hearing a Bird Seen at a Lady's Window," 82; "Literary Statesmen of Britain," 137; "More About the Civilized Indians," 179; "Mount Shasta," 87–88, 221, 225–26; "A Night Scene," 84; "The North American Indians," 188–92; "October Hills," 91; "An October Morn," 54; "Ode to the National Flag," 186; "Of Her I Love," 82; "Oppression of the Digger Indians," 134–35; "Poem," 147ff., 186; "Political Editing," 158–59; "A